COUNSELING

A
Modern
Emphasis
in
Religion

COUNSELING

*A
Modern
Emphasis
in
Religion*

LESLIE E. MOSER, PH.D.
Professor of Psychology
Baylor University

PRENTICE-HALL, INC.
Englewood Cliffs, N.J.
1962

Dedicated

to my mother,
Nettie Mae Moser,

whose Christian faith and example
have shaped the course of my life.

Preface

This book on religious counseling is written from the viewpoint of the psychologist. Counseling in religious settings should take cognizance of man's spiritual nature and needs, but psychology may serve a useful purpose in aiding the religious worker as he ministers to many varieties of human needs.

The religious counselor of today reaches out for any assistance in helping others. He has eagerly accepted the resources of psychology, psychiatry, and social work, although not without questioning the validity of their use in counseling. In general, he has seen these resources as additional tools to enhance but not to replace prayer, Scriptures, and various religiously oriented activities.

Having spiritual as well as psychological tools may make the religiously oriented counselor more effective; however, his task is sure to be more difficult. With every new tool comes the challenge of how it should be used. Furthermore, a new decision must be made for each parishioner, who presents unique problems and background. The religious worker has unusually strong motivation for study and self-improvement. He must learn to use judiciously both spiritual and psychological tools.

In attempting a psychological approach to counseling in the religious setting, an earnest respect for the time-honored methods of pastoral counseling should be maintained, based primarily on the spiritual aids of prayer, Scriptures, and the spirit-led intellectual activities of the man of God at work with his people. The aim of this book is to broaden the understandings of the church-related counselor by emphasizing the findings of psychology, a scientific study of the behavior of man. Man is a complex organism endowed with behavioral tendencies not easily understood. Psychological research has been able to give some new information about his behavior in the hope of assisting him to help himself and men to help each other.

This book is written, not for the clergy alone, but for all religious workers who have counseling tasks—the youth worker, the minister of education, the psychological specialist working in the church setting, and those who work in the church and church-school educational programs. Students who pursue formal courses in counseling in seminaries and divinity schools will find this book extremely useful.

Because those who read *Counseling: A Modern Emphasis in Religion* will represent a broad range of interest, some of the chapters pertain to "surface-level" problems and others deal more with a treatment of "depth" problems. Chapters I and II establish the frame of reference for the psychological approach. Chapter III offers material helpful in learning how to interview, with emphasis on interviewing in the religious setting. Chapters IV and V deal with methods of counseling those having personal and decision-oriented problems. Chapter VI treats some specifics of counseling persons having marriage and family-living problems. Chapters VII and VIII offer information concerning the most common theories and techniques of psychotherapy. Chapter IX gives helpful suggestions for all types of group work. Two full-length counseling interviews are used to illustrate techniques.

This book does not promote a certain religious viewpoint or doctrine. The religious concepts are very broad and apply to all religious workers who embrace the Judaeo-Christian system. As a strong proponent of religious counseling, I have served extensively as consultant to many clergymen and religious workers, and I feel that God's love for mankind is a strong factor in what transpires in the counseling office. The clergy and other religious workers have the most important role in helping man toward an abundant life, and I offer this book as a contribution to a work which I consider of utmost importance.

LESLIE E. MOSER

Table of Contents

COUNSELING

A Modern Emphasis in Religion

Counseling—A Developing Emphasis in Religion

A strong interest in counseling of all types and in all spheres has developed during the years since World War II. One has only to peruse magazines, newspapers, and college catalogues to believe this. Almost every slick magazine and newspaper carries a column or articles on counseling, psychotherapy, psychiatry, marriage problems, child care, or some other area of human problems. Television and the movies have capitalized on public interest in human problem solution. The role of the counselor, particularly the psychiatrist, has been glamorized and thrust upon an awakened and sensitive public.

Why so much interest in these matters? In the first place, journalists and those who promote entertainment media know the appeal of the presentation of human problems for those who have personal difficulties. Readers and viewers may identify with either the counselee or the counselor; and through vicarious experiences they are entertained, educated, and possibly helped. Secondly, the very humaneness of man turns his attention toward his troubled fellows.

Only the very naive, however, would believe that the counseling episodes depicted in mass communication media are highly beneficial. Without denying the humanitarian impulses of those who publish and produce, it is likely that their primary objectives are larger subscriptions and higher ratings for entertainment value and appeal. Except for the possibility that these productions may call attention in some cases to the available valid resources for help, they may be more harmful than helpful. While some educational values may evolve, much material of this type presents faulty information. That there are exceptions to the general rule is certain.

The broadening interest in counseling work has turned the attention of many students to seek careers in counseling. By and large, the desires of students who seek training in counseling theory and technique have superseded the capacities of the limited training facilities in the universities, seminaries, and medical schools.

As a result of many factors, including a sudden emphasis in counseling, inadequate training facilities, lack of legal status for qualified counseling workers, and a poorly educated public, the entire field is in a crucial state. Charlatans offer services under the guise of professionals; and many who have received the best training available to them are attempting things beyond their capacities.

Who Should Counsel

The consideration of who should counsel is a weighty question. One segment of critics holds that such work belongs only to the medical profession. Another holds that medical training is unnecessary but a doctorate in clinical or counseling psychology is essential. Still others see a need for counseling activity which demands all types and levels of training depending on the types of problems treated.

This problem cannot be solved easily or soon. It does seem wrong to withdraw all sources of help, however meager, from millions of people until such time as help may be available from counselors who have either Ph.D. or M.D. degrees. However, it is wrong to allow incompetent practitioners to deal with problems which may be made worse by improper counseling, no matter how well-intentioned the counselors may be.

Realistically, it is unthinkable that institutions such as schools and churches could fulfill their obligations without a counseling function. It is likewise unthinkable that parents, clergymen, teachers, and lawyers can refrain from counseling. So, while there are many arguments for vesting counseling functions only in the hands of Ph.D. and M.D. degree holders, practical considerations speak too loudly in favor of a multi-dimensional counseling function. Furthermore, it is unreasonable to expect that all counseling activity may be brought into a professional dimension. Complex modern society has tended to make parents and others inadequate for the counseling tasks they formerly handled with assurance; hence, the need for a professional counseling discipline has been accentuated. On the other hand, if parents relegated all counseling chores to the professionals, it would not be desirable.

In the professional sphere, the most hopeful approach to the problem of adequate training seems to be the training of counselors at several levels and in a number of approaches and dimensions. A part of such training would necessarily consist of a careful consideration of the types of problems to be dealt with by professionally trained people at various levels. Such training would also include meticulous instruction concerning the limitations of the several counseling groups and a scrupulous examination of referral resources upward and downward among the various professional levels of counselors. This approach to the solution of the problem of who should counsel and with whom seems to be gaining favor, although many individuals and groups are adamant in demanding sanctions and recognitions for their approaches. Such groups generally adopt a proprietary attitude toward all counseling work and see their special dimensions as panaceas.

Many groups have formed professional organizations and have set up training programs; and they are attempting to achieve professional status in the eyes of the public. Among these are school psychologists and guidance workers, social workers, industrial psychologists, clinical psychologists, marriage counselors, counseling psychologists, and counselors in YMCA and similar youth groups. All of these groups consider themselves professional counselors. But some of these groups and individuals within them are skeptical of the professional merits of some of the others.

That the multiplicity and variability of human problems demand attention through every reasonable approach is undeniable. That the unprofessional approach to the problems of human beings is often disastrous is equally undeniable. This dilemma may be solved only through emphasis on improved training in every sphere of counseling effort. It may be solved only through cooperation and free communication among all those groups which make honest attempts to define areas of work, to seek earnestly training conducive to competence, and to place human welfare above personal and even professional interests.

THE CHALLENGE FOR RELIGION

Counseling in Church-Related Circles

It is understandable that the school visualizes a strong emphasis on counseling as a means of accomplishing educational objectives. It is similarly natural to find that industry has turned to counseling as a means of solving not only its human problems but its production problems as well. On the other hand one may be amazed that schools, industry, governmental services, and others waited so long to see the relationship of counseling to the promotion of their objectives.

How much more surprising that churches and religious institutions have been slow to see counseling as a primary resource for accomplishing religious objectives! Of course, some churches have always promoted counseling through pastoral care and pastoral conferences. Some individual clergymen have developed and maintained strong programs of pastoral counseling. One has only to peruse religious literature to observe that the clergy has become critical of the use of the mass approach exclusively. However, writings of clergymen indicate that many religious institutions have been principally concerned with approaching the masses with sermons, inspirations, and remonstrance, and have neglected the personal and individual needs which may be served only as clergy or religious workers meet the parishioner or seeker in face-to-face encounter. As Kemp says:

> The minister should recognize that preaching is only one method of helping people face life's problems and live the Christian life. He should not attempt to do in the pulpit what should only be done in an interview, or perhaps in a series of interviews. . . . Some problems can only be dealt with face to face, when the person has the opportunity to express himself, to ask questions, and to relieve

his tensions; all of which is to say that preaching must be done along with pastoral work; it can never take the place of either pastoral counseling or pastoral care (11, p. 45).

There have been practical reasons for the emphasis on mass approach to religious objectives. Many churches have expected a single clergyman to fulfill all of the religious objectives of a church body composed of hundreds of people. The mass approach has seemed the most reasonable. It is certain that church bodies are seeing the enormity of the task the religious institutions face and are becoming adjusted to the idea that a church must be adequately staffed just as any business enterprise is staffed.

The traditional school was concerned with teaching the "three R's." This satisfied parents, teachers, and school patrons, generally. The modern school sees its task as embracing all the needs the student has, be they academic, social, vocational, or other. In much the same way, the church has moved away from the sole concern for man's salvation (still the primary concern) to a broader concern for his welfare in the various spheres of life. In the past, many church groups have been content to assist man in his search for a close relationship to God only to leave the newborn child of God to fend for himself. Few, if any, religious groups ignore the physical and psychological needs of the parishioners today.

Almost all religious groups continue to see the first task as bringing man into a satisfying relationship with God. Many churches now see this event as the beginning rather than the ending of the church's responsibility. The modern church should pledge its concerted and constant effort to assist not only its own members, but also humanity at large, to become happier, better adjusted children of God.

The modern philosophy of a broadened perspective for church involvement is evident in the number of schools, hospitals, and eleemosynary institutions operating under church auspices. Religious groups have evidenced a disproportionate concern for physical disabilities as compared to psychological and personal-problem solutions largely because of lack of resources for handling all problems. Man's physical disabilities are usually more conspicuous and demand attention first.

Much money and devotion have been channeled into medical missionary efforts, and close attention has been given to teaching functions both at home and abroad. The thinking is that people everywhere may be reached in the spiritual dimension if physical ills are treated first. Programs for relief of destitute peoples have been developed from a similar basis of thought. While this philosophy is undoubtedly sound and must be implemented more and more, there are other means of opening doors of opportunity which have been largely overlooked.

Although church memberships are large, many believe that relationships between God and man have grown cold. Could there be a better way to encourage a fuller spiritual dimension than by providing, under a church-guided program of counseling, a means of relief from personal and adjustment problems? This is among the considerations that have provided an atmosphere for the maturing of a counseling philosophy within churches.

It may be that religious institutions could suffer from a sudden overemphasis on counseling. In a sense, counseling has been thrust upon religious workers. A calm and careful consideration of the wise and prudent implementation of counseling service is imperative. Yoder (25) refers to counseling as "the theological specialty of the present generation." It is imperative that the clergy and religious workers gain the fullest understandings possible concerning this "specialty," which may be either the greatest boon or the greatest frustration that religion has been subjected to.

STAFFING THE CHURCH
COUNSELING SERVICE

The time available to the clergyman must be divided in many ways. As congregations grow larger, the work of the clergyman becomes more difficult and more demanding. He must have concern not only for the pulpit task, but also for problems of finance, staffing, promotion, and teaching, as well as for pastoral calling and visitation. Even though many of these tasks may be assigned to paid or volunteer staff, the clergyman is never free from any of them.

Regardless of his interest, the clergyman will not be able to do all the counseling that should be done, even in the small church. In the realm of counseling, there will be many problems that may be delegated to staff members; there will be many that will demand the clergyman's individual attention regardless of how many staff members may have a counseling function. Because of his position and the feeling people have for him, he is apt to be called upon for more counseling than he will have time for.

Although some parishioners will demand the individual attention of the clergyman, there is great logic in having staff members with specific assignments for counseling. The staff of a typical modern church consists of the clergyman, an educational director, a music director, a young people's worker, and in many cases a counseling specialist. In addition to these, there are the volunteer teaching and training faculties. Titles for these personnel will vary with the churches, but the functions implied in the above titles are typical. In smaller churches, some of the staff functions are combined and assigned to a single staff member.

Not only are staff members necessary for referrals from the clergyman, but, in the properly organized program, parishioners are likely to go directly to the counseling staff member. It is clear that the amount of counseling each staff member does varies from small incidental counseling involvement to full-time counseling practice, in the case of the specialist. Educational directors, music directors, and teaching faculties may be thought of as incidental counselors, while the specialist and the youth director have professional orientations. Specific counseling opportunities for the specialist and the youth worker will be indicated at a later time.

The Clergyman as Counselor

If the function of the clergyman must be summed up with a single phrase, the phrase should be "spiritual guidance." Most clergymen would prefer to think of all their humanitarian interests and activities as contributing to the spiritual welfare of mankind. Most spiritual guidance is achieved through encounter with the parishioner either in the mass or individual frame of reference. In a sense, almost everything the clergyman does in pursuit of his aim of spiritual guidance has a relevance to counseling.

The pulpit work of the clergyman may be thought of as group spiritual guidance extended individually to every member of the congregation. It may also lead to individual counseling.

The counseling function of the clergyman in no way conflicts with his age-old function of spiritual guidance. On the contrary, one reinforces the other. In sermon after sermon, the minister, rabbi and priest speak on the issues of life. If a clergyman's work with individuals has taken root, it can bear fruit in the acceptance his congregation gives these general messages. They will take on a new note of reality. People will listen with a new earnestness.

Looked at from another viewpiont, if each sermon rings with an understanding of life's many problems as people actually know them, the congregation will come one by one to the clergyman for the counseling they need (14).

Another sphere wherein counseling and pastoral work ramify each other is the clergyman's visitation efforts. These efforts are often referred to as the pastoral call. Dicks has much to say about the pastoral call (7). Hulme contributes as follows:

The pastor's calling ministry can also help to shape his people's opinion of him. It is something of a preview of the counseling process. Since his people are hesitant to come for counseling, they need this preview. The counseling ministry does not replace the calling program, since counseling grows out of calling. Just to call, however, is not enough; the preview may influence a person to stay away rather than to come. If the pastor is unable to keep a conversation moving, his parishioners may feel ill at ease in his presence. If he can talk freely but is not able to stimulate others to talk, his people may feel all the more incapable of expressing their problems to him. On the other hand, if the parishioner has enjoyed the visit and has participated in the conversation and found the pastor understanding and receptive, he is encouraged to make his problems the topic of conversation (9, pp. 13, 14).

A well-trained clergy is among the strongest assets a community has for mental health. Mental health and counseling go hand in hand. Counseling may bring about mental health; and mental health achieved through broad means, including spiritual values, is likely to make the counseling load lighter.

In a sense, each clergyman practices mental hygiene during all his hours of service. For generations, religious leaders have been working with the human personality, helping people to fight their own individual battles. With kindness and understanding, with insight and skill, the clergy has led people to a better adjustment to life, while never losing sight of life's larger ideals (14).

Ward and Jones (22), in their pamphlet *Ministering to Families of the Mentally Ill,* point out that "much of the clergyman's help will lie in the area of influencing the way people think and feel about mental illness." As the clergyman conveys his own attitudes toward mental illness in sermons and conversations, his people will adopt similar attitudes. An improved public sentiment concerning mental illness will be a great asset in bringing help to those who need it.

Perhaps the most comprehensive study of the clergyman as counselor has been made by the Commission in the Ministry, appointed by the New York Academy of Sciences in 1955. A report of this commission has revealed the religious or pastoral counselor as a person with many unique features as compared to other counselors. A part of this report follows:

> In functioning as a counselor, therefore, the clergyman always does so as a representative leader of a religious community. This works out practically in several ways:
>
> First, his responsibility to the total group limits the amount of time he can spend with any one individual, regardless of the amount of training he has as a counselor.
>
> Second, his right to choose or select his counselees is limited.
>
> Third, the clergyman is less free than other counselors to terminate his relationship to his counselees, inasmuch as he is enduringly related to them as communicant members of his congregation.
>
> Fourth, the fact that a clergyman-counselor functions in the larger religious framework may be both a help and a hindrance to therapy. It would be a help to the extent that it would enable the counselee to relate readily in terms of confidence in the counselor. It would be a hindrance if the counselor were to use his position as a clergyman to dominate the counseling situation.
>
> Finally, the clergyman's leadership of a religious community puts him in touch with situations that often would be considered "normal" by the psychopathologists, which nevertheless are severe problems to the person involved.
>
> In summary, then, the clergyman, although a true counselor and, in this sense, one making contact with other counseling professions is, nevertheless, first and foremost a religious counselor. This latter aspect characterizes his uniqueness as a counselor (15).

What types of problems most often are brought to the clergyman? This question was carefully considered by the Commission in the Ministry of the New York Academy of Sciences. They divide the parishioners who seek counsel from the clergyman into eight categories.

(1) Persons having religious conflicts, doubts, and questions. Marital conflicts, for example, often take a specific religious direction. People with such problems often seek help from their priest, rabbi, or minister.

(2) Persons who have committed sins of which they are aware come to the clergymen as representatives of God. They seek God's pardon and forgiveness. Included in this group are those whose difficulties are not manifestations of psychopathology.

(3) Convalescent psychiatric patients who feel the need to develop their religious dimensions in addition to the psychotherapy they are receiving are turning in increasing numbers to clergymen.

(4) Persons who have misgivings with respect to psychologists, psychiatrists, and psychoanalysts often seek the help of clergymen instead. This group includes those who are afraid to go to psychotherapists because they are uncertain as to the latter's attitude toward religion. This may be a rationalization for avoiding therapy, but it also may have some justification in fact as well.

(5) Patients who are receiving psychotherapy and have questions about the wisdom of continuing therapy bring questions to the clergyman in many instances.

(6) Persons for whom psychotherapy may not be indicated come to the clergyman. This would include older people who feel isolated and alone, and want to enter into a small group relationship. The church has natural groups already in action for such people.

(7) The fact still remains that persons who cannot afford psychiatric treatment still turn to the church for this form of help. The clergyman is in every town and hamlet, and he is often compelled by circumstances to assume the role of the poor man's psychotherapist.

(8) Finally, the clergyman in many instances gets the kind of person who has been unable to respond to counseling by other counselors. Such an unfortunate person expects a clergyman to perform a "miracle," or to act as his permanent crutch (15).

Although some of the parishioners represented in the above are characterized as normals, it seems clear that this list emphasizes those undergoing psychotherapy or who are deeply disturbed. One can easily believe that this list would fit the pattern of people who go to clergymen for whom no particular effort has been made to publicize his counseling function. Where the counseling function of the clergy is presented as pertinent to the everyday problems of normal people, it may be expected that the following categories would be added:

(1) Young people concerned about vocational plans with emphasis on religiously-oriented vocations.
(2) Those with marriage adjustment problems having no concomitant religious conflicts or psychopathology.
(3) Parents concerned with the academic and social problems of their children, from early childhood to adulthood.
(4) Young people seeking help with social problems, reassurance, and a sense of forgiveness for minor or major transgressions.
(5) Persons of all ages seeking religious meanings, with or without strong duress.
(6) Young people seeking pre-marital counsel.
(7) Church members desiring the prayers of the clergyman for others. Such parishioners may or may not share with the clergyman their knowledge of the problems of their friends and relatives.

It goes without saying that no list would include all the types of problems faced by the clergyman. It is certain that he must face a broader pattern of human difficulty than any other counselor.

The Counseling Specialist

There are many factors which justify the presence of a counseling specialist in the church setting. In the first place, the clergyman in a church of even moderate size cannot hope to do all of the counseling that is requested. He may benefit from having an assistant to carry part of the load.

Secondly, there is reason to doubt the wisdom of subjecting the clergyman to the rigorous training required of those who work with deeply disturbed people. The specialist may be trained in clinical methods including the use of psychological tests and psychotherapeutic techniques.

Many parishioners have problems which seem too trivial to require an appointment with the clergyman. Where a program of counseling revolving about a constantly available counselor is present, these ordinary but important problems may be dealt with. It is also true that some parishioners, who are reluctant to go to the clergyman with problems, would seek help from a specialist who was perceived as a nonjudgmental person. Most clergymen realize that there are a few people in their congregations who, for one reason or another, cannot feel free to approach them, especially with problems which may be thought of by the parishioners as uncomplimentary to them.

The counseling specialist may be an asset in church promotion. Some prospective church members are likely to be influenced toward joining a church which demonstrates progressiveness by recognition of the need of counseling. This factor is of greatest importance to those who have adolescents and young people in the family.

Until recently, the position of minister of education or its equivalent was found only in a few churches. Today, most churches of moderate size consider the educational minister an absolute necessity. It is probable that the position of counseling specialist will follow a similar trend; a considerable number of churches have this position now. A few years hence it will likely be standard for all churches who can afford to hire a specialist.

It is important to make a firm assertion that the specialist in counseling in the religious setting has not at this time come into broad recognition and acceptance. There are many negative aspects, especially in the thinking of the clergy. It is probable that most clergymen are skeptical (8).

The questions clergymen raise concerning the wisdom of having specialists in counseling are valid and reasonable. Many of them feel that counseling should be vested solely in a trained clergy. Then, there is the recognized difficulty in assuring that the philosophies and practices of the counseling specialist will coordinate and integrate with the aims and ideals of the church body. Many clergymen are justifiably afraid that the presence of the specialist will result in a loss of direct communication between clergy and the people as well as a scrambled interpretation of the purposes of the church to the people. Problems of policy determination and implementation as well as conflicts in ideals and personalities have been common between clergy and staff members as long as there have been staff members, other than the clergyman, in the church. For many years following the inception of the widespread use of educational ministers, there were conflicts between them and the clergy. As the work of the educational minister has become more standardized and stabilized, conflict between clergyman and educational minister is more the exception than the rule. If the specialist in counseling becomes widely accepted, it may be that stabilization of this position will result in a cooperative effort between clergy and specialist without the probability of dissension.

In 1955, the Commission in the Ministry of the New York Academy of Sciences agreed that the specialist in counseling was undesirable. These men deplored the formation of a "priesthood within a priesthood" (15).

Research needs to be done to determine the number of counseling specialists who are working in various church groups and the thinking of religious leaders on this point. The author read the report of the Commission with great interest in 1955, made a superficial survey, and found a very limited number of specialists at work. It is known that, since that time, scores of specialists have been hired and many churches seek specialists.

The specialists in counseling who are desired in the churches at this time are those who have strong religious training in the seminaries of the respective church groups. For the most part, these specialists are expected to be capable clergymen with extra training in counseling. They are often given status as "assistant clergymen." It may be assumed easily at this juncture that more emphasis is placed on theological training than upon psychological training for the counselor in the church. The time may come, but is not now, when clinical psychologists, counseling psychologists, social workers, and psychiatrists who have strong religious orientations but little theological training may be accepted widely as counseling specialists in the church.

To some extent counseling specialists in churches are recruited from the membership on either a paid or volunteer basis. Sometimes an individual who has established a strong reputation for earnestness and zealousness in the program and faith of a church and who has training in a counseling dimension roughly consonant to the demands may be assigned special counseling functions. These people may be trained in the dimensions of social work, school guidance, or may have Master's degrees in clinical or counseling psychology. Because of good relationships established with clergy and people over a period of time, these specialists may serve effectively.

The Youth Worker as Counselor

The youth worker is perhaps the staff member most common to all religious groups. He has a definite counseling function, and this is recognized by the clergyman and the congregation. At the same time, the negative appraisals of the psychological specialist do not accrue to the youth worker. The reason for this is that while the problems usually delegated to the specialist are considered for the most part depth problems, those brought to the youth worker are usually surface problems. The youth worker deals primarily with academic, vocational, personal, and social problems at a nontherapeutic level.

Training for youth work in the church is being recognized more and more as a specialty in seminaries and divinity schools. The successful youth worker must have not only a special kind of personality but also special training which many clergymen could not duplicate even if time should permit them to do an adequate job with young people. Youth workers are usually expected to have strong theological training; their formal training in counseling is often meager. They may bolster their counseling training received in seminaries and divinity schools with courses under psychological, educational, or social work auspices. They should have training in both individual and group methods of counseling.

THE TRAINING
OF THE RELIGIOUS COUNSELOR

Undergraduate Training

Most departments of religion in colleges, universities, and divinity schools include elementary courses in counseling for undergraduates. These courses serve two purposes. They are designed to orient the student to the counseling field preparatory to his specialization in graduate school or seminary. They are also designed to assist the clergyman or youth director who goes directly into service at the end of his undergraduate training or even prior to his graduation. There are a number of denominational groups which do not require seminary or even college training for the clergyman; but there is no denying that he needs elementary instruction in counseling whether in the large or small church, whether in rural environ or the city. For the most part, these undergraduate courses instruct concerning the counseling functions pertinent to the area of pastoral care. Every clergyman must visit the sick and infirm and must attend his parishioners during times of joy and sorrow.

Training in the Seminaries

It is difficult to assess the quantity and the quality of psychological training of religious workers in the seminaries and other graduate theological schools. Perhaps the best information we have has been furnished by Queener (17), who made a survey in 1952 of the offerings of 109 schools. This was done at the request of the American Psychological Association in an attempt to determine the nature of psychological training given in America's theological schools.

This survey revealed that 83 per cent of these schools offer one or more courses which they are "willing to call psychology." Taking into account the schools which did not answer the questionnaire, it is reported that "perhaps 60 per cent to 70 per cent offering psychology is a safer estimate for all theological schools."

It is of particular note that only 5 per cent of all the persons who teach psychology courses in these schools affiliate with the APA. According to the report on the research conducted by Queener that appeared in *Pastoral Psychology*, "To the extent that lack of APA membership reflects lack of training, then, the quality of instruction in these schools may be questioned" (17).

There is no reason why the quality of seminary training should be judged by such a criterion. Most seminary teachers have experience training which helps them in many areas where formal training in psychology would not. It would seem that courses offered in seminaries are able to train adequately in terms of counseling in religious conflict areas, in typical marriage and family problems, and in normal problems of youth. It is no doubt true that courses in seminaries are at present inadequate in training for clinical skills. Most seminaries are eager to utilize the courses in the departments of psychology on university campuses to supplement the training of religious counselors.

Clinical Training

A number of efforts have been made to provide for clinical training of clergymen in various short-term institutes. The Council for Clinical Training and the Institute of Pastoral Care have provided a number of training centers in general hospitals, mental hospitals, and in correctional institutions. Some 45 or 50 of these centers have provided from six to twelve weeks of intensive training for some 4,000 clergy.

Several denominational groups and The National Council of Churches of Christ in America have created media through which clinical training for clergymen is offered. The National Council has created a Department of Pastoral Services.

The Southern Baptist Convention organized the Southern Baptist Association for Clinical Pastoral Education in 1957 at the second annual Conference on Counseling and Guidance. Among the purposes of this Association are: (1) to encourage clinical pastoral education for persons entering a church vocation, (2) to provide clinical pastoral education for persons already engaged in church vocations, (3) to encourage the production of literature in the field, and (4) to provide a uniform system of accreditation for those working in the field of clinical pastoral education (4).

There is some danger that the clinical aspects of counselor training may be overemphasized because of the high interest most people have in the mentally ill. Religious counseling must focus on the broad range of human problems; the majority of those needing help are not mentally ill.

Opportunities for study and experience in pastoral counseling are multiplying rapidly. Mark Shedron (19) has rendered a valuable service in making a comprehensive analysis of existing opportunities.

THE CHURCH-RELATED CLINIC

Church groups have a strong interest in the maintenance of various types of clinics in the community. There are many types of clinics insofar as functions are concerned. These include marriage and family relations clinics, child guidance clinics, outpatient psychiatric clinics, general medical clinics, and many others. There are many types of clinics insofar as sponsorship is concerned. These include the privately owned clinic, the city-county-state welfare clinic, the community clinic under community chest and social work auspices, the court-related clinic, and the church-related clinic.

Religious leaders have led in the formation and maintenance of many of these clinics. Clergymen have been utilized on a volunteer basis in many community clinics and have served as chaplains in others. It is often the case that a group of clergymen will see a community need, activate the formation of a clinic, and then allow social service groups to take the clinic under control. A group of clergymen in Waco, Texas, having become concerned with the lack of a marriage and family clinic, have organized a clinic in that city.

The Ministerial Counseling Center of St. Louis

A somewhat recent trend has developed in which a church or group of churches set up various types of clinics to be administered and controlled by church forces. An example of this is the Ministerial Counseling Center in St. Louis which has been set up under auspices of the Metropolitan Federation of Churches. This is a general clinic and seeks to serve the entire community. Undoubtedly this effort will become a pilot study in the area of church-supported clinics.

Although it is not medically oriented, the Ministerial Counseling Center utilizes a psychiatrist as consultant with every client. With every intake, a staff conference consisting of a psychiatrist, at least one minister, a staff conference director, and the Administration Director is held. If psychiatric treatment is found necessary, the client is referred to a privately practicing psychiatrist; otherwise the counseling is done by a minister-counselor who is specially trained, who has a position in a local church, and who is "on call" for counseling work at the Center (5).

A study of the first 200 cases treated at the Center reveals the following breakdown in problem types: Marital problems, 112; "nervousness and tension," 21; behavior disturbing to the community, 16; decision and general conduct of life, 33; alcoholism, 5;

no special complaint, 9 (5). From this breakdown it may be seen that the majority of clients were faced with what may be termed "serious trouble." It may be hoped that church counseling clinics will be made to appeal to the normal people who need information, counsel, and orientation for facing ordinary problems. It is conceivable that church counseling centers could come to be utilized constantly by a majority of the membership; only in this way may stigmas now attached to clinic visitation be removed.

The Nature of Clinics

Clinics usually emphasize one of several basic approaches or dimensions. The clinic formulated with disturbed children in mind, the child guidance clinic, usually is maintained within the dimensions of psychiatry and psychology. Staffs usually consist of a psychiatrist, clinical psychologists, and psychiatric social workers. This type of clinic has not been sponsored by churches to any appreciable extent.

The marriage and family relations clinic is usually staffed by counseling psychologists and social workers, with social workers dominating. Although many marriage and family problems are therapeutic in nature, a counselor trained in the dimension of counseling psychology, of social work, or education is usually considered competent to handle the nontherapeutic problems and to recognize those which need referral. Marriage and family relations clinics are staffed by workers who have affiliations with the American Association of Marriage Counselors, the American Personnel and Guidance Association, or the American Psychological Association. The last named of these associations requires the Ph.D. degree for full membership; the other two emphasize training at the Master's degree level and beyond.

A church-sponsored clinic may serve to gain the advantages of the counseling specialist without the objectionable features discussed earlier. It is certain that such clinics must be closely supervised by a board of directors appointed or elected by the sponsoring church body. It is certain that a strong religious affiliation and orientation will be required of practitioners in the clinics. It is possible that such clinicians may have less theological training than that demanded for the religious counselors working in close alliance with an individual church.

It must be said that the role of the church-related clinic has not yet been clearly defined. There is no assurance that the trend for such clinics will grow. The clinic is a means by which church bodies may offer a broader community service than is possible with the ordinary program of counseling found in the individual church. It is likely that strong growth of church-related clinics must wait until more and stronger emphases on church-centered counseling develop. The clinic emphasis in counseling may be compared to the challenge felt by many church groups to go beyond their own doors in an effort to help humanity.

COUNSELING
IN THE CHURCH SCHOOLS

Many church groups organize and administer their own school systems. These schools may be known as church schools or as parochial schools and often cover the entire span of grades offered by public education. These school programs cannot logically succeed without a strong emphasis on counseling. School counseling areas emphasize academic, vocational, and personal-social problems. Although there are few specifics in this writing related to school counseling as such, it must be recognized that the church school comprises an area for a modified type of religious counseling.

Much of the counseling done in the church school is done by the clergyman, who usually assumes a supervisory role in the school. The clergyman is likely to do most of the counseling which is distinctly religious in tone; he is likely to depend upon the teaching staff for implementation of academic and vocational counseling.

Teachers in church schools usually gain competence in academic and vocational guidance through their own academic training programs in schools of education. Guidance services for the schools have become a strong emphasis in public education and this carries over to the church school with little modification. Teachers need training in the administration and use of psychological tests, the keeping and utilization of adequate record systems, the use of occupational information, and counseling techniques related to personal-social problem areas.

These areas are covered to some extent in this book in Chapters IV and V, where the clinical treatments of academic and vocational problems are emphasized as well as the nonclinical approaches to personal-problem counseling. All religious counselors should create opportunity for themselves to become acquainted with the fundamentals of guidance services implemented in both public and church school programs.

REFERRAL RESOURCES
FOR THE RELIGIOUS COUNSELOR

There are several reasons why referral is of great importance to the religious counselor. As long as the church program of counseling is conceived to treat parishioners who are "in real trouble," a large portion of those who come will be deeply disturbed. As the program comes to be conceived as an avenue of help for *all* of the people, the percentage of deeply disturbed will decrease. Because there will be little stigma, the absolute number of deeply disturbed coming to the counselor will increase. It is interesting to note that of the first 200 cases coming to the Ministerial Counseling Center in St. Louis, thirty-two were screened for psychiatric therapy (5).

This indicates that roughly one-sixth of those who come have difficulty beyond the capacity of the typical clergyman to help adequately. While this reveals much about the need for referral to psychotherapists, it is necessary to assert that not all who need to be referred are therapeutic cases. Pending the broader and more comprehensive training of religious counselors, it is probable that referrals should be made to counselors who treat problems in the normal range. Many religious counselors are incapable of good vocational counseling; and, if they are not, they should not hesitate to make referral to school counselors or privately practicing counseling psychologists. It would be better for the religious counselor to serve only as an adequate referral source than to counsel outside his competencies.

Regardless of his training, every religious counselor should carefully investigate, in the community, resources for referral which are acceptable to the religious group he serves. If at all possible, the persons to whom referrals are made should have religious orientations compatible with the religious group from which the counselees come.

The determination of who is an adequate referral resource person is not easy. The medical and psychiatric personnel to whom one might refer do have at least the minimum training required by law for such practitioners. While this is a distinct advantage in determining their competency to practice, it does not mean that every medical or psychiatric practitioner will be an adequate referral for a given parishioner.

In the areas of psychology and other professional counseling dimensions, one does not find legislative sanctions as guidelines in referral. It is true that some states certify psychologists; but to date, these certifying laws at best are vague in determining competency for the specific assignment of counseling and psychotherapy. Among professional counselors of less than Ph.D. status, there are no legislative sanctions.

It is possible to evaluate referral resources to some degree by checking professional affiliations. Competent psychologists almost always belong to the American Psychological Association, most competent school and vocational counselors belong to the American Personnel and Guidance Association, many marriage counselors affiliate with the American Association of Marriage Counselors, and so on.

Competencies may be determined in part by local reputation. In the long run, religious counselors will reserve judgment of complete adequacy until they have observed some first-hand results of the referral resource people in action.

It should be clearly understood that competency depends upon training and experience in specific dimensions, not on the degree held. Most psychiatrists are inadequate vocational counselors and undoubtedly many of them would be poor choices as marriage counselors. A person trained in school counseling would likely be more adept at handling a romantic problem of a teen-ager than would most clinical psychologists. The following may be helpful in determining competencies among referral resources.

The Clinical Psychologist

The field of clinical psychology has developed as a means of evaluating and treating persons having psychological deviations. This includes working with those having emotional distresses, deviational behavior patterns, and abnormal mental maturities. Evaluations are made by wide use of testing devices as well as by observation and inquiry. Emotional distresses and deviant behavior patterns are treated by a process of restructuring the attitudes and personality patterns of the client through a method known as psychotherapy. Psychotherapy consists of communications between counselee and counselor which, along with relationship aspects, produce changes in personality. Psychotherapy does not change or affect the organic conditions the client may have; its chief utility is with functional disorders.

It is usually agreed that the clinical psychologist capable of engaging in psychotherapy must have had extensive training, requiring supervised internship and formal learning experiences, which results in the acquisition of the Ph.D. degree. Clinical psychologists of lesser training may be capable of the testing and evaluation aspects. An adequacy in psychotherapy with functional deviants may be expected only of one who devotes a major portion of a lifetime in preparing himself for the task.

The Psychiatrist

The popular point of view is that the psychiatrist has the same training in evaluation and in psychotherapy as the clinical psychologist, and that he has added to this the understandings and skills of medicine and surgery. This is not entirely correct. The psychiatrist is first and foremost a medical doctor. He has a great deal of training in psychological concepts. His training in psychological testing of the types most often utilized by clinical psychologists is minimal. His diagnoses are usually based on behavioral and observational aspects, plus the psychophysical devices used in assessing organic neural disability. He is expert in diagnosing emotional disorder, inasmuch as such disorders are usually accompanied by concomitant physical changes.

Contact between clergymen and psychiatrists is much more common than between clergy and other psychological practitioners, inasmuch as both are often required to attend the parishioner and his family during periods of severe mental illness. For this and other reasons, the clergy and psychiatrists have developed mutual interests and cooperative attitudes. This is evidenced especially in the vast amount of writing done by psychiatrists on the subject of religiously oriented counseling.

The psychiatrist stands high among referral resources the clergy has, especially if the problem is one of psychopathology. The majority of psychiatrists recognize contributions made by religion to mental health and the treatment of the mentally ill, and they demonstrate a high degree of warmth and acceptance toward the clergy.

The clergyman needs to be aware, however, that psychiatrists in a given community vary not only in their cooperative attitudes but in their emphases in practice. Some psychiatrists specialize in working with children, whereas some are especially expert in dealing with alcoholics. Many psychiatrists are highly interested in treatment of the neurotic group by psychotherapy, and others are more devoted to the emergency treatment of the psychotic group.

In making referral, the clergyman needs to determine the type of practice a particular psychiatrist emphasizes. He may refer different parishioners to different psychiatrists depending upon his evaluation of the problems and of the psychiatrists. He may refer some parishioners to clinical psychologists for long-term psychotherapy; he may refer others to psychiatrists. The fact that psychiatrists are able to administer medicines where indicated must be taken into account. When the clergyman feels definitely that the parishioner needs medical as well as psychological help, he should choose the psychiatrist in lieu of the psychologist.

The clergyman may consider himself fortunate to find a clinic that emphasizes the team approach; but the very fact of the team approach, utilizing psychiatrist, psychologist, and social worker, does not in itself insure competence and a good referral resource for a particular parishioner. Many factors must be considered in choosing resource persons. Training, personality, and attitudes toward religious concepts are all important.

The Counseling Psychologist

The counseling psychologist is a relatively new addition to the roster of practitioners to whom referrals may be made. Counseling psychology has grown from the roots of vocational guidance, psychometric research, and psychotherapeutic methods. Counseling psychologists are committed to work in behalf of the personal development of average people having common everyday problems.

> Because it aims to contribute to the personal development of a great variety of people, counseling psychology does not concern itself only with the more extreme problems presented by individuals who are in need of emergency treatment. In other words, counseling psychology does not place special emphasis upon the development of tools and techniques necessary for intensive psychotherapy with individuals whose emotional growth has been severely distorted or stunted. Counseling psychology, then, leaves to other psychologists the major responsibility for the emergency treatment of psychological disasters (16, p. 283).

The clergyman and religious counselors will find the counseling psychologist a valuable referral resource for vocational problems, many marriage problems, and personal-social problems of many types. It is entirely reasonable that those who have made extensive study of the common problems would be better qualified to help with these than those who have trained to help the deviate and the emotionally-disturbed.

Counseling psychologists may be found in private practice and in institutional settings. The length of training and requirements for supervised practice for counseling psychologists are about the same as those for clinical psychologists. Both groups are strongly affiliated with the American Psychological Association.

The Marriage Counselor

The person who refers to himself as a marriage counselor may have training in any of several dimensions, or he may have no training at all. Clinical and counseling psychologists often accept this title. However, most psychologists who do marriage counseling prefer the psychological label. The greatest number of people who prefer the title, "Marriage Counselor," are trained in the dimension of social casework. This is true in private and in institutional practice.

The religious leader may find well-trained marriage counselors in private practice, but he should be cautious in ascertaining their training and affiliations. Those counselors working in community clinics, especially those affiliated with Family Services Association, usually must pass minimum requirements for training. A large portion of marriage problems necessitate adjustment but do not require psychotherapy. The clergyman should evaluate carefully, and then make referral to a marriage counselor having the qualifications necessary for the particular problem.

Vocational Counselors

The religious leader often needs to refer to a qualified person intimately familiar with the various aspects of vocational counseling. The complexity of the modern work scene is such that one must train specifically for vocational counseling. The counseling psychologist has this training; few clinical psychologists, psychiatrists, or marriage counselors do have. There are many counselors not called psychologists who are adequate vocational counselors, some of whom may be found in public schools and colleges, others in employment services and in vocational rehabilitation facilities. A few vocational counselors offer their services privately under this title, but the qualifications of these must be checked most carefully. The religious leader can usually find most adequate referral resources for vocational counseling among public school counselors, college counseling personnel, and counseling psychologists.

THE SCOPE AND NATURE
OF RELIGIOUS COUNSELING

Just what the scope and nature of religious, Christian, or pastoral counseling is or should be has certainly not been agreed upon. There is a variety of opinion ranging from the conviction that man has no problem except the spiritual and that all problems are functions of spiritual impoverishment to the feeling that all secular counseling, even that done by the atheist, is in reality spiritually oriented. Between these extremes are many intermediate positions.

The Ministry to the Spirit

In an early writing, Bonnell (2) speaks of "a ministry to the spirit and indirectly to the mind and body—a ministry which, therefore, necessarily goes beyond the practice of the psychiatrist or the physician." In this same book, *Pastoral Psychiatry*, Bonnell deplores the transforming of pastors into "fourth-rate psychiatrists."

It is probable that there has been a moving away from the concept of placing the basis of *all* adjustment upon a "right" relationship with God. At the same time, there are many clergymen who feel that the exclusive function of the clergy or religious worker is to aid in establishing and maintaining this God-man relationship. The intent is to have the client place himself within the will and purpose of the Creator and to yield himself to the ministrations of God. In some contexts this is referred to as a "surrender." The exact nature of this experience differs with the various religious groups, but generally consists of an act of confession, repentance, and consecration. These ends may be promoted by prayer, scripture study, and various religious rituals.

Within this framework of conviction, some see this type of ministration as sufficient to solve all of the parishioners' problems. Everyday trials of life as well as inevitable illnesses and death are thought of as trials which God has intended and which need no counseling ministration. An extension of this point of view is that man's basic problem is one of adjustment to the will of God, that he will have other problems, and that he may be able to receive help from various practitioners; but the task of the religious worker ends with the purely spiritual exercise of facilitating the God-man relationship.

Although the authorities in the field of pastoral counseling do not seem to accept this confining position for the clergy, it may well be that a majority of the clergy feel that the clergyman is overstepping his intended bounds in entering the broader area of problems suggested by most of the recent writings. It is also possible that many clergymen find this position a comfortable one and refuse to yield because they are afraid that the spiritual nature of their ministry must suffer from a broad emphasis.

Counseling on Conscious Religious Problems

In a sincere effort to restore order to the confusion surrounding the scope of the clergyman's counseling function, Bier (1) has advocated that the pastoral counselor restrict himself to people with "conscious religious problems." Bier believes that the work of the pastoral counselor should clear the way for the parishioner to "practice his religion as he desires." He is able to maintain a rather strong distinction between the secular and religious counselor.

> There is, therefore, no intrinsic connection between the work of the secular counselor and the better religious functioning; the contribution which the [secular counselor] has to make in this area is remote and dispositive only. With the pastoral counselor, however, the contribution to a better religious life is intrinsic and direct, since he frees the counselee of religious conflicts. . . . For the individual, however, with conscious religious problems, once these problems are resolved, the way is cleared for him to practice his religion as he desires (1, p. 12).

It is difficult to ascertain just what problems Bier would classify as "religious." Depending upon one's concept of the "conscious religious problem," marriage and family problems may all be excluded or all be included. The Protestant and Catholic views on the nature of "conscious religious problems" may not always coincide, for instance.

Leslie has answered Bier as follows:

> Others of us, however, while seeking to discover our distinctive role, do not find it useful to restrict our counseling to purely "conscious religious problems." There is a sense in which any problem of personal or interpersonal adjustment is "religious."
> . . . Rather than make distinctions between conscious or unconscious religious problems, I prefer to say that there is a religious dimension to any human problem; my task is to try to work effectively with those who chose, for reasons that are seldom wholly clear, to work with me, a clergyman (12, p. 54).

It is safe to say, however, that many noted clergymen support the basic contentions of Bier, especially in the direction of outlining a distinctive role for the clergyman in his counseling function.

Counseling—A Function of Love

There is a conviction among many of the religious writers today that any counseling activity proceeds out of a foundation of love and concern of one person for another, and that, inasmuch as this is true, the presence of a type of loving or caring gives spiritual dimension to counseling. Bonthius says:

> It appears to me that the counseling relationship can be one of love in profound measure. And that, when this is the case, the truth of God is received, though the idea of God is never mentioned (3, p. 74).

Wise says in this context:

> If the situation is one where the basic relationship is that of love in the sense of seeking the fulfillment of the personality of the counselee, then God does not have to be brought into the situation; God is in the situation (23, p. 154).

Rickel contributes as follows:

> The universal solvent is love, not scientific knowledge, and that love is the love of God. Hence therapy becomes a religious endeavor (18, p. 39).

It is difficult to envision any sustained counseling effort which is not predicated on some degree or some type of caring about the client. This idea is discussed at length in Chapter II.

SPIRITUAL DIMENSION AND COUNSELOR-CLIENT EXPECTATIONS

It is easy to postulate a spiritual dimension for all counseling endeavor. It is indeed possible that the work of a given counselor may have spiritual dimension without his conscious knowledge, his intent, or his desire. To include all counseling work under a spiritual dimension in this broad sense, however, does little toward helping us to evolve a distinctive function for the religiously oriented counselor.

This writer suggests that the distinction of pastoral, Christian, or religious counseling cannot be expressed as functions of problem types or of the existence of some level of loving or caring on the part of the counselor. Neither can such work be distinguished by the presence or absence of religious symbolism. To postulate that the role of the counselor is limited to a given type of problem would be to invite confusion concerning what types of problems have spiritual dimension. To postulate that the attitude of caring about the client determines religious nature of the counseling experience would be to assign religious intent to many who neither claim it nor wish their counseling to be so construed. To suggest that religious symbolism typifies religious counseling would be to enforce the promiscuous use of such symbols in the religious setting.

A more reasonable criterion is the expectations of client and counselor. Where the counselor expects to counsel within a religious framework or where the client believes he is participating in an experience which has at least religious undertones, then the task becomes distinctive as religious counseling. This would imply that some counseling work is religious because of the position of the counselor. Thus, the clergyman performs a religious function whenever he counsels, because both he and the parishioner expect religious undertones. On the other hand, the setting of the work may typify the counseling effort as religious, inasmuch as those who seek out religious workers in religious settings usually expect a counseling process having some religious orientations.

Even though the criterion of expectations be accepted, frames of reference for religious counselors may vary greatly. Some religious workers believe in a loving God who values His people intrinsically and individually. Others maintain a frame of reference which is distinctly sectarian in nature; and they endeavor to promote, along with the adjustment of the client, an acceptance of a usually narrow and specific set of doctrinal beliefs. Still others have concepts of a divine force which does not involve a god as a personal entity. Some think of God as a force in the universe, and some identify God as nature.

THE USE OF SPIRITUAL AIDS AND SYMBOLS

It has been designated previously that religious counseling does not require the use of spiritual symbols as a distinctive feature. Even so, it is true that many religious counselors utilize spiritual symbols and the aids of prayer, scriptures, and rites. It is agreed that such symbols and aids have a usefulness in religious counseling; but it is suggested that their promiscuous use would not be desirable. Bonthius (3) says, "To attempt to 'Christianize' counseling by diagnosing and prescribing in theological or evangelistic terms will be self-defeating to the extent that it blocks the individual's own communication of the problem." He goes on to relate an example of a woman under treatment who would not have profited by religious symbolism because of her negative attitude.

On the other hand, it is probably true that the majority of those who come to the clergyman expect him to utilize spiritual tools; and they would benefit from such use. The key to the situation is the previous experience of the parishioner as well as his present and immediately past attitudes.

It should be recognized that the use of religious symbolism and spiritual aids must be evaluated on a twofold basis. It may be acknowledged that at least a part of the value in the use of spiritual aids is psychological. Such aids may improve the attitude and develop a sense of security. Prayer and scripture reading may prepare the client for a calm approach to the problem; and various religious rites are capable of enveloping the parishioner in a sense of forgiveness and general well-being.

Few religious counselors would use spiritual aids because of their psychological effect alone. Rather, many counselors believe in the power of a loving God. They believe the religiously oriented performances of prayer and ritual both prepare the parishioner to receive the spiritual blessing and bring the Spirit forcefully into activity on behalf of the client.

COUNSELING—
A COOPERATIVE VENTURE

There is confusion concerning the place of science in the process of religious counseling. A number of authorities both of the spiritual dimension and of the scientific dimension have stated that psychological healing could be possible only when the seeker finds a satisfying relationship with the ultimate source of peace.

Among those who place great emphasis on religious values in maintaining mental integration is Carl G. Jung, the noted Swiss psychiatrist. He says:

> Among all my patients in the second half of life—that is to say, over thirty-five—there has not been one whose problem in the last resort was not that of finding a religious outlook on life. It is safe to say that every one of them fell ill because he has lost that which the living religions of every age have given to their followers, and none of them has been really healed who did not regain his religious outlook. This of course has nothing whatever to do with a particular creed or membership of a church (10, p. 264).

Tillich has said, "a real healing of a person as a person is not possible without a relationship to the ultimate" (21).

There are those, however, who are so intent on maintaining the spiritual emphasis in counseling that they would deny the appropriateness or the value of any scientific treatment, specific or accessory. Rickel not only emphasizes the place of love in therapy but speaks out in opposing the necessity of a scientific partnership in the counseling process.

> *It will not be the knowledge that modern psychology has made available to him that will enable him to help others; it will be the power and insight which his spiritual experience of rebirth provided him* (18, pp. 36-37).

Rickel has been answered by a number of authorities including Wise, Millet, and Dicks:

> While we can agree with many specific insights, such as the place of love in therapy, we cannot agree with the need to set the religious and scientific points of view over against each other as he does (23, pp. 40-41).
>
> Experience has shown that neither physician nor priest is necessarily the best therapist for the individual sufferer. The most successful therapist is the one who has come to a sufficient state of inner resolution to offer no threat to the sufferer, and who through his own struggle to attain it is capable of deep understanding of the sufferer's trouble. His is genuinely a religious gift in the true sense (13, p. 42).
>
> Spiritual resources and scientific knowledge do not constitute two incompatible entities. Nor is it an inconsistency to draw upon the

inner, spiritual forces that God has placed within the personality
and at the same time to employ psychotherapeutic techniques. The
combined use of religion and psychiatry in the treatment of the emotionally ill constitutes, rather, a total approach to the problem
(6, p. 43).

In giving credit to the contributions of secular psychology to
religious counseling Bonthius says:

> The conclusion here reached regarding counseling is that, though
> it has been developed in large part by secular therapists, it is an ap-
> proach to personal problems which can mediate divine love and pre-
> pare the individual for more meaningful understanding of the Chris-
> tian message (3, p. 78).

The vast majority seem to agree that scientific psychology and
religious concern for the individual must ramify each other in full
service to the parishioner. Tillich supports this view and further
indicates that scientists and clergymen have supporting, though
distinctively separate, roles.

> The minister exercises the pastoral function, and he should never
> become a little doctor or a little psychotherapist. He would not heal
> in this case, but would prevent healing. . . . On the other hand, the
> doctor or the psychotherapist, although he may be a bearer of much
> spiritual power, should not impose religious symbols on his patient,
> either Christian or non-Christian ones. He must remain in the realm
> of medical healing, even if indirectly he exercises pastoral healing
> (20, p. 26).

Counseling or Psychotherapy

The religious worker is concerned with spiritual problems in counseling explicitly presented as such by the parishioner.
He is also concerned with personal problems that are not specifically
spiritual. When the clergyman has pursued an adequate program
of training, he may also do psychotherapy. This is not usually the
case. According to Bier:

> The ordinary clergyman who engages in counseling should limit
> himself to the problems of normal people, leaving to the professional
> counselor or to the psychotherapist people with genuine personality
> disorders. Emotional problems which are realistically related to the
> circumstances of life, such as illness, death, or natural catastrophe,
> are the domain of the counselor, not those disturbances that are

irrational and unrelated to reality. The latter belong to the domain of psychological disorders and are properly reserved for the psychotherapist (1, p. 9).

As pointed out earlier, some religious institutions engage the services of a specialist for handling emotional disorders. Where this is not the case, the clergyman may resort to referrals of parishioners with emotional disorders.

This division of labor between clergyman and psychotherapist and the dichotomizing of normal and abnormal problems cannot be passed over so lightly. Facing the problem squarely, one must concede that the clergyman cannot limit himself to certain types of problems. He is the representative of God to all his parishioners. While it is true that he can successfully refer many to psychotherapists for treatment, he can never segregate himself from these even after referral. On the other hand, there are those who will not or cannot receive psychotherapeutic aid; and the clergyman will be forced to deal with them on some level and in some manner.

The psychological literature is replete with attempts to separate counseling from psychotherapy. This has never been successfully accomplished and the controversy need not be extended into this book. Suffice it to say that human problems occur along a continuum from the most surface-level to the deeply unconscious problems of psychopathology. The clergy should avoid becoming obsessed with abnormal problems to the neglect of the proximate problems of the parishioners. Religious workers should endeavor to deal in counseling with the basically normal folk and should call freely upon medical and nonmedical psychotherapy for assistance with abnormals. They cannot choose their clients as can other practitioners because of their unique position in the religious community. In the main, however, their role in working with the deeply disturbed can be supportive and accessory rather than purposefully psychotherapeutic.

References

1. Bier, William C., "Goals in Pastoral Counseling," *Pastoral Psychology.* February, 1959, pp. 7-13.
2. Bonnell, John Sutherland, *Pastoral Psychiatry.* New York: Harper and Brothers, 1938.

3. Bonthius, Robert H., "What Is 'Christian' Counseling?" *Journal of Pastoral Care.* Summer, 1959, pp. 69-79.

4. Burton, Joe W.(ed.), "Third Counseling Conference Planned," *Southern Baptist Family Life Education.* January, February, March, 1958.

5. Deitchman, Robert B., "The Evolution of a Ministerial Counseling Center," *Journal of Pastoral Care.* Winter, 1957, pp. 207-215.

6. Dicks, Russell L., "Is Psychotherapy a Religious Process?" *Pastoral Psychology.* March, 1956, pp. 43-44.

7. ————, *Pastoral Work and Personal Counseling.* New York: The Macmillan Company, 1947.

8. Hiltner, Seward, "Credentials for Pastoral Counseling?" *Pastoral Psychology.* January, 1961, pp. 46-50.

9. Hulme, William E., *How To Start Counseling.* New York: Abingdon Press, 1955.

10. Jung, Carl Gustav, *Modern Man in Search of a Soul.* New York: Harcourt, Brace & World, Inc., 1936.

11. Kemp, Charles F., "Life-Situation Preaching and Pastoral Work," *Pastoral Psychology.* October, 1956, pp. 35-46.

12. Leslie, Robert C., "Readers Forum," *Pastoral Psychology.* October, 1959, p. 54.

13. Millet, John A. P., "Is Psychotherapy a Religious Process?" *Pastoral Psychology.* March, 1956, pp. 41-43.

14. National Association for Mental Health, *The Clergy and Mental Health.* New York: National Association for Mental Health. n.d.

15. Oates, Wayne E., "Report on Commission in the Ministry," *Annals of the New York Academy of Sciences.* Volume 63, Article 3, 1955.

16. Pepinsky, Harold B. (Chairman), Committee on Definition, Division of Counseling Psychology, A. P. A. "Counseling Psychology as a Specialty," *American Psychologist.* June, 1956, pp. 282-285.

17. Queener, E. Llewellyn, "The Psychological Training of Ministers," *Pastoral Psychology.* October, 1956, pp. 29-34.

18. Rickel, William, "Is Psychotherapy a Religious Process?" *Pastoral Psychology.* March, 1956, pp. 36-39.

19. Shedron, Mark, "Opportunities for Study, Training, and Experience in Pastoral Psychology," *Pastoral Psychology.* January, 1961, pp. 11-30.

20. Tillich, Paul, "The Theology of Pastoral Care," *Pastoral Psychology.* October, 1959, pp. 21-26.

21. ————, "Is Psychotherapy a Religious Process?" *Pastoral Psychology.* March, 1956, pp. 39-40.

22. Ward, Archibald F., and Granville L. Jones, *Ministering to Families of the Mentally Ill.* New York: The National Association for Mental Health. n.d.

23. Wise, Carroll, "Is Psychotherapy a Religious Process?" *Pastoral Psychology*. March, 1956, pp. 40-41.

24. ————, *Pastoral Counseling in Theory and Practice*. New York: Harper and Brothers, 1951.

25. Yoder, Walter H., "Judgmental Attitudes in Pastoral Counseling," *Journal of Pastoral Care*. Fall, 1955, pp. 162-165.

II

Psychology
and Religion

TWO DISCIPLINES—
TOGETHER AND APART

Information from many sources (historical, ethnological, and archeological) points to the conclusion that religious experience has always been deeply rooted in man's nature. Through the ages, man has clung tenaciously to his religious concepts (8).

Man's quest for an explanation of his being and his destiny is a product of his superior brain. Man is a thinker; he must seek reasons for all things. In a sense, religion is the result of man's seeking for an explanation of the mysteries of life and death. In another sense, religion is the result of a search not only for meaning but for security.

Religion and psychology were once but a single discipline. Even in our Western culture, psychology, philosophy, and religion were placed together academically until the eighteenth century. We are told that in other parts of the world today (in countries embracing Hinduism, for instance) psychology and religion are the same subject and always have been so (8).

Psychology and Its Aims

The term "psychology" has a variety of meanings. "Psychology" in lay terminology seems to refer to the clever and subtle efforts of man to motivate and influence his fellows. This, indeed, is applied psychology. In the academic sense, psychology refers to the study of behavior. There is no reason to doubt that psychology has been in existence since the beginning of relationships between humans. Man has always sought both to influence and study the behavior of his fellows as well as other organisms. In this sense, psychology and religion came into existence together.

The distinct separation of psychology and religion began during the eighteenth century when certain scholars began to think of psychology as a science. These men began to question the validity of basing understandings of man's behavior on philosophy, inaccurate observations, and so-called divine revelations. A laboratory was set up in Leipzig, Germany in 1879, under the leadership of Wilhelm Wundt, with the aim of subjecting behavior to accurate observation and scientific experimentation.

The history of scientific psychology has been erratic, and many of the early concepts have been shown to be as unscientific as was the "armchair philosophy" which preceded them. However, rising out of these early attempts has come a psychology which deserves the scientific label. This is the psychology of the modern university and of the well-trained psychologist of our day.

Psychology has endeavored to study man's behavior through empirical approaches. In claiming to be a science, it studies man's behavior objectively. The methods of study may be subjected to rigorous evaluation, and the findings may be verified through repetition of techniques by a number of independently working researchers. These findings are largely devoid of subjective opinions and philosophizing by prejudiced workers. The scientific emphasis caused a separation of religion and psychology.

Religion and Its Aims

The separation of psychology and religion was not one of aims but of approach to the aims. During the early days of scientific psychology, the emphasis was on studying man's behavior and not on motivating it. At least a part of religious subject matter was and is the same as that of psychology, the nature and behavior of man. Religion has usually emphasized the motivation of behavior rather than the objective study of it. Religion has been content to depend upon other than scientific data for its understanding of the nature and behavior of man. Information concerning man has come to religion through supernatural manifestations. These have consisted of reported experiences, utterances of men said to be under divine inspiration, and the scriptures, among others. Religion has utilized observations in determining man's nature but without the careful controls typical of modern psychological research. Religion counts its source of truth as being from the supernatural God revealed in various ways.

Inevitable Conflicts

Thus, psychology and religion, although having some of the same aims, have separated in their methods of attaining them. Conflicts have become inevitable. The foremost thinkers in religious circles have sanctioned psychology as an objectified study of man's nature and behavior. It is true that the rank and file of religiously oriented people look with suspicion on psychology and believe that psychology seeks to discredit religion. Many psychologists, on the other hand, view religion as pure superstition and without basis in reality.

As psychology has pursued its investigations, various findings have been at variance with some of the beliefs established by religion. The undeniable truth is that many but not all of the findings of psychological research are valid; and this is acknowledged by the trained psychological researcher. Most thinking people also come to the conclusion that many of the supposedly divine revelations are valid and real while some are not. Since individuals in both psychological and religious circles make assertions, derived either from strong prejudices and biased judgments or from faulty research, suspicion and distrust between these two groups is widespread. This is an unfortunate circumstance.

Actually, psychology is a science devoting itself to searching after truth in much the same way as does the science of physics or chemistry. Psychology makes no attempt to disprove any religious concept or to contradict any statement purported to have come from God. In no sense does scientific psychology disclaim the spiritual elements of life, although it is true that some psychologists do not believe in a supreme being at all. Psychology as a science disclaims a primary interest in the spiritual because the spiritual affairs of man, whether real or fancied, simply are not within the scope of psychology except for their motivating influence on behavior. Religious experience is not the specific professional concern of the chemist; religious experience concerns the psychologist as a scientific researcher only because of its impact on behavior. So far as this impact is concerned, it leaves its mark on the behavior of the believer in spiritual affairs whether such affairs are real or fancied.

From all this, one may see that even scientific psychology cannot maintain complete separation from religious experience. Even so, there does seem to be advantage in maintaining the two disciplines, one to base its conclusions on objective research and the other on faith and supernatural leadership. Despite the conflict, there are many religiously oriented people who are able to accept the tentative findings of psychology without conflict. Likewise, some students of psychology are able to interpret their findings within a religious framework. It is encouraging to find that leading thinkers in each discipline have adopted a positive, accepting attitude one for the other.

Togetherness in Healing

The neat cleavage in channels of psychological and religious direction breaks down almost completely as the psychologist turns his emphasis away from his objective study of the individual toward the relief of his problems through counseling and psychotherapy. As stated earlier, religion has always emphasized motivating, influencing, and helping man more than has psychology. Since the end of World War II, psychologists have become intensely interested in counseling and psychotherapy. With this interest, the separation of religion and psychology has become much more untenable than before. Becker says:

> On the more theoretical side, psychology has found that the relationship with religion, which was neatly kept in check so long as the

psychologist was the detached, experimental investigator, has become all "muddied up" now that psychotherapists are deeply involved in the business of changing persons. The goals of psychotherapy and the real concerns of psychotherapists place psychotherapists in juxtaposition to the goals and work of religion relative to the individual person. Thus psychology and religion, which entered into a state of legal separation during the early part of this century in order to allow psychology to thrive as a science unfettered by doctrinal restraints, have fallen in love again and are at least cohabiting if not fully married to each other because of the influence of psychotherapy on psychology (1, p. 567).

A Value Orientation for Psychology

The pure scientific psychologist has been prone to deny a value orientation for his discipline. He has supposed that holding values would interfere with his objectivity. The psychotherapist cannot be a value-free practitioner. An amoral therapy is a contradiction in terms (17). Becker also contributes to this thought.

> What this paper is suggesting is that psychotherapy, by virtue of the obvious ethical implications involved in its "caring" for or "treating" persons and because of its unavoidable espousal of some view of man and some value orientation as to his true well-being, has brought psychology and religion into a contiguity and interlacing of work where it is no longer possible to distinguish neatly the psychologist from his religious colleague. . . . At this point it is enough to recognize that psychology and religion are linked arm in arm in the depths and in the implications of psychotherapeutic practice (1, p. 568).

What Becker has said concerning the similarity of the psychologist and his religious colleague is more true in relation to the aims and objectives of the two practitioners than in relation to the overt techniques used. The clergyman in particular will continue to use spiritual aids to counseling, but it is unlikely that the psychologist outside the religious setting will make use of them. It is true that the psychological specialist in the church setting may be completely indistinguishable from the psychologist in other practice, both from the point of view of aims and overt techniques.

Tillich (15) has said that religion is ultimate concern. The religious worker seeks the ultimate wholeness for those with whom he comes in contact. His concern for the proximate problems is overshadowed by his concern for the best that life may offer his parishioner both in this life and in the life he envisions for his parishioner after death (9). Is the aim of the psychotherapist different? As Boisen (2) indicates, a person who is mentally ill is profoundly concerned over the reasons for his existence, the meaning of life, and his ultimate destiny. Johnson says of mental illness and its treatment:

> It is, therefore, akin to religious experience, for the concern is ultimate enough to involve the whole life. As a major crisis, it may either make or break a person. There is no solution by evading the crisis in drifting or delusional defenses. Recovery comes like a religious conversion by facing the truth and honestly confessing it, then deciding upon a new and constructive way of life (11, p. 576).

From this there seem to be only two distinctions between the aims of the religious worker and those of the psychotherapist. The psychotherapist in his concern for the best life for the client and the improvement of society does not usually call into play the forces of a supernatural God. He does not usually extend his "ultimate concern" to the life after death.

Surface Problems and Religious Meaning

It should be remembered that this writing does not place sole emphasis upon the problems of mental illness. It is true that the deeper problems are more fraught with religious meaning than are the more surface problems. Even so, some surface problems may have imbedded in them a great deal of religious significance. Again we are indebted to Johnson who writes:

> Of course, no decisions are as trivial as they may seem, for they have deeper motivations than appear and farther reaching consequences than we often foresee. If a vocational decision is projected from a searching struggle with the meaning of human destiny and my responsible role in the larger context of eternal values, it will be religious in ultimate concern. It is in the crisis of dire need and acute distress, whether in illness or not, as decisions are weighed in the balance of great perspectives with devotion to ultimate values that we are religious (11, p. 577).

It is apparent that a counselor performing at any level may see his work as having religious value. The church-related counselor working with the surface problems of young people is, indeed, a full-time religious worker.

THE SPIRITUAL AND THE PSYCHOLOGICAL IN PROBLEM SOLVING

The Human Dilemma

In the complex modern society, man is confronted with many difficulties, which may be described in three categories. He may be physically ill or malformed, or he may have his tissues damaged in some manner; he may have anxieties proceeding from psychological and situational conflicts; and, he may be spiritually disturbed.

The human dilemma would not be so disconcerting should the individual's malfunctioning occur in strictly segmented fashion. To be physically ill or psychologically anxious would be disturbing enough. It is not unusual, however, for the human to have physical infirmities that bring about additional and concomitant psychological anxiety. On the other hand, psychological anxieties often cause physical illness of the psychosomatic type. The situation may be made worse still, if, in addition to coexisting physical and psychological difficulties, the individual experiences spiritual disturbance such as guilt or insecurity concerning his ultimate destiny. Not only may the human being have three varieties of troubles; each of the three may accentuate the other two.

Tillich offers valuable confirmation of the above views:

> There are three levels of healing: the medical, the psychotherapeutic and the religious. The three are distinguished but not separated. Although in principle they are different in function, they overlap in the actuality of the healing processes (16, pp. 25-26).

Curran (5) also sees the human dilemma in three dimensions, ". . . pastoral counseling incorporates this third dimension. The person has come for personal help certainly, but he has come too, to reorganize not only his relationship with himself and others but his relationship with God."

Treating the Whole Man

Since treatment of human problems must be related to the causes of disability, it would seem that the person must be helped as a whole person rather than as a segmented person, if he is to be adequately helped. As reasonable as this seems, one will observe the segmented treatment of human difficulty to be the rule rather than the exception. Most physicians treat physical ailments without due regard to the psychological stresses underlying them. Peptic ulcers are known for the most part to be caused by psychological tension; yet the majority of ulcer patients receive only a treatment consisting of diet and internal medicine. Some physicians do not regard psychological treatment as being valid and feel that the chances are good that the source of tensions will be removed automatically in time.

Many religious workers approach both physical and emotional distress using only spiritual aids. This is more true of emotional than of physical distress. Without taking anything away from the power of God, we may believe that psychological and medical treatment would enhance the chances of the parishioner to recover.

The relationship of spiritual and psychological approaches to emotional distress is very difficult to ascertain. Most religiously oriented people will assert that God is able to heal any infirmity, if He chooses to do so. Few people who believe in God deny His omnipotence. Thus, it may be asserted that, if God wills it, He can straighten a crooked limb or cause cancerous tissue to disappear.

There was a time when most people regarded the healing of physical infirmities as being the direct intervention of a divine power. Some groups still maintain that the only proper approach to healing of any sort is through divine intervention of a supernatural power called forth by the demonstrated faith of the sufferer or of those who intercede for him. These groups hold that, if faith is sufficient, miracles will be performed.

It seems safe to say that, even among religious folk, few believe God uses His power to bring about miraculous cures in the physical bodies of men. This does not deny that the ultimate source of healing power comes from God. Few people wait for direct intervention of a supernatural force to heal them; most accept the ministrations of medical science. Even those who frequent the tents of the "faith healers" have, for the most part, tried various medical approaches.

Most religious people view the ministrations of doctors and nurses as an indirect ministration of a divine force. Those who pray for God's help in time of illness usually ask Him to guide the doctors so that they may be instruments of God's power as they seek to help the patient. Those who embrace this concept also think of the development of new drugs and other aspects of medical science as being gifts of a benevolent God who desires that His people may have the instruments of healing. Most people, whether claiming a religious background or not, are willing to concede that many people are alive today who would not be alive except for the wonders of medical science.

Spiritual Aids in Emotional Illness

Although the rank and file accept the medical approach to physical difficulties, few have accepted psychiatric or psychological approaches to the relief of emotional stresses. Many people still are prone to regard emotional distress as arising from their wrongdoings and improprieties. Many are also prone to believe that the reasonable cure for psychological distress is to be forgiven for sin and to return to God's will. No one is able to say conclusively that God does not bring about both physical and emotional difficulties as a punishment for sin. The point is that most people accept physical illness as arising from definite factors in the environment, but they cannot accept emotional illness in the same way.

It is easy to accept the causation of a disease such as pneumonia as the presence of a microorganism, but it is still difficult for people to accept the causation of anxiety or depression as being an environmental factor. Surely it is true that antiquated notions concerning mental illness are among the chief deterrents to a faster progress in its control and treatment.

We may assert with some assurance that emotional distresses have definite causes arising from the environment, just as do physical illnesses. We may also believe that the relief of these distresses must follow a definite program of medical and psychological treatment. Should we follow these assertions rigidly, we could reduce the use of spiritual aids in the healing of emotional illnesses to the same category as in the physical. The doctors and psychologists could proceed to treat the patient along lines which have been proved scientifically valid, while friends, relatives, and religious leaders pray that God may guide the hands and intellect of those who minister to the sick and distressed. In this, as in the physical area of treatment, there is no denial of the power of God to heal.

Such a simple explanation of the relationship of spiritual factors to the treatment of emotional distress is far from sufficient. The truth is that although microorganisms cause physical illness and childhood and other events totally unrelated to the spiritual lives of people do cause emotional illness, other emotional distresses are brought about in whole or in part by the lack of conformity to religious principles.

There is absolutely no doubt that religious conflict, guilt, and other phenomena usually identified in the spiritual realm are able to bring about both emotional and physical illnesses in man. Lack of conformity to learned religious values almost always brings about distress.

Spiritual ills are, indeed, difficult to separate from emotional ills. The overt effect of both seems the same. The upset which comes from guilt, for instance, must be described as emotional. Actually, spiritual values comprise a part of the cultural background of the person who has been subjected to them. To violate spiritual values seems only slightly different from violating a cultural value which dictates that the child should love his mother. Thus, we should be able to see why some psychologists believe that there is no classification of spiritual illness. To them, there are only physical and psychological illnesses, since they believe the spiritual, as usually identified, to be only a phase of the psychological existence.

There may be a difference, however, in treatment. No one would be likely to expect good results from treating a virus with psychotherapy or from treating an emotional distress with a sulfa drug. To use purely psychological means of treatment when the cause of distress has come from a spiritual factor seems just as foolhardy.

Those who relate their difficulty as one of guilt, spiritual bereavement, or lack of spiritual security either suffer from such conditions in reality or think that they do. It is logical to base treatment methods on the difficulty as the client perceives it; thus, a spiritual approach for a perceived spiritual problem can hardly be a mistake. From all this, one may see that to place all emotional distress in a psychological context with no regard to spiritual effects is unrealistic. It is just as unrealistic to relegate spiritual aids to the position of accessory importance, as they have been relegated in the area of physical medicine. In the treatment of emotional distress, spiritual aids may in some cases occupy the front position. As a matter of fact, there are cases where the spiritual aid is sufficient for the problem at hand.

It is a rare problem that has only spiritual factors involved. Many basically psychological problems have spiritual overtones. The wisdom shown by psychiatric hospitals which employ chaplains is apparent when one is aware that psychological adjustment cannot be complete in the face of spiritual confusion or insecurity.

CONCEPTS OF HEALING

There is, perhaps, no issue in religion more controversial than healing. Bonnell (3) reminds us that "God is at work both in medical science and in the prayer of faith." Healing is an art, a science, and a ministration of divine love. The controversies about healing concern not only the place of divine love, but man's capacity for bringing such love into the pattern of his efforts to aid his fellow man.

There are a number of concepts of healing among medical, psychological, and religious practitioners. These concepts are seldom mutually exclusive, and they defy efforts at categorization. This author feels that concepts of healing may best be brought into a pattern by studying them as extensions of systems of belief in a supreme being.

It is simple to say that a belief in a supreme being is requisite to any concept of healing that includes a spiritual element. To attempt to discuss concepts of healing under the twofold heading of the believer and the nonbeliever may be an oversimplification. However, one should be aware that belief and nonbelief are not like darkness and light. With every individual there are many shades of what he believes and many gradients of strength with which he believes. So, we must hope that if what follows here is somewhat superficial because the believer and nonbeliever cannot be separated easily, it may at the same time be valuable in delineating some *basic* differences in the spiritual concepts of healing.

In an attempt to sharpen some understandings and at the same time encourage intelligent thought on a subject which has few absolutes, a fourfold treatment, including the concepts of the nonbelieving secular therapist, the believing therapist, the spiritually oriented counselor, and the faith healer, follows. Inasmuch as the religious worker moves among practitioners having many and diverse concepts of healing, he may benefit from such review.

The Nonbelieving Secular Therapist

Those critical of religion have not been able to ignore religion as a fundamental human drive and as a springboard to action. Thus, all who study man's nature and behavior must come to grips with the reality of religion as a force in the lives of those who profess it and as a deep-running all-pervasive cultural force in the lives of everyone, whether or not he acknowledges a religious viewpoint. The therapist who does not believe in a supreme being deals with religious concepts in his fellow human beings as though they were nothing more than psychological manifestations.

This therapist sees man as a psychophysical system and not as a psychological-physical-spiritual being. To the nonbelieving therapist the area of existence referred to by the believer as spiritual is only a subsystem under the psychological area.

The nonbeliever sees every motivation in his client as coming from natural sources. He admits no supernatural possibility. Even so, he cannot escape the fact that his counselees think they are driven and guided by supernatural forces. To him they are driven by unconscious motives springing not from God but from the desire to have a God. Feifel says:

> Psychologists and psychiatrists critical of religion take two major positions: (a) that it is an escape from reality, a residue of fanciful formulations of natural events by which primitive men comforted themselves during their ignorance of these events; and (b) that it represents a mere repetition of infantile experiences (8, p. 565).

In repeating infantile experiences, the counselee is thought to be seeking a father substitute in the person of a supernatural God.

Most practitioners of this type regard religious faith and experience as distinctively helpful to the mental balance of their clients. While they do not believe in a supernatural, they feel that it is beneficial for their clients to believe. Some therapists actually seem to desire a capacity for belief in God, and they realize that life is highly meaningful to many who do believe.

Such persons generally have achieved a humility that comes from long and tedious study. They realize that they have only a little of the vast storehouse of knowledge. Many, if not all of them, accept the possibility that others may have understandings beyond their own. They usually do not deny the possibility of a supernatural, but they have not been convinced by the evidence that there is such.

Most nonbelieving practitioners utilize the purely psychological tools in counseling. Few, if any, enter into argumentation with the clients concerning religious convictions. Even when there are unhealthy or pathological manifestations, such argumentation is not thought to be helpful. In general, the therapist believes the client has a right to his own religious convictions. He is inclined to believe that as factors of personality malfunctioning are relieved by psychological approaches, the client will experience relief also from what he has identified as spiritual stresses. As Feifel says:

> Whether we view religion as wish fulfillment with God as a projected father image of humanity, a collective obsessional neurosis with the God-belief as its center, or man's attempt to approach and understand a transcendental God—regardless of our own religious or nonreligious commitments or attitudes—we need to accept and understand the individual's religious situation as a significant area of his life (8, p. 565).

There is strong resistance to the nonbelieving counselor among those who have religious frames of reference. Most clients do not have the same resistance to nonbelieving physicians; indeed, few medical patients even raise the question concerning the religious concepts of the physician.

The highly trained nonbelieving therapist may utilize psychological approaches to the relief of human problems with very good results. He may be a tool of God without believing in God in the same way that a nonbelieving physician may be. At the same time, one must see that the analogy between the counselor and the physician can go only so far.

It is undeniable that many nonbelieving therapists have not been properly trained in regard to the exclusion of religious nuances from the counseling sessions. Without doubt, they are unable to stay clear of religious issues and may be prone to attack the religious concepts of the client in subtle ways without conscious intent.

The truth is that many nonbelievers are confused about religion and attempt to clear up their own confusions by projecting these into the counseling sessions. In all fairness, however, it must be said that some religious counselors handle some of their confusions in the same way.

The Believing Therapist

While the academic approach in psychology is value-free, it has been shown that this cannot be true of the psychotherapist. This does not mean, however, that every psychotherapist is a believer in a personal God or even in a divine power. It means that all psychotherapists seek the ultimate good for their clients; that is, they demonstrate ultimate concern for their clients. There are, however, many therapists who believe in a supreme being who rules the universe. This may be especially apparent when one observes the vast number of therapists who began as students of the ministry. There is also a surprising proportion of psychologists and psychiatrists who have fathers or brothers who are clergymen (8).

The believing therapist sees man as having motives that are natural and others that may be supernatural. Thus, he believes that his clients may be directly aided and benefited by the ministrations of God; he also believes that the client may benefit if God gives strength and guidance to him, the counselor. The believing therapist usually thinks that all power and motives are vested in God and feels that God can provide extra power at will. The natural forces are thought to be those common to mankind, but the believing counselor concludes that the supernatural may at times oppose and transcend these natural forces.

The believing therapist may be found working as a psychological

specialist in the religious setting. He is often found in private practice, in a clinic, or in a hospital. He may be identified to the public
as clinical psychologist, counseling psychologist, psychiatrist, or
simply as professional counselor.

The believing counselor as envisioned here usually does not utilize
the spiritual aids in counseling. If not in the religious setting, he
is usually restricted from a practice of spiritual nature by the institution in which he works. Most schools, hospitals, and clinics would
be unlikely to sanction an outwardly religious approach. The counselor will be like the believing physician who prays for God's guidance in his treatment of the patient, but who usually does not resort
to prayer and scripture reading with him. The counselor may discuss spiritual values in very broad terms, but he will almost never
coerce or exhort the client into specific religious channels.

The believing counselor will employ basically psychological means
of helping the client adjust. He is likely to see himself as a servant
of God working through psychological approaches to problem solving. It is not essential that the counselor agree with all the suggestions of scientific psychology. He will select and use psychological approaches that do not oppose his own religious convictions.

This counselor understands the pertinence of a well-ordered spiritual frame of reference for the mental health of his clients. He
may encourage his clients to strengthen their spiritual ties, and he
may often refer his clients to ministers and priests in the community so that they may receive direct spiritual counsel. Within
the community, he will seek out practitioners of all types for referral
and will likely refer his clients to other believing counselors and
physicians.

The psychologist who believes that man may be motivated by
a power that is supernatural faces a larger task in evaluating the
client than does the psychologist who ascribes all things to natural
causes. It is much less complex to explain man's behavior as derived
altogether from natural motives than to approach the same task
believing that man may be motivated by a combination of what
is natural and what God has superimposed on the natural. For example, a young man may present himself to the believing counselor
saying that God has called him to do social work. The counselor
administers tests and other evaluating devices all of which show
that the young man is summarily unqualified for the work to which

he believes God has called him. The counselor's task is difficult because he must integrate what may be supernaturally derived motives with natural motives. The nonbelieving counselor would quickly assume that what has been termed the "call" is either confusion or pathology.

The Spiritually Oriented Counselor

The spiritually oriented counselor, as depicted in this writing, represents the counselor who utilizes spiritual aids in helping others to solve their problems. In the religious setting, such a person may be any of the staff members mentioned earlier. Those who are most apt to use spiritual aids are the clergyman, the minister of education, and the youth worker. The specialist working in the church setting is less likely to resort to spiritual aids, but the minister or priest will use spiritual aids consistently.

Most counselors who are spiritually oriented are capable of seeing the problems brought to them as being caused by a variety of factors, and therefore deserving a variety of attack. Most such counselors do believe that there are human problems which are nothing more than spiritual. They wait for the parishioner to express himself; and, if he does indicate a spiritual bereavement, the clergyman moves along purely spiritual channels. Other problems may be expressed as situational conflicts, as psychological tensions, or as decisions. Techniques suitable to the problem are then used.

Almost all spiritually oriented counselors resort to prayer with the seeker and, perhaps, to intercessory prayer for him in private. They often encourage the parishioner to pray for himself. As a general rule, the spiritual counselor feels that benefit accrues if prayer precedes each counseling session. He may also feel that prayer is indicated at the end of the sessions. Some clergymen utilize various religious symbols and rites which are meaningful within a given religious framework. There are those incidents, to be sure, when even the spiritually oriented counselor senses that prayer and symbols would be disturbing. In such case, he may resort to private intercessory prayer.

It is typical that spiritually oriented counselors place more faith in the ministrations of divine power than upon their own efforts or upon psychological aids which they may supply. Nevertheless, many, if not most, spiritual counselors are becoming trained in the use of psychological approaches to counseling. Since they almost invariably see themselves as instruments of God, they endeavor to become the most effective instruments possible.

Needless to say, the spiritual counselor appeals widely not only to church people but to people of all kinds. People are apt to feel that this person has a high sense of moral responsibility and a capacity for caring, which supersede those qualities in other counselors.

The Faith Healer

The author hesitates to include the faith healer as one in a list of counselors because he is widely unpopular among most religious groups. Although the faith healer probably deserves no recognition among professional counselors, he does have a frame of reference for his work which lies at one extreme of a continuum and is therefore included. On the other hand, the religious worker often comes in contact with those who have been to the faith healer and would benefit from reviewing some of the psychological implications derived from a study of faith healing.

The frame of reference of the faith healer is one placing complete trust in divine intervention in the problem of the seeker. Faith healers seem more interested in physical illnesses than in psychological distress, but they have demonstrated some success with certain emotional problems.

In order to understand what happens in the faith healer's tent, it is necessary for one to understand the nature of certain physical and emotional distresses. In the first place, there is the hypochondriac, whose illness is purely imagined. There is no organic basis for the hypochondriac's complaint. Through faith and the emotional impact of the faith healer's ministrations, the imagined illness may subside, either temporarily or permanently.

A psychosomatic illness such as asthma or peptic ulcer is brought about by tensions, but these tensions have caused organs to be susceptible to irritation, inflammation, or disease. There is, therefore, tissue damage in psychosomatic illness even though the original cause was psychological stress. The faith healer may, through engendering faith in the seeker, bring about at least temporary relief for the sufferer by making it possible for the individual to control his tensions.

The hysterical group of maladies are those that have a physical manifestation engendered by a psychological conflict. Many paralyses are hysterical. If the paralysis is prolonged, there may be atrophy of the muscles. Blindness and deafness are often hysterical conditions; there is no organ deficiency, but the seeker does not wish to see or hear. These conditions often yield to the faith healer's ministrations, unless atrophy is advanced.

The physical conditions brought about by accident and disease usually do not yield to the faith healer's methods. If and when they do yield, there seems to be a clear revelation of the power of God to heal directly.

Few people deny God's power to heal, but many doubt the efficacy of the faith healer. Although many faith healers are charlatans, many are sincere believers in God and in their own powers through God. To deny the ability of faith to heal is foolish. It will undoubtedly affect the hypochondriac, the hysteric, and the sufferer of psychosomatic illness. Whether one chooses to accept the psychological explanation and deny the intervention of God through the psychological means or to accept the psychological means of cure as a tool of the divine God must rest with the individual. The sincere faith healer believes in the power of God to heal; he believes that when the seeker is not healed, God has not willed it to be so.

The majority of writings on the issue of faith healing reaffirm the power of faith to heal, but do so within a context of reasonableness. For instance, Fairbanks questions the reasonableness of equating illness with sin, he suggests that various difficulties are the common lot of man, and he emphasizes the concern of God for his people. "Therefore we can approach God with full confidence that He cares and that He will listen and that He will understand" (7).

Ikin sees a revival of the ministry of healing in the church but emphasizes that healing will take place through earnest efforts of the clergy and psychiatry, not by various magical processes.

> Today, the revival of the ministry of healing within the Church, and the development of psychotherapy within the medical profession, indicate that if we can join forces and work in harmony, it should be possible to tackle the problem of disease more effectively

and so fulfill the gospel command more adequately than has yet been feasible (10, p. 44).

Perhaps the most comprehensive treatment of faith healing is given by Salzman (14). In his article, he differentiates faith healing (achieved through belief in the healer) and spiritual healing (achieved by the exercise of faith within a religious context). Both kinds of healing may be highly suspect on occasion, and the possibility of unscrupulousness on the part of charismatic leaders is great. Healing by faith as promoted by the minister seems most desirable.

> Although inquiry should be directed to any reputable claim of healing, I believe that most emphasis should be placed on the least spectacular but most reliable agent of spiritual healing, the minister, who, by his devotion to the whole man, encourages his fulfillment as a natural, spiritual, and existential being (14, p. 155).

DETERMINISM VERSUS
FREEDOM OF THE WILL
Is man free to choose his direction or has this already

been determined for him by his environment? This controversy is an old one which will always be a source of contention among those who study man's nature and behavior. It is a question of such great importance to the field of counseling that it must be discussed briefly in a chapter on psychology and religion.

The Psychological Position

Needless to say, the basic psychological position favors determinism. It is only reasonable that those scientists who have studied man's behavior objectively, without taking into account the possible presence of a divine force operating in the lives of men, should arrive at the conclusion that man's behavior is determined by his experiences and his heredity. The philosophy of determinism maintains that man can only do that which has already been determined for him by his heredity, his environment, and his earlier experiences. Thus, he has no freedom of choice. When a situation that seems to imply choice for man arises, he searches for an answer to his decision-provoking situation; but even in search-ing, it is already determined what he shall do.

Determinism differs considerably from fatalism. Fatalism holds that the individual cannot escape a fate that has been predestined for him. The philosophy of determinism allows for the possibility of interference. Thus, a child may be prone to choose bad conduct but is deterred from doing so by hearing his Sunday school lesson taught. Determinism may be varied by events up to the instant of decision; but, theoretically, the individual himself has no power of determining.

While the above represents the basic psychological viewpoint, it is incorrect to say that all psychologists are in agreement. Few believe in determinism as an unswerving and unmodifiable force. Many psychologists believe that basically man's behavior is de-termined or at least is strongly directed by past experiences, but that man's superior intellect may obviate the effects of earlier ex-periences. Undeniably, man has the greatest brain potential of any organism; he may, therefore, be able to reason out the consequences of his behavior and at least dilute the effects of experience. Yet, even in this framework, the sharp thinker may discern that the intellects of men vary, and that the possession of this or that power of intellect is in itself a determiner of the direction adopted by the individual. The person who is fanatically devoted to the theory of determinism can usually win in debate over all who oppose.

The Religious Position

There is little doubt that the Scriptures establish man as a creature with freedom to choose, at least on some issues. While it is natural to expect that those who study human behavior from the purely objective and natural point of view would adopt deter-minism, it is also to be expected that those who believe in super-natural forces dwelling within the human would believe in freedom of the will. In this context, man is something more than an animal; he has a spiritual being as well as a physical body. This spirit in man may lend him a power to "will" his behavior in opposition to past experiences.

Some say that the human goes toward freedom because of an indwelling spirit of God; others say that man's behavior is determined by his heredity and also by his present and past environment. The entire implications in the question of determinism versus freedom of the will cannot be consummated on the above duality. The controversy has continued for centuries and will continue, and few of the participating writers demonstrate complete loyalty to either side. Jonathan Edwards (6), a classic proponent of freedom of the will, does not claim an unmodified freedom for man. Neither are the concepts of Albert Outler (13) in favor of unqualified freedom. These and others do believe that there is a human capacity of freedom of the will, which has basis in an elevated level of existence.

Pertinence of Determinism to Counseling Theory

Why is the question of determinism or freedom of the will so important to counseling theory? It is because the culpability for conduct revolves with the question. Basically, blame may be fixed upon an individual who acts against society's codes only if he has freedom to choose; but if his actions are already determined, he is not culpable and should not be judged for his behavior. According to an unmodified determinism, if a man steals, it is because of heredity and earlier experiences over which he has no control; and if he kills he is not to be blamed. Those who believe in determinism accept punishment for crime only as education for other would-be criminals and as protection for society. Punishment becomes a determiner of future action on the part of the criminal being punished and on the part of others who are aware of the punishment.

There seems to be a growing conviction among men everywhere that those who offend are not altogether to blame for their actions. Such philosophies tend to accent the educative and preventive means in the solution of such problems. Operationally, the chasm presumed to exist between those who embrace determinism and those who believe in man's freedom is not as wide as some believe. For instance, if one believes in determinism, he must believe that the effect of present motivations may change the pressures exerted by past experiences. Thus, a juvenile who sets out to rob a store must wait thirty minutes in the alley for the policeman to walk this part of his beat. While waiting, he has time to contemplate;

and having contemplated, he decides not to go through with it. His action has been determined by his thinking, the policeman's presence, and other factors. The freedom-of-the-will point of view is that the juvenile exercised his power to choose between right and wrong.

Almost everyone believes that the past influences present decisions. The emphasis placed on training the young assures us that most people believe present instruction influences future actions. It is possible that man has the original inclination toward evil. It is possible, as some believe, that some men or all men have either spiritual beings or spiritual relationships which aid them in overcoming evil inclination and make it possible for them to choose the positive direction rather than the negative one. It is possible that man has one free choice—to accept the indwelling spirit of God or to reject it.

What are the exact truths about these things? We cannot know; but we do know that these thoughts have challenged man for ages and that his tentative conclusions concerning these matters have had much to do with the evolution of theories of counseling.

The philosophy and the technique of the individual counselor may be immeasurably influenced by his concept of determinism. The chief effect of a greater emphasis on determinism has been to focus attention on the evolution of theories and techniques in counseling which emphasize the nonjudgmental, amoral, and accepting attitudes on the part of the counselor.

On the other hand, nonjudgmental attitudes may be achieved by one who holds to freedom of the will. This counselor may believe that regardless of whether or not the client has exercised his choice in a positive rather than in a culturally designated negative direction, a nonjudgmental approach in counseling is the correct one. Judgment and moralizing may create barriers to positive action in counseling because of the hostility they induce. One should realize, however, that the nonjudgmental attitudes of the counselor who believes strongly in freedom of the will differ in quality from those of the counselor who really believes the client is blameless.

Every counselor ultimately develops his own philosophy relative to this issue. Once developed, the philosophy is not apt to remain static; continued careful consideration of this and other issues usually results in revised philosophies. This is as it should be. No counselor, religious or otherwise, should ever rigidly compartmentalize his thinking.

Fortunately, there are many middle-of-the-road positions on the determinism issue. It has been established that man is strongly influenced by his past, and it is undeniable that man has some qualities that set him apart from the lower organismic forms. Perhaps a modified capacity for "willing" his behavior in opposition to environmental determinants is one of these qualities.

SYSTEMS OF PSYCHOLOGY COMPATIBLE WITH RELIGION

In the last century and a half, many systems of psychology have evolved. Some of these have been completely refuted and abandoned. Others have been modified with new information and continue in favor with certain groups of psychologists. A system may be abandoned because the chief tenets have been found invalid; but, for the most part, systems are considered neither right nor wrong. Systems are generally thought of as points of view for explaining human nature and behavior.

Some systems of psychology have been incompatible with most religious concepts; others have corroborated religious concepts. Wayne Oates (12) has indicated that some types of psychology are compatible with Christianity. The student of psychology and of religion will benefit from some of these thoughts.

The Gestalt Psychology

The Christian understanding of personality is most compatible with those types of psychology which emphasize the wholeness of personality. The Christian understanding of personality is set over against any psychology which would attempt to explain personality by dividing it into its real or supposed component parts (12, p. 284).

The wholistic view of personality has largely supplanted the atomistic psychology of Wundt and Titchener. Wertheimer, Koffa, and Kohler have won the following of the majority of modern psychologists in their emphasis on wholeness of structure and of behavior.

Man in Conflict

The Christian understanding of personality abides at home, in the second place, with psychologists who take the basic conflicts of men seriously. Whereas personality is essentially a totality, both biblical and psychological estimates in increasing number of his nature portray him existentially in conflict with himself (12, p. 286).

Basically, it has been the self-theorists who have accented the drive for self-consistency, for self-improvement, and self-actualization. These are represented by Prescott Lecky, Carl R. Rogers, and Gordon Allport. These strivings within man which propel him forward toward integration, consistency, and wholeness may be likened to religious strivings.

Man in Relationships

The social nature of man may be the most significant fact in explaining his behavior. Man does little outside direct or indirect relationships with other people.

A Christian understanding of personality, therefore, gives careful attention to nature and quality of fellowship between persons and to the disruptive disharmonies within personality and between personalities (12, p. 288).

Psychologists who have emphasized man in relation to his fellows include Harry Stack Sullivan, Karen Horney, and Gardner Murphy. Christians are strongly motivated and made secure by the fellowship which they have through their relationships to Christ. The Christian concept of security is based almost completely on "right" relationships.

Mature Man and a Capacity for Love

Some psychologies see love as selfish need-satisfaction. They see the human being as having the same capacity for love as does the animal.

The distinctly Christian understanding of personality is founded upon an unconditional love for rather than an instrumental use of persons. Therefore, it joins forces with psychologists who see men as

persons rather than as things. . . . The Christian understanding of
personality is at one with those psychologies of personality which
accord to the capacity of love the highest place in measuring of the
mature person (12, p. 294, p. 296).

From what has been said before, concerning the capacity for
"caring" among psychotherapists, it seems likely that those psychologists who have deep interest in counseling and psychotherapy
would find acceptance among Christians. Among those who do
emphasize love, acceptance, and "caring" we find men like Men-
ninger, Angyal, and Erich Fromm. Each of these emphasizes love
as a human quality and one marking the maturing of the person.
Love is the outstanding theme of the Bible and the outstanding
tenet of the Christian faith.

Man Responsible for His Decisions

The Christian understanding of personality leaves man at last
"face to face with a choice and venture . . . actively in the sense
of *a decision.* . . ." He moves as he decides to move or not to move
(12, p. 303).

This statement does not necessarily demonstrate a Christian concern for the doctrine of freedom of the will. Man must make his
own decisions and suffer the consequences of them. Whether or not
he has freedom of choice is not the consideration here.

This understanding is in juxtaposition to that promoted by nondirective techniques and philosophies in counseling. Many psychologists have contributed, including Rogers, Snyder, and Porter. The
nondirective theories of counseling have great pertinence to the
field of religious work because of the compatibility of these theories
and the Christian concepts of responsibility. As a matter of fact,
the nondirective or client-centered theories are highly compatible
to most of the Christian understandings of man.

In discussing compatibilities between systems of psychological
thought and the Christian understanding of man, it is necessary to
observe that a given system may be compatible in some respects
and incompatible in others. This is especially true of the self-
theories that undergird the nondirective system of counseling. There
is little or nothing in the stated theories that violates Christian
thought; there is nothing at all in the technique that seems contrary

to a religious interpretation of life and growth. One must recognize, however, that most of the contributors to self-theory align themselves with the humanist philosophers who visualize man as the ultimate. Christian understanding of man can never support the concepts of humanism, but it can make use of many of the contributions of humanists.

A PSYCHOLOGICAL APPROACH IN RELIGIOUS COUNSELING

This writing attempts a discussion of counseling in the religious setting with emphasis on a psychological approach. It seems necessary to define the intent and to set forth the semantics of the term "psychological approach" before proceeding further.

In a general sense, the psychological approach in counseling is the application of techniques that have evolved from scientific studies of man's behavior. This author joins with Bonthius (4) in believing that secular counseling techniques are in harmony with Christianity's ministry. There is nothing in the psychological approach to counseling that is in disharmony with the aims of religion; nor does the use of religious symbols, performances, and rites violate any of the techniques of secular psychology. Despite recognized disparities between some psychological theories and Christian philosophy, techniques of counseling are equally applicable in secular and religious settings.

The approach suggests that every religious counselor learn all he can about techniques of counseling as developed by scientific psychology. Then, each religious counselor should apply these unless he feels there is conflict with his religious beliefs. Believing himself to be a representative of God, he should seek wisdom and guidance in utilizing the spiritual aids to counseling, integrating these as best he can with psychological techniques. Undoubtedly, under such an approach, the counselor will vary both psychological and spiritual aids with the individual client. It is conceivable that only spiritual aids may be used with some counselees and only psychological aids may be used with others. The following chapters will present the ideas about counseling which have bases in psychological research. To some extent, suggestions will be made concerning possible situations where psychological techniques and spiritual aids may be integrated.

In the long run, each counselor must judge the relative merits of spiritual and psychological aids during each instant of counseling action. The religious counselor in the Judeo-Christian framework believes in God; if there is to be a psychological approach to religious counseling, the belief in God and the power of God to motivate both counselor and counselee must be respected. Such respect is paramount in this author's concept of "a psychological approach to counseling in the religious setting."

This author feels, moreover, that the proper utilization of psychological techniques in the religious setting under the sought-after aura of the Spirit of God will become more than the summation of two values. There will be new dimensions. The author agrees with Outler who says specifically of psychotherapy:

> I believe that, first of all, it would be discovered that psychotherapy can be as rigorously and unswervingly scientific when undertaken in a Christian context as it has ever been in the secularist world view. . . .
>
> But, I also believe that a Christian context for psychotherapy would add new dimensions to the relation between therapist and patient which would deeply affect the basic attitudes of both to each other and to themselves . . . The love and self-respect of the therapist would be established in his awareness of God's love and he would be conscious of God's will for men to love one another, without possession or coercion. . . .
>
> Or, again, the psychotherapist working in a Christian perspective would be able to understand and reinterpret the religious and ethical aspects of his patient's problems as the secularist never can. . . .
>
> What is called for—and what seems to me clearly possible—is a *division of labor,* on the one hand, and a *synthesis of goals,* on the other. The professional therapist cannot do the work of the Christian minister, nor can the minister replace the therapist. But both could do their proper work with the same assumptions and goals derived from a basic Christian faith and commitment. . . .
>
> Psychotherapy can become one of man's most notable services to man, and through man, to God. The Christian Gospel is God's fullest manifestation of His love and concern for man—and Christianity is commissioned to that service, in every area and dimension of human life. There is, then, no justifiable basis for rivalry between the two as if they were *both* religions!
>
> . . . But if a good science makes way for an honest alliance with high religion, and religion opens its eyes ungrudgingly to the grow-

ing light of good science, we would then have a notable alliance and collaboration, in which men of faith and fine intelligence might freely join in common devotion to God who made man's mind to praise Him, and in common service to mankind, in which we may show forth our love of God (13, pp. 139-140, pp. 261-262).

References

1. Becker, Russell J., "Links Between Psychology and Religion," *The American Psychologist*. October, 1958, pp. 566-568.

2. Boisen, Anton T., "Religious Experience and Psychological Conflict," *The American Psychologist*. October, 1958, pp. 568-570.

3. Bonnell, John Sutherland, "Faith Healing Valid Today," *Pastoral Psychology*. January, 1951, pp. 7-10.

4. Bonthius, Robert H., "What Is Christian Counseling?" *Journal of Pastoral Care*. Summer, 1959, pp. 69-79.

5. Curran, Charles A., "A Catholic Psychologist Looks at Pastoral Counseling," *Pastoral Psychology*. February, 1959, pp. 21-28.

6. Edwards, Jonathan, *Jonathan Edwards on Evangelism*, Carl J. C. Wolf (ed.). Grand Rapids: Eerdmans, 1958.

7. Fairbanks, Rollin J., "Religious Healing: A Meditation," *The Journal of Pastoral Care*. Spring, 1958, pp. 44-47.

8. Feifel, Herman, "Introductory Remarks, Symposium on Relationships Between Religion and Mental Health," *The American Psychologist*. October, 1958, pp. 565-566.

9. Havens, Joseph, "Psychotherapy and Salvation," *Pastoral Psychology*. February, 1961, pp. 10-18.

10. Ikin, A. Graham, "The New Testament and Healing," *Pastoral Psychology*. May, 1956, pp. 33-34.

11. Johnson, Paul E., "Discussion, Symposium on Relationships Between Religion and Mental Health," *The American Psychologist*. October, 1958, pp. 576-577.

12. Oates, Wayne E., *Religious Dimensions of Personality*. New York: Association Press, 1957.

13. Outler, Albert, *Psychotherapy and the Christian Message*. New York: Harper and Brothers, 1954.

14. Salzman, Leon, "Spiritual and Faith Healing," *Journal of Pastoral Care*. Fall, 1957, pp. 146-155.

15. Tillich, Paul, *Dynamics of Faith*. New York: Harper and Brothers, 1957.

16. ————, "The Theology of Pastoral Care," *Pastoral Psychology*. October, 1959, pp. 21-26.

17. Watson, Goodwin, "Moral Issues in Psychotherapy," *The American Psychologist*. October, 1958, pp. 574-576.

III

The Counseling Interview in the Religious Setting

The interview is a useful medium in many areas of human relations. Many businesses, professions, and disciplines make use of it continuously, some as an adjunct to broader pursuits and some as a fundamental tool of their endeavor. Among those who use the interview widely are salesmen, accountants, executives, and consultants of many kinds. Lawyers, physicians, teachers, and personnel administrators make extensive use of interview techniques, as do public opinion surveyors and social researchers.

Some of the people listed above employ the interview as a method of counseling people, but most of them have other uses for it. Naturally, its nature will depend largely upon the purpose to be accomplished. Interviews are for purposes of information getting, opinion surveying, and direction giving. Many are promoted in a probing manner, some in a persuasive or conciliatory manner, others in a manner designed to bring comfort and encouragement. Many interviewers are interested in the techniques solely as an aid to themselves—as a means of selling a product or promoting a business.

The interview in all its forms and uses has long been a legitimate interest in psychology, and many studies have been designed to improve interview techniques. Some studies have aimed at improving effectiveness from the standpoint of gain for the interviewer with only secondary consideration being given for the interviewee. Other research has aimed at enhancing the benefits for the person being interviewed.

There is no sphere in which the interview is more widely used than in pastoral and other church-related work. Aside from his public appearances, the clergyman has no greater responsibility than that of meeting the church members in face-to-face encounter.

The same is true of all religious workers, including youth workers, Sunday School teachers, volunteer visitation workers, and fund solicitors. Almost every phase of religious endeavor is highly individual and personal; and personalized contacts vary widely, from the earnest approach of the clergyman in trying to bring the individual into a right relationship with God to the meeting between the lay budget solicitor and the would-be contributor.

THE NATURE
OF THE COUNSELING INTERVIEW

Benefits to Client

All of the interviews in church work are not of a counseling nature, but it is safe to say that most of them have a modified counseling orientation. The distinguishing feature of the counseling interview as compared to other types is that it is always aimed at providing benefits for the client. Thus, Erickson (9) has defined the counseling interview as a relationship in which one person with a problem turns, in search of assistance, to another person with a background. Although there may be benefits to the counselor in terms of money received from his work, it is worth repeating that the client is the person for whom the interview is conceived and planned.

A Variety of Purposes

Although the broad aim of any counseling interview is to aid the client, interviews do differ in their immediate purposes.

Some are designed to elicit information about the client; this may be the highly structured interview in which the counselor takes the lead and asks questions and the material obtained is used in a later interview of an unstructured nature. An example is the intake interview in a clinic setting as well as the clinical diagnostic interview.

It is true that what transpires in an interview will be determined largely by the basic philosophy of the counselor and the techniques which he favors in counseling. There are some counselors who would be unlikely to use probing interviews or to derive case histories because the techniques used do not require advance information about the client. In discussing the counseling interview, it will be necessary to center the discussion around factors which are common to many methods and theories of counseling rather than to try to discuss specifics of interviewing within various methodologies. Actually, these specific variations will be discussed in future chapters which treat some methods specifically. There are many common ideas which may be subsumed under the title of the counseling interview. It shall not be the purpose of this chapter to discuss only those ideas which have universal acceptance in counseling, but rather those things which are most generally accepted.

Interviewing is undoubtedly the heart of the counseling process. Indeed, some claim could be laid that the interview is the embodiment of counseling. No counseling method exists that does not utilize an interview situation, but it would be inaccurate to state that there is no more to counseling than the interview. In the fullest sense, counseling consists of the interviews, the things that precede the interviews in a preparatory sense, counselor activity which may follow the interviews, as well as counselee activity motivated by but taking place outside the interviews.

A Medium of Communication

Of the artistic and scientific aspects of counseling, the interview accentuates the artistry of the counselor. The scientific aspects of the counseling process may be carried out in the interview to some extent as the counselor draws upon his systematized knowledge of human behavior. A large part of the scientific aspects of the counselor's training will be relegated to the extra-interview activities of testing and evaluation of the client. His art-istry in handling people will be demonstrated in the face-to-face interview situation.

The counseling interview is a verbal interplay between counselor and client, but it is much more than that. As a process of com-munication, it involves more than verbal exchange. Sullivan (16) has described the interview as a "vocal communication in a two-group, much of which is non-verbal as intonation, rate of speech, enunciation, and other indications of meaning which are crucial in understanding the problems of interpersonal relations." Ross (13) has further emphasized the communicative aspects of tone of voice, movements of body, gestures, sighs, breathing, laughter, dress, grooming, tears, blocks in conversation, silences, bearing, handclasps, and other bodily manifestations, as well as the un-conscious relating of the therapist and the patient. Blum and Balinski (5) suggest the importance of the things not said, omitted, or avoided in addition to the verbal aspects of the interview.

THE PHYSICAL SETTING OF THE INTERVIEW

Privacy

Proper setting is important for any type of interview, and the astute salesperson is sensitive to this factor. Some sales are best made in the home, some in the business office, others in the store or display center. Salesmen in the direct-sales field make extensive studies concerning the opportune time and place for making the sales contact. Time, place, and setting for saleswork depend upon the product to be sold and upon the pre-sales ap-praisal of psychological factors influencing the sale.

In the counseling field, the setting is especially important, inas-much as the task to be accomplished is likely to be involved, in part, with the emotional life of the client. Practically every coun-seling activity demands privacy; and this is a function of many factors, some physical, some psychological. In general, it is more related to how the client feels than to purely objective factors. Privacy does not imply secretiveness or furtiveness. It is not necessary that the counseling office be removed from the heart of activity, only that privacy be insured once the door to the office is closed.

It should not be considered enough to remove the client from the eyes and ears of the world; the counseling session should be uninterrupted by trespassing of any type. Although usually the client does not desire to be secretly closeted with the counselor, most clients desire *uninterrupted* interest and attention of the counselor once the counseling session has begun. If someone comes to the door, knocks, and demands the counselor's attention, privacy has been invaded, even though the door is opened only a crack and the trespasser does not see the client. The most common invader of the privacy of the counseling session is a telephone or buzzer. A counselor may be able to justify, as necessary for public relations, a telephone conversation carried on during counseling interviews; but he cannot justify it for client relations. Proper handling of counseling interviews will demand that the counselor devote the full assignment of time to the needs of the client.

There are special difficulties in this area to be reckoned with by the clergyman. He finds it difficult to remain incommunicado even for a short period of time. The nature of his service to his parishioners more or less demands not only a twenty-four-hour assignment to call, but also an obligation to be available at any instant. The counseling specialist in the church setting may instruct his secretary that he is not to be disturbed during an hour of consultation with a client; but the clergyman finds extended periods of privacy difficult to maintain. Even so, the clergyman should not accept interruptions as inevitable or refuse to insist on a reasonable degree of privacy. He may educate his congregation concerning his need for privacy during stated counseling hours; and with proper publicity of his counseling schedule, there will be fewer demands both by staff and by parishioners during those times.

The clergyman will not be able to maintain a rigid schedule of counseling hours as easily as will the specialist. Many occasions arise in which the parishioner wants and needs help immediately. Thus, the clergyman may find it necessary to come to counseling quarters in the church at odd hours, even as he finds it necessary to make calls in homes and hospitals at a moment's notice. Even so, there is advantage in announcing and adhering to a stated schedule for counseling.

There is something to be said for the wisdom of insisting that the parishioner come for counseling at the counseling office rather than receive the clergyman in the home. Privacy is usually difficult to achieve in the home setting, especially if there are children. It is often true, also, that parishioners will call the clergyman to come to the home immediately following an emotional encounter between members of a family; and insistence that the counseling session be held at the church may permit a subsiding of emotion and insure better success. Each situation must be judged on its individual merits in this regard, since there are instances in which the clergyman should go to the parishioner with dispatch.

A Warm and Permissive Atmosphere

It is unfortunate that most church buildings constructed as much as a decade ago do not provide adequate counseling quarters. The trend in present-day church architecture is to provide ample space for counseling by all members of the staff. There is no reason why special rooms must be provided for counseling; however, the clergyman's office or study and the usual "cubbyholes" provided by most churches for staff members are seldom adequate.

There is reason to believe that a room especially planned for meeting with individuals and another arranged for groups would be wise investments for most churches. The individual counseling room may be shared by all those staff members who have distinctive counseling functions, and the group conference room could be used for the many varieties of staff and promotional meetings of the modern church as well as for group counseling. Where one special room for individual work is provided, counselors in the church may need to stagger their counseling hours for maximum utility. Even so, each office should be equipped for some usage as a counseling room.

Whatever the arrangement, the modern church must reflect a central position of the counseling function in its provisions for counseling space. Effective counseling will require special consideration; it will be necessary to spend money to provide for adequate counseling space just as money is required for an adequate music program.

Counseling quarters in the church or church-related institution should be comfortable and attractively decorated and furnished. Most counseling relies on producing expression on the part of the client, and a warm and homelike atmosphere seems best suited to uninhibited conversation. The counseling office should be quite different from the business office, the physician's office, or the legal office. The furnishings and appointments in these offices are chosen to present a smoothly operating, highly efficient, and somewhat hurried atmosphere. Most businessmen, physicians, and attorneys desire to motivate clients toward economical and time-saving handling of appointments. The clergyman or church-related counselor may feel some need to hurry, at times; but he should present his client with an atmosphere conducive to an unhurried, calm, and relaxed approach to the problem.

Adequately furnished counseling offices utilize carpeted floors, attractive draperies, and well-matched accessories such as lamps, paintings, and growing plants. In addition, counseling quarters in the religious setting will reflect the context by use of some religious symbols consonant with specific religious faith.

Most counseling quarters have desks, but it is better for seating arrangements to provide a situation where counselor and client may sit apart from the desk. It may be that in some instances, with specific clients, the counselor may wish to sit behind the desk; but it should not be mandatory in the seating arrangements that he do so. This suggests a spaciousness usually not found in a study or in an office, and is one of the reasons for including special quarters for counseling in the building plans. Although the term "counseling office" is in constant use, counseling quarters should not have the appearance usually associated with offices.

Great care should be exercised in choosing chairs for the counseling office. Upholstered chairs utilizing warm fabrics rather than plastic coverings are beneficial in promoting a relaxed atmosphere. Fastidious planners of counseling offices may be attentive to the smallest detail. So far as chair arrangements are concerned, it is well to arrange a choice of seats for the client at the desk as well as in the area apart from the desk. A chair across from the counselor and one nearer to him at the side of the desk seems a wise arrangement. Even the selection of the desk may affect the atmosphere. Counselors' desks which are very broad present an expanse of space which becomes a barrier with every communication, if the client chooses to sit across the desk from the counselor.

The use of color has come into a place of great importance in creating atmosphere (4). It has been demonstrated that greens are restful as compared to yellows, oranges, and reds. These warm colors, on the other hand, spur efficiency in business offices. Blues are both relaxing and cooling. Wall colors are especially important because of the necessity for making eye-level contact with walls as the client and counselor look directly at one another.

It is obvious that attention to producing a desirable atmosphere could occupy the continuous concern of the counselor who is attentive to small but important details. Actually, there is need for research in this area. Unfortunately, many counselors must work under such definitely sub-standard conditions, that they are not apt to be highly motivated in seeking out the small details of atmospheric determinants.

PLANNING THE INTERVIEW

Review Available Material

The type of information the clergyman and others in the religious setting usually have concerning the prospective counselee differs considerably from that obtained by counselors in other settings. The ordinary counselor receives referrals from varied sources as does the church-related counselor. However, the chief sources of referral in the church setting are other church members.

When a member of a congregation refers a fellow member to the clergyman or to his co-workers for counseling, he is typically impatient that something be done. The ordinary counselor acknowledges a referral and then waits for the client to make his appearance; he rarely coerces the client. There are several reasons why the clergyman in particular cannot always await the coming of the client.

General counseling theory emphasizes that little help can come to the client unless he actively seeks it. In the church setting, there is typically more than one person involved in the problem referred; and the clergyman cannot feel free to jeopardize the welfare of several because the prospective client will not appear. For instance, if a wife reports that her husband is drinking heavily and asks the clergyman to talk with the husband, the clergyman may wait for a time. He may attempt to motivate the husband to come through the wife's solicitation, or he may write a letter inviting the husband to come. In the final analysis, the clergyman may be forced to go to the husband and insist on discussing the problem with him. The clergyman is unique among counselors in this respect.

The church-related counselor is apt to have much more opportunity for learning in advance about his client than do other counselors. Most of the counselees will be church members; and, unless the church is very large, there is much common knowledge available. On the other hand, the prospective counselee may enter counseling with more than the ordinary knowledge about his counselor. Having advance information about the client is usually beneficial; having a client who is familiar with his counselor is beneficial in some ways.

Ross (13) indicates that the counseling interview actually begins with the letter or telephone call to the counselor rather than with the face-to-face meeting. The client is involved in the interview from the time he decides to present himself to the counselor, and the counselor is involved from the time he makes the appointment to see the client. There are several things which should be done in planning for the interview. The amount and direction of planning will depend on whether the interview is the initial one or one in a series. In case the interview is the first one with a particular client, there will be less planning than is usually true of an interview in a series. Even so, there will be some planning necessary, particularly in those situations in which the counselor has access to records about the prospective client. In most school-counseling situations there are records which could be perused. In many clinical situations there is material about the client which may be gained from questionnaires, from social workers' reports, or sometimes from intake interviews. At any rate, the counselor should review all of the available material about the client before the initial interview.

If the interview is one in a series, then the counselor should take a few minutes before each interview to familiarize himself with major aspects of the case. He should review notes made at previous sessions and think back over the developments of previous sessions. If a case history is available, this should be reviewed, as well as test material for the client.

Arrange for Test Administration and Contact Referral Source

It may be that the nature of the problem to be discussed will be known by the counselor. In this event it is possible that the counselor may make arrangements for the administration of various tests which are somewhat standard for vocational or educational counseling. Testing in the church setting has not become as widespread as it is likely to be in the future. Both public and church schools depend heavily on psychological testing for information to aid in counseling youth. Clergymen may learn about tests by taking several graduate courses; for the most part, the use of psychological tests in religious counseling will come within the province of the counseling specialist in the church.

In planning for the interview, the religious counselor may wish to talk with the referral source. This is especially desirable in the church school where contact is easy to arrange with referring staff members. It is often the case that a public school administrator, teacher, or counselor will refer to the religious counselor students who have vocational problems related to religious work. In such cases, it is not unusual for the public school to share with the religious counselor test scores and other data accumulated at the school.

It goes without saying that some interviews come about without benefit of appointment or prior knowledge on the part of the counselor. Such interviews cannot be planned properly. The clergyman, in particular, faces a quandary concerning appointments for counseling. To insist that all counseling be done on an appointment basis may cause the parishioner to feel that the clergyman is unapproachable. To schedule counseling hours without appointments may result in having people wait for long periods of time. As a general rule, those who come to the clergyman for counseling desire a high degree of secrecy, perhaps even more so than persons undergoing psychiatric treatment. The close fellowship among members of a congregation and the nature of problems brought to the clergy (especially marriage problems) are factors which urge privacy, and this is difficult to achieve when parishioners must sit and wait for the clergyman. Privacy without furtiveness may be enhanced by counseling on the appointment basis.

Each Interview a Unique Situation

In the long run, learning to interview can be accomplished only through practice. This does not deny, however, that some instructions for beginning counselors is valuable. Most books on interviewing present long lists of activities for the beginning interviewer to study. There is some indication that good interviewing may be accomplished by an outlined approach in which one does a number of things in succession in order to accomplish the desired results. Such outlined directions are valuable and will be found in this writing also. The religious counselor should understand thoroughly that no two interviews can be handled alike; each is a new experience in dealing with the particular problems of a unique human personality.

Even if standardized interviews were general in other situations, they would be improbable in the religious setting. As pointed out earlier, the religious counselor often uses spiritual aids, but he cannot use them promiscuously. Not only is he faced with a greater range of problem types; he has more tools from which to choose.

Each counselor will develop basic techniques on which he relies heavily. The counselor is a unique personality and may have unique philosophies. His techniques will be outgrowths of his personality and his philosophies, but these techniques should be flexible enough to allow for personality and problem variants in his clients.

The field of medical psychotherapy provides a statement which is appropriate in this context. Deutsch and Murphy state:

> A technique is good only when it is handled in such a manner that no one is aware that it is a technique. The uniqueness of each individual case will defeat any attempt to succeed with a stereotyped approach. While there are general principles to follow, their blending is dependent essentially upon the common sense, versatility, and experience of the therapist. With reticent and uncommunicative

patients, it may be necessary to talk and be fairly active during the initial interviews, i.e., until the case develops. As the patient becomes more communicative, the therapist is able to play a less active role (8, p. 18).

Lists of suggestions for promoting the aim of the interview which are found intermittently in this chapter may be utilized by the student of religious counseling in studying typical interview proceedings. After the student has had some experience as an interviewer, he may use these as checklists immediately after a counseling session to ascertain what might have been done to make the session more profitable and orderly.

THE OPENING PHASE OF THE INTERVIEW

Although it is not unusual for the ordinary counselor to see his client for the first time when he enters the counseling room, this is not nearly as likely in religious counseling. The clergyman in particular has a chance to know his clients in other relationships. He has an opportunity through his public messages and through his appearances before various groups in the church to display his personality, as well as to know personally many of his future counselees.

For these reasons, the opening phase in religious counseling may vary considerably from other situations. It is most probable that the parishioner comes to the counseling session with a high degree of confidence in the counselor.

This favorable aspect carries with it some disadvantage. The client may enter counseling expecting more than the counselor can deliver and with a level of familiarity not conducive to good results.

Rapport

Perhaps no term in psychological literature has been more overworked than "rapport," but it is not possible to write a comprehensive treatment of the counseling interview without giving attention to this all-important concept. Rapport may be defined as a mutual feeling of warmth, comradeship, and trust existing between two individuals. It is usually assumed that rapport should be gained as a preliminary to entry into the problem area. This may be a necessity with some reluctant and uncommunicative client; it may be necessary to work specifically for rapport. In the general case, rapport building will be a continuous enterprise in the counseling interviews.

There is little question that the task of rapport getting is closely related to the artistry of the counselor. The religious counselor who is warm and accepting, friendly and personable, yet without superficiality, will be able to develop a feeling of warmth and trust in the client with considerably more ease than will a counselor who is not endowed with the traits conducive to friendly relationships with all types of people. Allport points out the value of the "social gift" in the interviewer:

> The interviewer . . . must possess the "social gift," for his function is most complex: he must listen quietly and yet probe, encourage frankness and yet never seem shocked, be friendly and yet reserved, patient but prodding, and through it all never seem bored (2, p. 516).

It is possible, however, that too strong a case has been developed for the effluent counselor who by virtue of the weight of his personal charm is able to win people to a warm and trusting relationship with himself. "Loosening up" the client with "glad hand" methods or a "good sense of humor" as well as attempting to become conversant with the client about his interests and current events need closer scrutiny. It may be that the real artistry of the counselor will not be evidenced by his friendliness and his ability to make the client feel relaxed and "at home," but by his judgment of how much of this type of thing is desirable with the given client. The client may be so burdened with his problem and so ready to attack it, that a frivolous-minded counselor would be a most unwelcome obstacle to his unburdening. Some counselors are able to promote such an aura of charm and good will that the client may feel guilty of having a problem at all in such a "beautiful world."

Ideally, the clergyman and his co-workers should be mental telepathists with additional powers of being able to read, in a glance at the client, the future as well as the past. They are not at all likely to possess these qualities; but it is reasonable to suppose that they would be sufficiently perceptive to interpret from the client's demeanor, his actions, and his expressions just how much rapport-building is necessary. Their artistry, scientific understandings, subliminal interpretations, and intuitions may all serve toward determining a course of immediate as well as of continuing action with the specific client.

There is questionable value in developing a set of rapport-building principles to be used with each client. Davidian summarizes as follows:

> If we believe in the need for rapport, we must divorce ourselves from the idea of consciously creating this state. What, then, is a possible answer? The most effective method of attaining this feeling of ease might be in developing an aura which is conducive to rapport. Counselors can develop through their own actions and principles of living a healthy way of life which will prompt them to be sought after by clients with problems. Would not this be the best possible type of rapport? It is not super-imposed, it is not artificial, it is not turned off and on at the counselor's door. This self is built by living a life which promotes respect, trust, and confidence. This self makes itself known in the lives of students, and rapport is established before there is any notion of a counselor-client relationship. Too often counselors have placed so much conscious effort on techniques and tools that it is forgotten that we, as individuals, are our most valuable instruments (7, pp. 469-470).

Among counselors everywhere, the clergyman occupies the best position for creating this type of respect and concomitant rapport. Other religious counselors occupy positions almost as advantageous.

Suggestions for the Opening Phase

The following suggestions for the opening phase of the interview are based on the idea of a first meeting of counselor and client; but many of these suggestions have value for subsequent interviews with the same client. The beginning religious counselor is urged to study these suggestions during his early training, and then to dispense with standard suggestions. He should train himself to proceed in interviews without a conscious effort to follow a list of rules, but with specific attention to the developing needs in the specific situation.

1. Greet the parishioner warmly as he enters the door; be natural,

superficiality is easily recognized. The student or beginning counselor may find it difficult to know just how to handle this first meeting. As a rule, the handclasp is standard for men, but is optional on successive occasions. When the client is of the opposite sex, the most general policy is for the male counselor to wait for a sign from the woman client indicating that she expects to shake hands. A woman counselor seldom makes the first move to shake hands either with men or women clients, but she follows through if they seem to desire or expect it.

2. Indicate that the client has a choice of seats. If he chooses to sit across the desk from the counselor's chair, this is a good indication that he would like to move slowly into a close relation. If the client chooses a chair at the side of the desk, near the counselor's chair, it is probable that subsequent interviews may be held in that part of the office away from the desk, where arrangement of chairs permits a true face-to-face seating arrangement.

3. Be sure that the client is comfortable. This may involve removal of topcoats or placing an ash tray where he can reach it.

4. Try to judge the level of anxiety in the client. Depending upon this, the counselor will determine whether or not the problem area should be entered immediately or after some delay. Generally speaking, the problem will be opened immediately if the level of anxiety is either very high or very low. The parishioner who is highly anxious usually benefits from immediate problem discussion; and the person with little anxiety has no need to delay. Parishioners with moderate anxiety may benefit from achieving a relaxed attitude before the problem is presented.

5. Relieve the client of the burden of making the first conversation. The counselor should be prepared to carry the conversation until the client has his bearings. Opening conversations may center around something of interest to the client—something he is wearing, something of particular current interest, or even the weather. If there has been a referral by a mutual acquaintance, he may become a good conversation topic for a few moments.

6. Give the impression of ample time. If the client is highly overwrought, he may have need to express his difficulty at once. If this is necessary, the catharsis should be allowed; and then a return to an unhurried pace in the interview should occur.

7. Avoid paternalistic, authoritarian, and superiority roles. This admonition is more pertinent to the specialist in the church setting than to the clergyman. The clergyman is often thought of as a father figure. Since he is looked upon by his parishioners as an authority, it may be that he will be forced to play this role to an extent. He should be aware, however, that such a role makes the client dependent on him. At least, it can be said that counselors other than the clergyman will do well to avoid these roles in the interest of creating independent action in the client.

8. Avoid humorous stories in rapport-building. The client may be deeply disturbed and in no mood to laugh. If he is forced to laugh in order to be polite, he may be unwilling to move abruptly from laughter to the problem area.

9. Avoid supportive gestures. Supportive measures are questionable at any time, and are definitely undesirable before the client has had an opportunity to reveal the problem. The problem may be a minor one, and efforts at support and reassurance may be misinterpreted by the client as an opinion on the part of the counselor that the difficulty is serious. Here again, the clergyman may have to modify his actions because of the cultural role in which he is cast. The clergyman is often thought of as a comforter and many parishioners come for the express purpose of receiving that comfort. Nevertheless, the hurtful aspects of support must be considered.

10. Move to the problem area at the earliest reasonable time. There is little doubt that the client is anxious to proceed. It is entirely possible that good rapport may be established and then allowed to depreciate because the counselor did not allow the problem area to be entered at the opportune time.

THE EXPLORATORY PHASE OF THE INTERVIEW

Presenting the Problem

Assuming that the need for developing rapport has been perceived and acted upon, the time will ultimately come during the counseling interview when the problem must be presented. As a general rule, the obligation for determining this rests upon the counselor; therefore, there must be an exercise of judgment concerning the time for bringing up the problem. Many factors will enter into such a decision. In some counseling situations, there is an unspoken understanding that the counseling experience must begin and end in one interview. In other cases it may be presupposed that the client will come again and again, if necessary. If the counselor ascertains that there will be only one interview, he will wisely shorten the rapport-building section in order to give more time for the problem. In such a case, the parishioners will likely be motivated also toward an early expression of the problem. In other cases, it is possible that the entire first interview may profitably be devoted to rapport-building discussions. It should be understood that rapport-building does not usually end with the expression of the problem; but in the typical interview there does come a time when the counselor and client purposefully turn from general conversation to the problems at hand.

When this time comes, the counselor may lay the groundwork for the client's expression of the problem by saying, "Now, what did you especially wish to talk about this morning." If the case is one of referral, the counselor may say, "I believe you came to see me at Dr. Woodrow's suggestion." Such expressions as these are usually sufficient to bring about an expression of the problem by the parishioner, unless he is severely upset.

Reluctance of Client to Express the Problem

The client may find it easy to express the problem, or he may find it very difficult. This will, of course, depend upon the nature of the problem and upon the personality of the client, as well as the level of rapport which has been developed. Personal problems in particular are difficult to express; and the client is apt to say, "Well, I don't exactly know where to start." The usual requirement for problem expression, if the problem is a difficult or an embarrassing one, is a quiet, accepting, and calm attitude on the part of the counselor. Assurances may be given, but may serve to distract the client. Logically, the client came to express the problem and will do so if the counselor is patient and accepting.

The typical parishioner does not barge directly into the basic problem area. He makes a few remarks somewhat related to the problem, perhaps, but at a comfortable distance from the real issue and in an effort to feel out the acceptance of the counselor toward him as a person. This is a critical time for the counseling experience if the problem is of a personal nature. The counselor's unperturbed demeanor is an absolute necessity for complete revelation of the problem and for opening up communication about it. Tyler (19, 20) emphasizes the necessity for a feeling of acceptance as a prerequisite to understanding. She indicates that the typical client fears understanding unless he has felt acceptance. This is especially true in the relationship between church members and their clergymen. Unless the member feels that the clergyman accepts him, he may be afraid to have the clergyman understand his motives and feelings.

Williamson (21) feels that the counselor should anticipate a reluctance on the part of the counselee to express his problems. Such reluctance is most likely to be apparent during the first meeting. The parishioner will probably divulge only peripheral components of the real issue at first.

One of the most common mistakes of beginning counselors is to be impatient with the client. The counselor may say, "Now, why don't we get down to the real problem." He may even say, "Now, why don't you quit covering up. You know there is something bothering you that you are not revealing." Such mistakes on the part of the counselor often cause the client to become reticent and the real issue may be lost entirely. If the counselor is patient, accepting, and courteous, the real issue will be revealed in time.

As a matter of fact, it is quite probable that the parishioner does not understand the real issues involved, otherwise he might not have needed help in the first place. Most clients do not know the factors underlying their difficulty. These factors may be unconscious or otherwise blocked off from the awareness. The chief function of counseling often is to make the client understand the source of difficulty; this must be achieved slowly and painstakingly. Such insight usually is frightening to the client.

Structuring

Once the parishioner has expressed his problem, most counselors are likely to engage in a process of structuring the counseling process. Realistically, it may be that the counselor will have to tell the client that he is not able to provide maximum help. If the problem expressed does come within the scope and competencies possessed by the religious counselor or clergyman, then it will be necessary for the counselor to explain the type of approach that is common for the type of problem presented by the parishioner. This type of structuring is confined to the initial interview, but it is usually a most important aspect of the first meeting of parishioner and counselor. The religious counselor may feel that structuring should include a statement of the possible use of spiritual aids. If prayer is to be used, the time following the structuring seems a very desirable time for it. Thus, the blessings of God may be requested before actually engaging in aspects of problem solution.

Most parishioners in need of therapeutic counseling expect to obtain the help they need in a very short time. Therefore, it may be necessary in structuring the counseling process to indicate to the client that the help he needs may take a considerable amount of time and effort. The client has a right to be told in general terms the processes and time to be spent in his relief. Then, he will be able to decide whether or not he wishes to pursue the outlined program. Many parishioners are not willing to pursue a lengthy process; and some may feel after the structuring that they should seek help elsewhere.

Structuring need not reveal the intricacies of methodology. Typically, the parishioner neither needs to understand detailed method nor could understand it fully. Indeed, there are reasons for believing that if the client is highly informed about methods, he will be so intent on seeing them applied that his benefits from counseling may be jeopardized.

If the philosophy of the religious counselor is essentially nondirective, the client should be made aware of his own responsibilities in promoting the counseling aims. If tests and case histories are to be used, the general nature of their application to the problem may be explained.

Pursuing the Problem

It is not the intent in this chapter to discuss different methods of counseling. Naturally, different methods of pursuing the problem will become functions of different basic philosophical approaches. The counseling interview is different in several respects from other types of interviewing; and yet, there is much variation in handling the counseling interview. For instance, some counselors pose as authority figures and others do not.

It can be said that the counseling interview, regardless of basic theory followed, differs from other interviews in that client expression is always considered important. Expression of any type on the part of the client is considered relevant in counseling. Every method encourages this and attempts to bring about self-understanding and insight on the part of the client. In opinion polling, by comparison, the interviewer is interested only in certain structured responses.

Although much diversity in method accompanies the explanatory and insight-development phase of the interview, the following suggestions comprise common ground for all counselors. The student of religious counseling should study these; but he should utilize the list of suggestions only until they may become incorporated into his individual approach to interviewing.

Suggestions for the Exploratory Phase

1. Demonstrate acceptance of the client. He must feel accepted before he will reveal his problem, especially if there are derogatory elements to the revelations. In order to demonstrate acceptance of the client, the counselor must feel it; and this includes accepting him as he is without judgment, blame, or criticism. Demonstrating acceptance is especially important for clergymen. Since they have been called upon to condemn wrongdoing and improprieties from the pulpit, the parishioners are prone to see them as judgmental. They must struggle even harder to overcome this negative appraisal.

2. Maintain a calm and relaxed manner. If a person must make supreme efforts in order to be calm, he should not be a counselor. The client watches for and senses counselor perturbance as he

reveals himself. If the counselor demonstrates excitement, the client likely will withdraw and find communication difficult.

3. The counselor must maintain high interest. The client deserves his undivided attention. Some client expressions may be boringly dull, but the counselor should remain wide awake. He must defer his own plans and problems until he is free from his counseling obligation. Clients can easily sense boredom and lack of attention.

4. Listen carefully and painstakingly. The counselor should be aware that his primary job is to listen, not to talk. The amount of talking the counselor does will depend on the philosophy of counseling he embraces, his choice of techniques for the particular client and situation, and the urgency implied in the client's presentation of the problem. It is safe to say that most counselors talk too much and are not as good listeners as they ought to be. The clergyman, in particular, usually finds it difficult to refrain from overtalking. Advice and verbalizing are expected of him; it is difficult for him to differentiate his roles as counselor and as preacher.

The counselor should be especially watchful for inconsistencies in the client's material; he should watch for avoidances and resistances. He should watch for changes in emotional inflections as the client discusses various matters. He must listen for the overtones and undertones in the client's statements. All of these things have meaning, but they may not be understood by surface-level listening. Annette Garrett (10) suggests that the counselor should "listen to what the client means as well as to what he says." There is no doubt that some of the things the client says have meanings which he does not understand.

5. Assume the "internal frame of reference." The "internal frame of reference" is a term more closely related to some counseling methods than others, but all counselors are interested in seeing the world through the eyes of the client. Only in this way can reasonable understanding take place.

This requires a constant effort on the counselor's part to keep before him the broad areas of the client's situation, since the situation of the client affects the way he sees things. When one is able to see the world through the client's eyes, he is not likely to be judgmental. He may be able to see the reasonableness of the client's actions and feelings.

Such a point of view does not compromise behavior that is

"wrong" according to society's codes or religious concepts. An understanding of the reasons for behavior will enhance the possibility that the clergyman or other counselor may help the client avert a similar "wrong" behavior. It is possible for a clergyman to be nonjudgmental of the person while being judgmental of the action.

6. Be slow to break silences unless the parishioner indicates discomfort. Most silences are beneficial to the client. Strang (15) describes the counselor as a "catalyst for the student's thought processes." A catalyst acts quietly, and the counselor may be performing a definite function even though he is saying nothing. Of course, silences must be broken when it becomes evident that the client is not using the silence for constructive work.

7. Allow emotions to subside. Parishioners who become emotional usually are not lastingly embarrassed about it if they are allowed to control themselves before they continue expressions. Sympathy usually prolongs the emotional period. The counselor should wait quietly; and if he says anything it should be such as, "You should take as much time as you need to gain control. We are in no hurry."

8. Avoid promiscuous reassurances. If the counselor reassures the client, it may have a wrong effect. It may cause an emotional outbreak. If the counselor assures the client that "everything will be all right," he may be inviting doubt on the part of the client. The client may feel that the counselor doesn't know what he is talking about, or that he has little ability if he thinks everything is going to be all right (10). Reassuring in the framework of asserting God's concern for His people deserves the same careful consideration as do other types of reassurance. At the same time, spiritual aids are very helpful and appropriate at times.

9. If questions are asked the client, let him answer them. A common failing of counselors is to ask too many questions. Some questions are permissible, to be sure. However, many counselors ask questions in such a way as to dictate the answer in advance in order to prove a point. The counselor may ask, "You don't like mathematics very well, now, do you?" The client may answer, "No," or he may say, "Well, not very much." He really has a hard time answering, "Yes, I do," if the question has been posed as above.

10. Avoid entering problem areas which the parishioner does not suggest. Quite often it is apparent to a counselor that a client has

a problem in an area altogether different from the one he consulted the counselor about. Bordin (6) cautions against the counselor's being quick to assign emotional overtones to decision-oriented problems. The interview should be adapted to the client's expectations; the client should not be forced into an area he wishes to avoid.

THE CLOSING PHASE
OF THE INTERVIEW

The body of the counseling interview can usually be divided into three parts which may be labeled (1) The opening phase—rapport-building and getting acquainted, (2) The exploratory phase—developing insight into the problem area and bringing about self-understanding, and (3) The closing phase—summarizing of things accomplished and setting plans for any future interviews. The summarizing is typically a joint undertaking of counselor and parishioner. The client is usually invited to return for continued pursuit of the present problem or for consultation on other problems which might arise. Closing the interview requires considerable diplomacy in most cases. The interview usually is closed because of time limits and, if this be the case, it will be necessary that the counselor keep track of time. He should bring the insight development phase of the interview to an end with time to spare for the summary and the closing activities before the interview must end.

The task of closing interviews on time will require considerable practice for the beginning counselor. Some clients are not inclined to end the interview at the time chosen by the counselor or dictated by the time element. Usually, the counselor should stop the forward progress of the interview some ten minutes before actual closing time, saying, "I see that our time is about up and I wonder if we might take just a minute to review what has been accomplished." After client and counselor, working together, summarize the session, the counselor might say, "Now, our time is up for today. I wonder if you feel you would like to come back and pursue this problem further." Most clients will make preparations for leaving when the counselor rises; and the interview can be terminated without difficulty. Other clients have to be reminded that the time is up and that someone else is waiting for an appointment.

It is always difficult to present ideas about the conduct of the interview because stereotyped plans seldom work out. It is often the case that a client is engaged in a series of interviews, perhaps of a therapeutic nature, and the question of returning is settled from the beginning. In cases like these, the exploring and insight development phase of the interview may continue right up to the last minute. As counselor and client become more used to their respective roles in an extended series of interviews, more of the interview hour can be spent on highly valuable pursuits. This is not to say that summarizing is of small value, but much time can be saved from structuring and closing phases of the interview. The following suggestions for the closing phase of the interview should be studied toward the end of making these activities spontaneous elements of the counselor's interview technique.

Suggestions for the Closing Phase

1. Avoid abrupt closes. In order to avoid hurried and abrupt endings for interviews, it will be necessary for the counselor to begin the ending phase early enough. After one or more interviews with a given client, he should be able to ascertain the amount of time which would be profitable in closing the interview with this client. Even so, the length of the ending phase will depend in part upon what needs to be accomplished—upon how much material needs to be summarized and upon predicted involvements in the closing summary.

2. Urge the client to participate in summarizing. The summary of the interview has many values; and it may elicit additional responses. The client should be able to clarify any erroneous understandings which have carried over to the counselor and by so doing will bring more clear-cut understandings for himself. Actually, it is a good idea to suggest that the client do the summarizing, with the counselor supplying missing details.

3. Determine unfinished topics. Assuming that there will be another interview, it is well to indicate which topics deserve continued discussions in future interviews. These items should be entered in the counselor's notes.

4. Indicate subjects for the client's consideration between interviews. All counseling methods will be conducive to gains for the

client during the time between sessions; in fact many theorists claim that the work done by the client between sessions is more important than any other. All counselors do not suggest to the client that certain topics might profitably be given thought between sessions, but this is a favorite technique of some.

5. Have a clear understanding about client's return. If the client is to return, the appointment time should be made definite and should be entered in the counselor's appointment book. The time of the next appointment should be impressed upon the parishioner in a casual manner.

There has been no resolution of the question concerning the wisdom of appointment-making by clergymen. Certainly, there will be some cases where the clergyman will not wish to encourage the type of relationship that may grow out of a series of designated appointments. The reader is referred to "The Consultation Clinic," in *Pastoral Psychology* where this subject is discussed by Bletzen and Bruder (18).

Some clergymen dislike definite appointments because their work is demanding and strong pressures develop as a result of holding specific times open for counseling. On the other hand, specific appointments serve to assure that counseling activity will not be crowded out by other pressing matters.

6. Be firm but courteous in dismissing the client. The specialist in the church who counsels for several hours every day will experience little difficulty in terminating the counseling session. Most parishioners will not be extremely sensitive to rejection at the hands of the specialist. The clergyman will have more difficulty and will need to be extremely careful not to make the parishioner feel rejected. Every counselor should realize that if he allows a talkative client to stay overtime once, he will have difficulty every time this client comes for counseling.

7. Do not solicit the parishioner to return. The counselor must leave the impression that he is completely willing to meet the client again to continue discussing the problem; but it should be the client's decision to return. This would not always be true with clients undergoing psychotherapy, since some of these people are unable to know what is best for them.

8. Complete records immediately. The religious counselor and

the clergyman cannot afford to be less meticulous than other professional counselors. No counselor can remember all he should about counseling sessions; therefore, some form of recording is highly desirable. All materials should be filed immediately against the possibility that they may be read by the curious.

9. Exercise spiritual prerogatives. Without wishing to dictate to the religious counselor concerning spiritual tools, the author suggests that likely there would be no better time for intercessory prayer than immediately following the departure of the parishioner. It may be, also, that the situation might indicate a prayer with the parishioner before his departure.

10. Review session, seeking self-improvement. Time does not always permit this step. If the counselor cannot perform this task with each interview, it is suggested that he make a survey of his day's activities to ascertain his development as a counselor. The United States Air Force suggests a twelve-point self-evaluation for counselors serving Air Force personnel:

1. For each counselee, was there sufficient time allowed for adequate exploration?
2. Was I sufficiently sensitive to the counselee and was my approach one to inspire his confidence?
3. Did I motivate the counselee to take the responsibility for his part in the interview?
4. Was the conversational exchange "free" to the required degree?
5. Was my objectivity unhampered by "set" opinion?
6. Did any personal bias enter the decision?
7. Were the "leads" furnished by the counselee recognized by me?
8. As the interview progressed, did the counselee become positive and decisive?
9. At any point, did I fail to have the needed occupational information?
10. Was there evidence of increasing insight on the part of the counselee?
11. Was the counseling process, in itself, a satisfying experience?
12. Was there experience value in each interview? (1, ch. 2, p. 7).*

Such a self-evaluation process would benefit any counselor.

---

* Courtesy of Air Training Command, United States Air Force. Taken from ATRC Manual 35-1, *A Manual for Counselors* (now out of print).

RECORDING THE INTERVIEW
MATERIAL

There are many reasons why counseling interviews should be recorded. First of all, it is necessary for records to be kept in order that the counselor may be able to review his many interviews; it is unrealistic to believe that any counselor would be able to remember all that he should concerning his clients. It is necessary that he maintain a record so that he may review the events of past sessions from time to time.

Then, too, it is true that records may be able to bring out factors which the interview itself did not reveal. During the interview, words come so rapidly that neither counselor nor client is able to understand the full relationships of facts and expressed attitudes. Upon a close scrutiny of the printed records and upon listening to recorded interviews, things often fall into place and become more meaningful to the counselor.

On the other hand, it is quite possible that the client may at a later time seek help elsewhere, and it is well to have some records of the interviews to pass on to the new counselor. Although records are more important in some circumstances than in others, they should be valuable in any type of counseling activity.

Kinds of Records

Different counselors have various methods for the task of keeping records. Many prefer to take notes during the interview, but such a practice has both advantages and disadvantages. The question that arises is whether or not a person is able to give the undivided attention he should give to the client's expression if he tries to take notes on the developments. On the other hand, the counselor may be able to accomplish the dual task of listening and writing, but he may violate the client's feelings on the matter. Many clients sense that the counselor is not giving his full attention if he is writing during the interview.

Some counselors have been able to perfect a type of shorthand notetaking which allows a great deal of freedom from the writing function and still permits them to get the salient points of the interview. Usually, they are able to expand their notes in an after-session minute or two to include most of the important things covered. It is unlikely, however, that any counselor can take down a statement-by-statement account of events in a counseling session. The best he will be able to do is to get the *ideas* expressed on paper. Most counselors agree that they are able to understand and follow the client's thoughts better if they do not have to be concerned with notetaking.

Aside from the fact that notetaking influences the interview negatively in terms of the atmosphere created by the counselor's divided attention, it is disconcerting to some clients to have people take down the things they say. They may feel inhibited in expressing themselves if they know that everything is being taken down. For this reason, it is always in order for the counselor to seek the permission of the client before he takes notes on the conversation.

Most counselors ask if it is all right to take notes and suggest that the client may wish to see them occasionally to see what has been said. Although few clients really ask to see the notes, it is a good gesture for the counselor to agree to make them available to the client upon his demand. The obvious disadvantage in this is that the counselor would be able to take more voluminous notes in a manner that would be understandable only to him, if he did not have to allow the client to see them; and the possibility of being asked to see the notes forces the counselor to make more readable notes, and this means fewer notes. Most counselors do occasionally record impressions and evaluations they do not wish the client to see, but this can be done after the client has departed.

The tape recorder has come into rather wide usage by many counseling people, but it is a fallacy to suppose that the tape recorder will solve all problems inherent in record-taking. Many factors are involved. The first, as in notetaking, is the reluctance of some clients to having their conversations recorded; and there definitely seems to be more resistance to tape recording than to notes taken on paper. As a matter of ethics, it is wise to ask permission of the client to tape-record the interviews. Many clients say that it is all right with them, but this does not mean that they will be uninhibited with the recorder. Most counselors become aware that some of their clients are much more uninhibited without it. It is possible, of course, that any client would adjust to the recorder in time.

Even if the client agrees to tape recordings, and even if the client responds well in the presence of the recorder, there are other problems involved. Cost of tapes and recording equipment is an important factor. Few counselors are able to retain tapes, for filing purposes, on all interviews. It becomes necessary to record one interview over the other, usually, and thereby the record is lost unless a typescript has been made. The ideal situation would be to tape each session and have secretarial help transcribe each tape, and the typescript could be filed permanently. Although ideal, this situation is quite unusual if not unprecedented.

Once the tape has been made, it presents difficulties to the busy counselor who hopes to review a previous session in a very limited time. Tapes require the same time to play back as they require to make. If a counselor desires to review *completely* an hour's session, he must have an hour in which to do it. By comparison, he could glance over a page or two of concise notes in a minute or two.

As to hiding the microphone from the client, it has already been said that the recording should not be made without his consent. It is possible to gain the client's permission to record generally, and then to switch the microphone on at times without his knowledge. With such an arrangement as this, the microphone is, of course, hidden from view. This method may raise a question of ethics, inasmuch as some deceit may be involved.

The final choice of a method of record-keeping will depend on the feelings of the individual counselor about the matter. This writer feels that the best solution is a very fragmentary record kept by the counselor, as unobtrusively as possible, to be expanded by him the moment the session is finished and before he loses some of the valuable material he may have in mind to set down. This record could well be supplemented by using the tape recorder occasionally, especially in cases where psychotherapy is being used. The counselor can often sense that the session will be a highly productive one, and he will be able to make an occasional tape which he will likely review completely for valuable clues that he may have missed in the session itself. In cases where an occasional tape is very meaningful, it may be filed. Some counselors use the tape playback as a method of impressing insights on the client.

One of the greatest difficulties experienced by the average counselor in the taking, expanding, and use of notes is finding sufficient time to do all these things. Usually the counselor manages to get one client out the door just as another is ready to come in. If he is to expand his notes, he must do so immediately before they get "cold." Should he take time for this, he would not have the time to study notes and materials for the interview he must undertake just ahead.

The most ideal situation for a counselor who typically spends an hour in an interview is to have a full-hour period between interviews, to allow time enough for expansion of notes and preparation for the subsequent interview. Unfortunately, few counseling jobs allow the counselor to be so leisurely.

Keeping Records in the Religious Setting

The Consultation Clinic, a feature of *Pastoral Psychology*, deals comprehensively with the matter of "keeping records in counseling situations" in the religious setting (17). Among those contributing are Fairbanks, Southard, and Rutledge, all of whom are highly experienced in church-related counseling.

There are several important ideas which run through these discussions. One thought is that all members of a congregation need to be represented in a file wherein pertinent data may be kept on cards or in folders. This may be merely census data, but it may include records of contributions, of special events such as baptisms, and so forth. Several writers suggest that each entry in the file be assigned a code number.

The code number then may be used to identify those persons who need a more confidential filing arrangement. This second file would consist of materials dealing with counseling situations which deserve a measure of confidentiality. This second file might well be of the folder type so that written accounts of home visits and office counseling sessions could be slipped into it.

Rutledge, in particular, recognizes and discusses succinctly the problems pursuant to the secretarial phase of record-keeping and the important consideration of confidentiality assured by a well-trained staff:

The entire staff should understand that information about any person, including whether he has been or is being seen, must not be given to anyone, whether a relative or a professional person, without the express permission of the client—*and then only by the pastor or counselor in charge!* (14, p. 47).

LEARNING TO INTERVIEW

The student will be interested in the ways of learning to become adept at interviewing. To be sure, the best way to learn an activity is to participate in it, but there are other aspects of learning to interview than practice. Actually, one may practice doing a thing in a poor manner and may hurt his chances of learning the best procedures.

After the student has familiarized himself with principles and techniques of interviewing through reading widely in the field, he should be ready for some type of active-experience training. There are several good films depicting the counseling interview, and these may be used in conjunction with reading. Classic works in interviewing include books by Bingham and Moore (3), Garrett (10), and Kahn and Cannell (12).

Observing Counselors in Action

Several studies have been attempted with the idea of allowing student counselors to observe actual counseling scenes through one-way mirrors. Such observations would be an ideal source of first-hand information; and, together with criticism of the sessions, they should be a very good method for learning. The obvious disadvantage in this is the fact that the client's assurance of privacy is violated. Kadushin (11) found in an intensive study that a majority of a group of counselors rejected the observation method in teaching. There is reason to believe that observation of religiously oriented counseling sessions would be even more objectionable. In addition to the question of confidentiality, there may be the feeling that observation violates a sort of sacred trust the parishioner has in the religious counselor. No situation demands privacy as much as when two people join in prayer or when other spiritual aids are used.

Studying Tape Recordings

As a means of improving counseling technique, the tape recording, studied carefully, is an invaluable aid. Counselors at every stage of training and experience are often amazed at the obvious blunders they make. By listening to one's own tape recordings of counseling sessions, there is no violation of ethics.

Practically every counselor-trainer on university and seminary campuses has tape recordings that would be invaluable for demonstration of techniques to students. These may be used provided the permission of the counselee is obtained. There may be logic in promoting a plan by which counselor-trainers at different universities and seminaries could place some tapes in a circulating library to be loaned on request.

Training by Role-playing

Kahn and Cannell (12) have suggested role-playing as being a most valuable tool in counselor-training. The techniques of role-playing were developed as an aid to psychotherapy; however, the same dynamics which aid the individual in developing insight into personal problems also make him aware of his mistakes and shortcomings as an interviewer.

In the application of role playing to interviewer training, one member of the group plays the part of the respondent, identifying himself with some actual person whom he knows, and responds to the interviewer in terms of the role which he is playing. One of the other members of the group plays the interviewer. . . . When the role playing session ends, there is a general discussion of the techniques which the interviewer used, the problems posed by the respondent, and the strengths and weaknesses which were demonstrated.

The trainee who plays the interviewer role gets the benefit of practicing directly the words and techniques he must use in the interview situation. He also gets the experience of facing real problems without real penalties; the game has reality, but he is not playing "for keeps." As a result, he is freer in his approach and more able to observe himself than he would be in an actual interview situation (12, p. 337).*

---

* Reprinted with permission, from Robert L. Kahn and Charles F. Cannell, *The Dynamics of Interviewing*. New York: John Wiley & Sons, Inc., 1957.

A variation of this procedure is for the trainer to assume certain counselee roles and to be respondent with first one then another of the members of the practicum group. In this way, the trainer may bring about structured problems he may wish to demonstrate to the viewers. Thus, the trainer may play the role of the effusive talker and, at another time, that of the shy and reluctant client.

Role-playing activity is one which is typically dreaded by the student in the beginning. Most students are likely to be reluctant to demonstrate their abilities before their peers. However, once the "ice" has been broken, practically all student counselors gain much from such experiences. Under pressures of criticism from the group, a student may give up some habit in which he might otherwise persist for an entire lifetime. For instance, most beginning counselors talk too much. Group criticisms can make such a habit an uncomfortable one; and the counselor in training may receive an everlasting benefit from the role-playing experience.

It should be understood that the playing of the role of respondent is such an important one that the practice of casting the student as the counselor while the trainer plays the respondent should not be an exclusive situation, to say the least.

> The trainee usually gets as much out of playing the role of respondent, however, as he does out of playing the interviewer role. As a respondent, he can perceive where the interviewer failed to get information that was potentially available and when the interviewer used techniques that were irritating. Analyzing his own reactions to being interviewed, and experiencing directly the effects of different interviewing techniques, sensitize the trainee to reactions of respondents. Meanwhile, the trainees who are observers have a chance to see the performance in a more detached way and to plan the elimination of errors in their own interview techniques (12, pp. 237-238).*

Using the Tape Recorder

Most universities which attempt counselor training maintain some type of clinic where the trainees may participate in supervised practice. The respondents are either college students

---

* Reprinted with permission, from Robert L. Kahn and Charles F. Cannell, *The Dynamics of Interviewing.* New York: John Wiley and Sons, Inc., 1957.

or people from the community. In some other situations, it is possible to place the trainee in a community clinic under supervision either in a practicum training or an internship.

A most valuable method of training in any of these situations utilizes the tape recorder. The counselor-trainee is first made familiar with the recording instrument and is encouraged to gain experience with the device outside the training interview. Then, certain cases, which have been picked to accommodate the level and training of the trainee, are turned over to him for counseling. He obtains permission of the client to record the sessions, does so, and brings the tapes to his trainer for review and criticism. Usually, the trainee indicates to the client that his supervisor will be the only one, except himself, who will have access to the tapes.

The use of these tapes can be most beneficial to the training of the counselor; however, there are some hazards and obstacles to be overcome. In the first place, the trainer should be cognizant of the excessive amount of time involved in listening to and criticizing the interviews. This writer has found it almost impossible to listen to the complete tapes of his trainees. It is perhaps advisable to listen to one or two tapes all the way through, to discuss the strengths and weaknesses with the trainee, and to point out implications in the personality dynamics of the client. In this way, the trainee may be taught what to look for in his own tapes. After a few such operations, it may be that the trainee may be entrusted with reviewing his own tapes without benefit of trainer collaboration. He would then bring in specific questions concerning certain features of the tapes and he may wish to play parts of the tapes for the trainer's comments.

In the last stages of training with the use of the tape recorder, it may be that the trainee should be asked to transcribe those parts of his tapes which he thinks have specific meaning and to present the typescript to his trainer for criticism. It is obvious that typescript can be handled faster than electrically recorded material. In all of this, the trainer must satisfy himself that the trainee is developing enough competency that he may be allowed to proceed under less and less supervision. To set the trainee free from supervision and dependency is the ultimate aim of the trainer and should come about gradually.

Training under Visual Supervision

It is probable that the trainee's first counseling interviews should be held under visual supervision of his trainer. This may be accomplished by having the trainer enter the counseling room with the counselor-in-training and sit as an observer. This is admittedly a somewhat awkward arrangement in which the presence of the third party must be explained to the client, but it may be justified without embarrassment by explaining to the client that such an arrangement is a part of the process of training for the student trainee. If the client accepts the actual presence of the trainer, he will not object to having the trainer watch and listen to the subsequent sessions by remote control, through the one-way mirror, or over an intercom system.

This entire area is one calling for diplomacy and highly ethical strategy. In the first place, it is probably unwise to allow a student counselor to pose as anything other than a counselor-in-training. On the college campuses, these situations are usually understood and accepted by the students being counseled. Since the student counselor is not usually entrusted, in the training stage, with problems having great depth, it is unlikely that too much resistance will arise concerning visual supervision or recording of interviews. The entire situation may be summed up in this way: (1) The student counselor should not be allowed to counsel in early stages of training without close supervision, either visual observation or review of tape recording; (2) The student counselor should be gradually emancipated from the supervision by his trainer; and (3) Ethical standards should be observed as rigidly under training practices as under actual professional-level counseling.

Rating Scales

Kahn and Cannell (12) provide some rating scales to be used by the supervisor as an aid to the interviewer-in-training. Although these particular scales are not as applicable to the counseling interview as they are to information-getting types of interviewing, they do point up the values of having some methods worked out by which the supervisor may be somewhat explicit in his evaluations. To say the least, the supervisor should devise some method for making his criticism relate specifically to the actual events in the interview rather than being vaguely critical of unidentifiable mistakes.

Group Effects upon Training

The values of utilizing the group in training are great. It is highly valuable if a group of counselors-in-training can be molded into an interacting group for purposes of discussing training objectives, of formulating plans, and of criticizing counseling interviews. This idea has already been described relative to role playing, but should be used broadly in the training of counselors.

The specific value to be attained in group attack upon training problems and upon recorded interviews is the value of feedback, the criticism of one's efforts by the group. As a counselor-in-training listens to his own tapes, he is incapable of properly evaluating his progress or shortcomings. If the group has been developed in such a way as to eliminate the needs of the individual to defend himself against criticism, he will benefit greatly from criticism. A criticism which is defended against either verbally or mentally does little good.

Directors of training programs for counselors should plan specifically for the evolvement of a strongly knit group of trainees. It is too often true that the trainees are not encouraged to meet as a group; and in many practicum and internship situations, there is no meeting as a class. It is clearly evident that a most valuable aid to training is provided by some type of group meeting in which counseling protocols are discussed, role-playing is done, and opportunities for group discussion are promoted.

Ethics demands that permission be gained from the client in order to play his tape before a group. Such permission, sought after the tape has been made, is usually granted.

References

1. Air Training Command, *A Manual For Counselors.* ATRC Manual 35-1, June, 1952.
2. Allport, Gordon W., *Personality, A Psychological Interpretation.* New York: Holt, Rinehart, and Winston, Inc., 1937.

3. Bingham, Walter and Bruce V. Moore, *How to Interview*. New York: Harper and Brothers, 1941.

4. Birren, Faber, "Color in Your Plant," *Factory Management and Maintenance*. February, 1954, pp. 111-112.

5. Blum, M. L. and B. Balinski, *Counseling and Psychology*. Englewood Cliffs, N.J.: Prentice-Hall, Inc., 1951.

6. Bordin, Edward S., "Implications of Client Expectation For the Counseling Process," *Journal of Counseling Psychology*. Vol. 2, 1955, pp. 17-21.

7. Davidian, Elizabeth V., "Rapport and the Human Element," *Personnel and Guidance Journal*. April, 1955, pp. 469-470.

8. Deutsch, Felix and William F. Murphy, *The Clinical Interview*, Volume II. New York: International Universities Press, Inc., 1955.

9. Erickson, Clifford E., *The Counseling Interview*. Englewood Cliffs, N.J.: Prentice-Hall, Inc., 1950.

10. Garrett, Annette, *Interviewing, Its Principles and Methods*. New York: Family Service Association of America, 1942.

11. Kadushin, Alfred, "Interview Observation as a Teaching Device," *Social Casework*, 37, 1956, pp. 334-341.

12. Kahn, Robert L. and Charles F. Cannell, *The Dynamics of Interviewing*. New York: John Wiley and Sons, Inc., 1957.

13. Ross, Josephine H., "The Initial Interview," *Psychoanalysis*. Winter, 1957, p. 46.

14. Rutledge, Aaron L., "The Consultation Clinic," *Pastoral Psychology*. February, 1956, pp. 43-48.

15. Strang, Ruth, *Counseling Technics in College and Secondary School*. New York: Harper and Brothers, 1949.

16. Sullivan, Harry Stack, *The Psychiatric Interview*. New York: W. W. Norton, 1954.

17. The Consultation Clinic. "Keeping Records in Counseling Situations," *Pastoral Psychology*. February, 1956, pp. 43-48.

18. ————. "Should the Minister Make Weekly Appointments?" *Pastoral Psychology*. March, 1957, pp. 47-49.

19. Tyler, Leona, "The Initial Interview," *Personnel Guidance Journal*. April, 1956, pp. 466-473.

20. ————, *The Work of the Counselor*. New York: Appleton-Century-Crofts, Inc., 1953.

21. Williamson, E. G., *How to Counsel Students*. New York: McGraw-Hill Book Company, 1939.

IV

Nonclinical Approaches to
Personal-Problem Counseling

THE SCOPE
OF PERSONAL PROBLEMS

Those who approach the clergyman or other religious workers for counseling usually have problems which may be categorized in three groups: (1) decision-making problems, (2) conditions involving personality structure necessitating psychotherapy, and (3) surface-level personal problems which do not specifically involve decisions and do not require psychotherapy. Having arbitrarily set up this division of problems, the author freely concedes that there is no clear-cut line between them. For instance, decision-making problems may have therapeutic root structures; and surface-level personal problems may be founded upon faulty decisions.

There is need, however, for separating human problems for purposes of discussion. Only by a somewhat segmented approach may readers grasp the variations of counseling methods that deal with the type of problem under attack. In a very real sense, church members do present their problems to the religious worker as being specific in one area or another. The counselor is faced with problems which are perceived by the counselee as related to certain easily identified areas of experience. The religious counselor must consider problems and methods used in aiding the client to solve them in a somewhat segmented manner, realizing all the while that the human organism reacts as a whole to all of life's situations.

There is no denying that when human beings have difficulty they are troubled "all over." Thus, problems of decision affect the dispositions of people and bring about problems of interpersonal relationships. A man who is dissatisfied with his job may become dissatisfied with his wife also; and such a man seeking counsel would probably relate the difficulty with his wife immediately, and might not reveal his job difficulty at all. A high school boy who has been jilted by his girl friend would be "crushed" by his personal problem; but he would not likely consider the possibility that his basic problem is one of being uninformed about social graces.

This student would present his problem to the youth worker in an unrealistic manner; and the youth worker would accept the problem as stated, but realizing all the while that there might be other involvements. Yet, every counselor must learn techniques of dealing with problems as presented. He must be prepared to counsel the individual toward a solution of the presented surface problem. He must be willing to terminate the counseling effort at this point if the counselee so desires. He must have the tools for handling a problem of decision, if it arises, even though this may not have been the presented problem. He must be prepared to enter the therapeutic area or to refer the case elsewhere, should the nature of the problem so indicate.

The aim of this chapter is to indicate some theories and methods related to the solution of surface-level, nontherapeutic personal problems. Whether or not these surface-level problems lead to other problem types is beside the point here; attention is given elsewhere to theory and methodology for decision and therapeutic problems. As the problem area may shift, the counselor will be inclined to vary his techniques to accommodate the new emphasis.

It is probable that the majority of problems brought to the clergyman, youth worker, or other religious worker are personal problems; and it seems certain that the greatest need for training in counseling techniques among religious workers is in this area. It is true that personal problems, when neglected, may become increasingly serious, but the church-related counselor is often in a position to deal with problems before they reach this stage. He should make every effort to learn methods of counseling which will be helpful at the surface level where problems are typically presented. Every religious counselor should learn methods of treating personal problems at the surface level and should learn how to prevent the surface problems from becoming more serious than they already are. In addition, every counselor should learn how to avoid agitating the problem at a deep-running personality level while he seeks to provide some help at the surface level.

Undeniably, there are some individuals with whom the wise religious counselor will be reluctant to work in any capacity. In some cases, even if psychiatric or other help is unavailable, it is best to leave the problem alone.

Admittedly, this is a difficult philosophy for the clergyman to accept. He has much less choice than others concerning whom he shall counsel. When parishioners request help, the clergyman is compelled to listen. If he perceives in the parishioner personality characteristics that clash with his own, he is often forced to enter counseling against his better judgment.

If the clergyman finds the parishioner mentally ill and beyond his capacities, he may wisely refer the parishioner to competent psychiatric help. But he should realize that immediate referral, especially of some mentally ill people, often brings feelings of rejection.

The clergyman does have the prerogative of using only a spiritual approach to helping a client with whom he is reluctant to deal in psychological counseling. He may wisely utilize spiritual approaches for several sessions, until such time as he may suggest referral without severely upsetting the parishioner. A great weight of judgment rests upon the clergyman in making a decision whether to work with a given individual with psychological approaches, to utilize only spiritual approaches, or to refer him to someone else.

Examples of Personal Problems

In attempting to give examples of personal problems as conceived in this writing, it is necessary to reiterate that any problem listed may involve the other two arbitrarily designated divisions of human difficulty, decision-making and personality deviation. Thus, marriage problems are thought of primarily as personal problems. Marriage problems may, of course, entail decision related to divorce or therapeutic treatment of one or both marriage partners. Because such a preponderance of the problems presented to the religious counselor are marriage and family problems, a special chapter is devoted to them.

Other examples of personal problems as identified here are financial problems, sex adjustment problems, problems involving hetereosexual relations of young people, personal mental and physical hygiene, bad habit alleviation, and social ineptness. Although there is a distinctiveness in problems expressed by the parishioner as "spiritual," this writer would list spiritual or religious problems in the personal problem category. The distinction of these as personal problems is made because they do not necessarily involve either decision-making or psychotherapy.

As pointed out in Chapter I, many parishioners come to the clergyman because they distrust psychological counselors. Among those who are in need of therapeutic treatment, many present their problems as being in the range of normal personal problems such as those enumerated above. As an entry is made into the problem area, the clergyman often sees other involvements and shifts to treating the difficulty as a problem of decision or as a therapy problem. Most counselors differentiate techniques based upon the nature of the problem.

Development of Theory
and Personal-Problem Counseling

As the student examines the history of theories which have contributed to counseling method, he will understand that the broad category of problems identified as personal problems was late in receiving attention. Before 1940, two large areas of human problems had been under attack, and considerable progress had been made in their treatment. The field of vocational guidance, activated in 1908, was implemented through research in testing following World War I. Large-scale advances were made, and vocational guidance quickly spread to encompass the field of educational choice. Thus, the main areas of decision-making were brought under sustained study.

The field of psychoanalysis and psychiatry also entered large-scale development following World War I, as did clinical psychology. Freud's influence in America, which was first evident in the early part of the twentieth century, was bolstered by the works of Adler, Jung, Rank, Horney, White, Sullivan, Alexander, French, and others. Thus, a well-ordered spearhead of attack upon the problems of the deeply-disturbed was organized and implemented. More recent conquests in the area of drug approaches to treatment of the deeply disturbed have made the treatment of neurotics and psychotics more promising.

So we see that the problems of the normal person, who had personal difficulties not connected with choice situations, were largely overlooked. In the schools, much work had been done to aid the student in vocational and educational choices; but little theory and practice had been formulated to aid in personal-problem solution before 1940. Those people who had marriage problems, religious problems, family difficulties, financial problems, and a host of others were in great need; but methodology was lacking.

During the late 1930's, clinical counseling developed. These methods were aimed primarily at difficulties of college students including vocational and educational maladjustment; and they were highly directive and not very applicable to most personal-problem areas. Clinical counselors, clinical psychologists, psychiatrists, and psychoanalysts posed as authority figures who were capable of directing people to solve their problems in manners devised by the counselors. The clinical method, which utilizes case history, testing, diagnosis, interpretation, and direction, was employed almost indiscriminately with all types of problems including decision, therapeutic, and personal problems. The clinical method has proved to be most valid in decision-making and in therapy with some types of difficulties; but it is summarily insufficient for working with personal problems.

The Advent of the Nondirective Method

During the late 1930's, unrelated efforts were promoted toward the same end in the areas of personnel management in industry and in clinical psychology. These two developments were destined to have lasting results in the field of personal problem counseling, since both efforts resulted in understanding the values of warmth and acceptance in human relationships. One of these efforts was carried on in the Hawthorne Plant of Western Electric Company. The work began as an attempt to study the effects of varying physical factors upon production. The most valuable end product was an emphasis on personnel counseling. Through a long series of experiments in interviewing and in counseling with employees, research specialists came to understand that people respond to warmth and permissiveness (4). The Hawthorne studies emphasized the ability of individuals to cooperate, to improve themselves, and to make valuable suggestions for company policy if given a measure of freedom and the indication on the part of their supervisors, bosses, and counselors that their ideas and expressions were looked upon with favor, understanding, and acceptance.

Working independently and in a different sphere, Carl R. Rogers, a clinical psychologist, was making discoveries related to the improvement of psychological problems of children, adolescents, and adults. He was motivated to raise the question concerning the validity of the authoritative concept of counseling. The usefulness of permissiveness and acceptance as opposed to authority, diagnosis, and direction was brought out strongly in 1942 with the publication of *Counseling and Psychotherapy* (6).

For a full decade, the question of the comparative merits of directive and nondirective methods was debated, not only in periodicals but also by verbal argumentation and demonstration. The student needs only to look through the periodicals of this period to find a multitude of articles debating the issue. The charges were hurled back and forth; extravagant claims were made by both sides; and each side tended to support their own doctrines as panaceas for all the ills of counseling method. Argumentation caused the nondirectivists to support claims of validity of their method in areas of decision-making and vocational guidance. The so-called directivist forces made counterclaims as to the validity of the clinical method in solving the personal problems of normal people.

From the weighty mass of literature concerning the controversy between the directive and nondirective forces, the student may wisely choose to read representative works by Thorne (11), Raskin (3), Snyder (9), Rogers (7), and Hahn and Kendall (2).

The battle has not been won by either side, but apparently the controversy has resulted in many values since it forced some definitive thinking upon all counselors everywhere. More than anything else, the controversy has led counselors to believe that no methodology is sufficient to deal with all types of human problems. Stone (10) reports, "The conflict between 'directiveness' and 'nondirectiveness' is being resolved in terms of appropriateness to the situation, and timing, rather than as an either-or choice."

So far as this author is aware, no specific method has been developed to treat personal problems. The nondirective revolt seems to have been formulated in opposition to the clinical counseling method on the one hand and to conventional clinical psychology, psychoanalysis, and psychiatry on the other. This author feels that the need for a basic theory and methodology to deal with personal problems was a large impetus for the development of the nondirective method. In this sense, the development was not conceived to combat any existing method, but was motivated by a need which was not being fulfilled by other methods of counseling. Essentially, the nondirectivists were revolting against the use of clinical methods and authoritativeness in working with personal problems, where such methods did not apply very well. From the beginning, nondirective methods were aimed at personal-social-emotional problems. It is true that a method of therapy has grown out of the original concepts of nondirective counseling. This is called client-centered therapy and is treated fully in Chapter VIII. The client-centered method utilizes nonauthoritarian concepts and does not claim proficiency in working with disoriented and incapacitated neurotics or psychotics.

This chapter aims to present a review of the basic theories and methods which seem most appropriate to the religious counselor as he strives to aid the parishioner in solving personal problems. Such a presentation draws heavily on nondirective theory and method. However, the author makes no claim of presenting puristic concepts of any counseling method in the discussion which follows.

THEORIES AND METHODS FOR
PERSONAL-PROBLEM COUNSELING

The Atmosphere

One who comes to the clergyman or other religious worker for help with a personal problem benefits from an atmosphere considerably different from the atmosphere that is conducive to directive therapy or decision-making. Not all personal problems are embarrassing in the usual sense; but they do always cause tension. The client is likely to be ashamed that he has been unable to handle his own difficulties. Those who are overcome by personal problems have suffered a blow to pride and to their confidence in themselves. Most of them regard coming for help as an admission of failure.

In personal-problem counseling, the best help does not seem to come through the counselor's further robbing the client of his self-confidence by assuming the role of a benefactor. Little good is likely to come from a method which emphasizes the ability of the counselor to establish causes and to offer advice and direction to the end that self-direction is thwarted. In the first place, the handling of the entire counseling chore should aim at helping the individual become more self-supporting and give him confidence in approaching future difficulties. This is best accomplished by having the client feel at the end of the counseling task, whether it consists of one or many sessions, that he has really solved his own problems, and that he did not have to rely upon the support of someone older, wiser, and more gifted than he.

All of this may be accomplished only if the counselor really feels that his clients *do have* abilities to help themselves. No counselor has been highly successful in fooling his clients into thinking that he (the counselor) believes in them when he really does not. This means in effect that the religious counselor must have implicit faith in the abilities of parishioners, who come for help with personal problems, to help themselves. A counselor who believes in his client as one who has the ability to direct his own life, cannot at the same time believe that he (the counselor) has ability to determine what is best for others.

The clergyman and religious counselor will accept this basic truth even though they may be unable to accept the dogmatism with which these ideas have been expressed. Dogmatic points of view serve to make counselors aware of ideas which need to be entertained, evaluated, and integrated into a workable and reasonable synthesis. The following quotation from Rogers focuses attention upon basic questions of interest to the religious counselor:

> The primary point of importance here is the attitude held by the counselor toward the worth and the significance of the individual. How do we look upon others? Do we see each person as having worth and dignity in his own right? If we do hold this point of view at the verbal level to what extent is it operationally evident at the behavioral level? Do we tend to treat individuals as persons of worth, or do we subtly devaluate them by our attitudes and behavior? Is our philosophy one in which respect for the individual is uppermost? Do we have a need and a desire to dominate others? Are we willing for the individual to select and choose his own values, or are our actions guided by the conviction (usually unspoken), that he would be happiest if he permitted us to select for him his values and standards and goals? (8, pp. 82-83).

These ideas entail an acceptance of the client as he is. But in the treatment of personal problems, acceptance must go further than that. In therapy, the defendable aim may be to abolish the neurotic fears of the client, to change him drastically for his own good. In personal-problem counseling, the client is the one who must decide whether or not he wishes to change. Thus, the religious counselor needs to accept the client as he has been, as he is now, and as he wishes to be in the future. Such acceptance is necessary in order to develop and maintain an atmosphere which is permissive, warm, and free from threat to the client (1).

The emphasis here is on accepting the right of the client to be and to become what he chooses. In this, there need be no acceptance or condoning of conduct. Neither will it be necessary that the religious counselor anesthetize his convictions of right and wrong.

There is no doubt that this frame of reference is foreign to the thinking of many religious workers. These workers feel a commitment to instruct folk in the ways of righteousness and in the manners of life deemed desirable by society in general and their church group in particular. A difference must be considered between the *instructing* which the religious worker does from the pulpit, in Bible class, and in youth organizations, and the *counseling* in face-to-face encounter with the individual. The religious worker can hardly be true to himself or to his congregation if he fails to instruct where instructing is called for. But if he is to be successful as he attempts to counsel, he will need to be accepting and non-judgmental.

The author presents here a line of thought which has come from psychological research and which has been widely applied in psychological counseling. It would be most foolhardy to suppose that the same ideas may be transposed to the religious setting without variation. The religious counselor is often inclined toward being critical of some behavior for very good reasons. He may feel strongly that God would have him speak out in counseling sessions concerning the conduct of the counselee, and it is his right and obligation to vary accepted counseling techniques as he feels led to do so. The religious worker may not choose to adopt entirely the permissive and amoral atmosphere. The author is no evangelist for these theories; but he does feel that the theories have merit and should be examined by the religious worker.

The attitude of the counselor is the most important aspect of the permissive atmosphere. His noncritical, nonjudgmental, amoral, understanding, and friendly attitudes together with physical aspects of the office which suggest freedom and permissiveness should be conducive to a free expression by the client and a self-examination which has never been possible before.

The chief reason why the client is able to see his problems and himself more clearly in the permissive and accepting atmosphere is that he no longer needs to be defensive. In the usual everyday life situation and in the authoritative counseling situation, the client is under constant tension. He defends against tension by constantly covering up his true feeling and by assigning false values to his actions. Thus, the husband who has agitated his wife by working late at night may face the realities of the situation when he feels that he is not on trial and does not feel the threat of accusal. He may admit to himself for the first time that he really does not need to work so much at night and that the real reason for this late work is that he doesn't like the noise and confusion of his home where his children romp and play. When he sees the truth about his late hours and understands the reason for his actions without the necessity for defense or guilt, he will come to realize that his wife is justified in being angry with him. On the other hand, the wife may come to see, in permissive counseling, that she has been untidy and has not made the home as attractive as she might have. Faced with an authoritative situation, she would be sure to throw up a screen of defenses to hide behind. She would claim that she could do better if her husband were more considerate, she would say that no mother with two children could have time for self-improvement, and she would state a number of other reasons for her actions. In the nonthreatening permissive atmosphere, where she may be able to examine her motives freely for the first time without defending against the threat, she may gain insight into her actions. She may admit, for instance, that the real reason why she keeps such an untidy house is that she does not care to please her husband, who thinks so little of her as to spend every night away from home.

It would be quite impossible to overemphasize the value of the permissive atmosphere in bringing about the client's understanding of his reasons for doing things as he does. It would seem that the development and maintenance of such an atmosphere would be easy to accomplish, but there are many pitfalls; and the ability to maintain such permissive atmosphere comes only through concentrated practice. For instance, the client himself does not understand fully the purpose of the permissive atmosphere and is not likely to cooperate in the formulation of it. The typical client seeks constantly to gain the support of the counselor to his way of seeing things. He seeks to get the counselor to agree to his interpretation of events. The complaining wife will be desirous of getting the counselor to agree that she is being maltreated. The distracted husband will want to know if the counselor thinks he should give up his job just because it involves night work, about which his wife complains. The counselor must be aware that the moment he agrees or disagrees with any client on any subject, he has set himself up as a judge and the permissive atmosphere begins to dissipate. If the counselor agrees by word, expression, or nod of the head that the husband is right, then the husband has been supported in his defense against the actual truth; and the possibilities of the client's gaining a clear insight about his behavior are lessened. So the counselor must remain noncommittal but accepting. The difficult part is that he must remain noncommittal without seeming passive or unmoved by the client's difficulties.

The typical counselee who has a personal problem desires a counselor who will tell him what to do. This seems to be an extension of the childhood feelings of wishing to rely upon parents for direction. Even if the counselor has abilities sufficient to bring about the complete relief of the client's difficulties, such a procedure would be unwise. Our society places emphasis upon self-sufficiency; and this is what the counselor must attempt to instill in the client. He must aid the client in solving his own problem and thereby build up in him a feeling of self-sufficiency and the ability to solve future problems. Rogers says:

> This newer approach differs from the other one in that it has a genuinely different goal. It aims directly toward the greater independence and integration of the individual rather than hoping that such results will accrue if the counselor assists in solving the problem. The individual and not the problem is the focus. The aim is not to solve one particular problem, but to assist the individual to grow, so that he can cope with the present problem and with later problems in a better-integrated fashion. If he can gain enough integration to handle one problem in more independent, more responsible, less confused, better-organized ways, then he will also handle new problems in that manner (6, pp. 28-29).

Techniques for Client Understanding

The assumption for the personal-problem counselor must be that the client can solve his own problem, since he must do so eventually, and that the reason he has been unable to solve or accept his problem is that he does not have sufficient understanding of himself or the facts concomitant to his problem area. Although there are some facts which the counselor may be able to supply and some learnings which he may be able to pass on to the client, it is usually assumed that the only means by which a person may come to understand himself and his problem involvement adequately is to express his feelings relative to himself, his fellows, and his environment. So, the essential task for the counselor becomes one of aiding the continued intelligent expression of feelings by the client. Rogers says:

   . . . Certainly one of the significant goals of any counseling experience is to bring into the open those thoughts and attitudes, those feelings and emotionally charged impulses, which center around the problems and conflicts of the individual. This aim is complicated by the fact that the superficial attitudes, and those easily expressed, are not always the significant and motivating attitudes. Consequently the counselor must be skilled indeed in providing release for the client in order to bring about an adequate expression of the basic issues in his situation. The counseling relationship itself, as has been pointed out, aids in this process. . . . (6, p. 131).

Reflecting techniques are most important in keeping the client busy expressing himself. By subtle handling of reflections, the counselor is able to keep the counselee discussing himself, his associates, his problems, and his environment. The basic method is for the counselor to mirror back to the client his expressions in a manner designed to lead him into further expressions. Some counselors feel very strongly about adding new material to the counselee's expressions. Others feel that new material keeps the client moving forward even though it may not always be accurate. For instance, a client may say, "My mother never would allow us boys to go out with a girl unless she knew something about the girl and her family." One reflection designed to keep the client expressing himself might be, "Your mother was quite strict about your dating activities." The client likely would say, "Yes, she was . . ." and would move on to new expressions. This reflection could be thought of as a "content" reflection since it does not deal with feelings at all. Another reflection of the same client's speech might be, "You feel that your mother was unfair in keeping you under such strict surveillance." This statement reflects feeling as well as content and would likely result in more emotional expression by the client. Neither of these counselor expressions necessarily adds new material, provided, of course, that the feeling reflected was accurate.

The counselor might have said, "I believe it is evident that your mother has caused you to be a shy person." This would be definitely interpretative and would, of course, add new material to the discussion. The counselor likely will handle each client differently and also will vary his approach with the problem and over-all situation; but he should be fully conscious that when new material is forced into the interview, there is a change in atmosphere. The atmosphere automatically is less permissive since the interview has taken an authoritative tone. Rogers asserts:

> . . . When the counselor responds on an intellectual basis to the ideas which the client expresses, he diverts expression into intellectual channels of his own choosing, he blocks the expression of emotionalized attitudes, and he tends wastefully to define and solve the problems in his own terms, which are often not the true terms for the client. On the other hand, when the counselor continually keeps himself alert not only to the content which is being stated, but to the feelings which are being expressed, and responds primarily in terms of the latter element, it gives the client the satisfaction of feeling deeply understood, it enables him to express further feeling, and it leads most efficiently and most directly to the emotional roots of his adjustment problem (6, p. 141).

Advice-Giving

It is questionable whether any counselor can defend the practice of giving advice to people with personal problems. He should ask himself if he is ready to take responsibility for the resultant action following any advice he gives a client; but if counselors give only that advice for which they are willing to shoulder the responsibility, they will give little advice. Actually, it is unfair for the counselor to give advice unless he has seriously considered all the possible repercussions. The client is the person who must suffer the consequences of his actions; it is only right that he should make the decisions for these actions, assuming of course that he is in a proper condition for doing this.

If advice-giving becomes indefensible, then one should consider the defensibility of offering any type of comment that may be designed by the counselor to bring about a decision by the client and that arises from an evaluation of the problem by the counselor. A counselor who is interested in the welfare of his client will no more offer comment designed to motivate him toward an action which he (the counselor) feels the client should take than he would give direct advice. Consider the differences between, "I advise you to divorce your husband," and "It does seem that your problems are insurmountable, doesn't it?" Either of these comments may lead to a divorce. In the first instance the wife would have every reason to blame the counselor should she seek divorce and later be sorry.

In the second instance she would not be likely to blame the counselor, but the counselor would be to blame nevertheless.

Interpretations always change the atmosphere of the counseling situation and they usually have a directing force on the client's future actions; so it is best that the counselor be aware that these things are true. Such awareness does not always mean that the counselor will avoid all interpretation. Interpretations may be done in such a way as to cause the client to consider aspects of the problem situation that had gone unobserved. Suggestions for client consideration may not actually be interpretations although they are interpretative in a sense. The counselor may say to the high school girl, "I wonder if you have ever considered that your mother is doing this because she really loves you." Bringing forth new ideas for client consideration has as a base the eager explorations of the counselor. He must be most careful in doing this in order to keep his own individual sense of values from becoming involved in his explorations and his suggestions to the client. He must be extremely careful in suggesting ideas to the client so as not to convey, along with the suggestions, his own judgment of the state of affairs.

ADVICE-GIVING AND INTERPRETATION IN RELIGIOUS COUNSELING

The foregoing discussion of advice-giving and interpretation has drawn heavily from nondirective thinking. The ideas may be wholly acceptable by the religious counselor and may be considered by him as sufficient to his needs. He may, on the other hand, react in violent opposition to these ideas.

It goes without saying that neither all psychologists nor all religious leaders will agree with these ideas. Not all accept the supposition that the client knows what he wants and what is best for him. Some may feel that the superior wisdom of counselors who have had experiences and who have seen the results of the experiences of others should be utilized to aid the parishioner. In addition, the religious leader may feel the leadership of God in offering advice and interpretation.

There is no reason why the years of experience of the clergyman or religious leader should not be utilized. Since God is able to direct the clergyman in other areas, the same power will abide in advice-giving. The religious counselor must be careful not to confuse God's leadership with his own needs for ego-bolstering. If God leads and if assessments and evaluations made by the counselor are accurate, advice and direction-giving may be very helpful to the client. It behooves the counselor, because of the great danger of improperly given or improperly taken advice, to be careful in the area of advice-giving and direction-giving.

Realistically, it must be admitted that the clergyman has a more difficult time parrying urgent requests of his parishioners for advice than does the ordinary counselor. Under the pressure of demands made by the parishioner, the clergyman will sometimes give advice with trepidation. He will be forced at times to make "snap" judgments; he can only hope (and perhaps pray) that what he does will work out to advantage for his client.

In the long run, the clergyman and religious counselor must be eclectic. The counselor must carefully consider, during each instant of the counseling process, the best technique for handling each client's unique problem. He may utilize the nondirective framework as his base of operations, but he is almost certain to vary from this framework at times. The most difficult aspect of any counselor's work is the constant judging of what technique, what approach, and what level of personal involvement is best for the client. Having God's leadership might conceivably make the clergyman's choices easier. Inasmuch as he must struggle to be sure what God's leadership is, his task may not be easier but more difficult because of the added factor of divine leadership.

THE INTERNAL FRAME OF REFERENCE

Traditional clinical methods of counseling usually utilize an external frame of reference. The counselor studies and evaluates the client through case history evaluation and testing. He applies his systematic learnings to the situation and evolves an interpretation based upon understandings of human functioning gained from studying humanity en masse. Personal problems are usually expressions of individual reaction to stimuli, and their treatment may not benefit by an analysis from an external frame of reference.

The best method of understanding an individual is through attention to his own ways of perceiving the world—from an internal frame of reference; therefore the counselor must make a concerted effort to place himself within the personality of the client. By so doing, he will understand the client better; and more than that, the client will react to the counselor in a manner that may make self-understanding more likely for the client. The value of adopting the internal frame of reference is adequately explained by Rogers.

Let us try to restate this idea in another way. In the emotional warmth of the relationship with the therapist, the client begins to experience a feeling of safety as he finds that whatever he expresses is understood in almost the same way that he perceives it, and is accepted. He then is able to explore, for example, a vague feeling of guiltiness which he has experienced. In this safe relationship he can perceive for the first time the hostile meaning and purpose of certain aspects of his behavior, and can understand why he has felt guilty about it, and why it has been necessary to deny to awareness the meaning of this behavior. But this clearer perception is in itself disrupting and anxiety-creating, not therapeutic. It is evidence to the client that there are disturbing inconsistencies in himself, that he is not what he thinks he is. But as he voices his new perceptions and their attendant anxieties, he finds that this acceptant alter ego, the therapist, this other person who is only partly another person, perceives these experiences too, but with a new quality. The therapist perceives the client's self as the client has known it, and accepts it; he perceives the contradictory aspects which have been denied to awareness and accepts those too as being a part of the client; and both of these acceptances have in them the same warmth and respect. Thus it is that the client, experiencing in another an acceptance of both these aspects of himself, can take toward himself the same attitude. He finds that he too can accept himself even with the additions and alterations that are necessitated by these new perceptions of himself as hostile. He can experience himself in this way without guilt. He has been enabled to do this (if our theory is correct) because another person has been able to adopt his frame of reference, to perceive with him, yet to perceive with acceptance and respect (5, p. 41).

COUNSELING AND LEARNING

It is often the case in personal-problem counseling that a large part of the difficulty is present because the client lacks certain information. Oftentimes the counseling may be consummated by a teaching and learning process. If the counselor has information which he may pass to the client either by word of mouth or by printed matter which will aid in the solution of problems, it is not reasonable that he should withhold the information. Marriage problems are often agitated by the lack of sex information. The social problems of adolescents and young people are often solved by training and instruction in the social graces. Financial worries may be eliminated by furnishing information concerning loans, scholarships, or other provisions which are available but unknown to the client.

The personal-problem counselor should endeavor to become informed concerning the problem areas with which he is most often confronted. He should provide for his clients a source of reading materials which may be helpful for a variety of personal problems. He should consider it part of his obligation to keep abreast of situations and to keep his reading list current. He should never suggest a source of information for his clients which he has not checked for accuracy and for professional validity. He should evaluate every printed page he suggests for his clients. The religious counselor should accumulate good reading material of inspirational and spiritual nature. His evaluation of these should include a realistic appraisal in terms of a "true to life" religious approach which is not falsely reassuring to the parishioner.

Personal problems usually evolve from a lack of understanding of self or others, or a lack of knowledge in terms of factual information. As a client comes to understand himself better, he usually understands other people better. As he himself is accepted by the counselor, he learns new facts and new skills in dealing with his environment; and many of his personal problems are solved.

PROBLEMS WHICH CANNOT BE SOLVED

Unfortunately, there are many personal problems for which there are no solutions. Some clients receive help through the acceptance of their situations and the realization through examination of their difficulties in the counseling interview that there is nothing that can be done. The wife, who has an invalid husband whom she loves, must accept restriction in her social life. Parents who have subnormal children have to learn to accept them as they are. Many financial problems must be accepted as inevitable. While some human problems can be partially solved and partially accepted, others cannot be solved and must be completely accepted. Acceptance of a disability, especially in a spiritual framework, may result in complete adjustment to living with the difficulty, and a concomitant feeling of closeness to God.

In such cases as those suggested above, the counselor is likely to experience a feeling of futility. Actually, there may be considerable help involved in counseling an individual toward an acceptance of an unchangeable problem area. The religious counselor will not fail to help his suffering parishioners to a realization that their weaknesses are complemented by God's strength, and that the fullness of their lives and their services to His work may bring blessings to others.

CATHARSIS

Catharsis is often experienced by the parishioner in discussing problems, whether they can be solved or not. The pouring out of problems does nothing to relieve the cause of difficulty, but may give enough release of tension to help the client gather strength for an attack on his problem.

The religious counselor should realize that cathartic release is most likely when the individual perceives understanding and acceptance in the counselor. Sympathy and pity usually are unkind to the sufferer as these reactions make the client sorry for himself.

Many parishioners are seeking a source of strength to help them bear their difficulties. They come to the religious counselor because they believe he has either strength in himself or access to the strength they desire. While the counselor may make the strength of God more easily available to the client through spiritual aids, he must be cautious in offering an arm to be leaned on and a shoulder to cry on. The source of strength issuing from a divine power must ultimately be vested in the individual. If such strength comes to the client through ministrations of the clergyman, well and good; but if the clergyman presents himself as the ultimate source of strength, he is encouraging dependency upon himself.

Free expression of feeling in a permissive atmosphere provides a beginning place for solving problems and for gaining understanding and acceptance of oneself—a prerequisite to internal strength. The strength which comes from self-understanding and self-acceptance is graphically described by Rogers.

> An opportunity for free expression also enables the client to explore his situation much more adequately than, in most instances, he has ever done before. Even where emotional factors are at a minimum, talking about one's own problems, in an atmosphere calculated to make defensiveness unnecessary, tends to clarify the adjustments which one must make, to give a more clear-cut picture of problems and difficulties, to give possible choices their true values in terms of one's own feelings.
>
> Not only is the situation thus clarified, but also the client's understanding of self. As he talks freely about himself, he becomes able to face the various aspects of himself without rationalization or denial —his likes and dislikes, his hostile attitudes as well as his positive affections, his desires for dependence as well as independence, his unrecognized conflicts and motivations, his wishful as well as his realistic goals. Amid the pressures of real life situations, it is almost never possible to do this. Some sort of defensive "front" must be maintained in every situation. But in the counseling relationship, freed from any necessity of being defensive, the client for the first time has an opportunity to take a frank look at himself, to go behind the "front" and make a true evaluation.
>
> As he finds that this unconventional self, this hidden self, is comfortably accepted by the counselor, the client is also able to accept this hitherto unrevealed self as his own. In place of anxiety and worry and feelings of inadequacy, the client develops an acceptance of his strengths and weaknesses as being a realistic and comfortable point of departure for progress in maturity. Instead of striving desperately to be what he is not, the client finds that there are many advantages in being what he is and in developing the growth possibilities which are genuinely indigenous.
>
> It is these values in catharsis which make it truly therapeutic in counseling. The counselor endeavors to create a releasing atmosphere in which the individual may express himself. The client finds that expression leads also to the releasing of new forces within himself, forces which heretofore had been utilized in maintaining defensive reactions.

Even if counseling goes no farther than this phase of free expression, it is helpful and constructive. . . . (6, pp. 171-172).

TESTING AND PERSONAL PROBLEMS

Undoubtedly, testing is an aid to some types of personal-problem counseling. Any testing which aids self-understanding can be helpful for problems which occur in the general area covered by the test. For instance, a high school student whose problem is getting dates may benefit from information which may be derived from any of a number of personality tests which derive norms on traits such as friendliness, introversion, withdrawing tendencies, and so forth. Scores from sociometric tests may demonstrate how the youngster is regarded by his fellows and may reveal tendencies on his part to confine his interests to only a few people.

Self-rating scales are available covering a vast number of social traits. These may reveal why individuals fail to be accepted. Attitude scales have been devised which give opportunity for individuals to learn about themselves in terms of their prejudices. Clients are often surprised to find that they are narrow-minded and intolerant. A knowledge of these things may help one to change himself into a more acceptable and conformable person. A number of scales have been devised to determine whether or not a person is a good marriage risk; and at least one instrument has been devised to study the source of fault in discordant marriages.

This writing has presented a number of ideas which may be generally useful in working with surface problems. It is felt that the suggestions concerning atmosphere and methods for eliciting client expression have broad general utility. As mentioned earlier, all problems are personal and should be treated as such until a turn is made toward decision-making or psychotherapy. This writer feels that the counselor is wise who enters every counseling experience endeavoring to build the permissive atmosphere and to utilize methods designed to bring about client expression without direction from the counselor. As evidence is presented to show that the problem is more than a surface personal problem, then the counselor may turn toward other theories and methods, perhaps of a more directive and clinical nature. When the counselor perceives the problem as one that is more amenable to other types of attack than those basically nondirective methods that have gained wide acceptance for counseling with personal problems, he may be certain that the effort given to promoting warmth and permissiveness will be beneficial to any other framework of counseling which may be entered.

References

1. Clifford, Paul Rountree, "The Theology of Acceptance," *Pastoral Psychology*. February, 1961, pp. 19-22.

2. Hahn, Milton E. and William E. Kendall, "Some Comments in Defense of Counseling," *Journal of Consulting Psychology*. April-May, 1947, pp. 74-82.

3. Raskin, Nathaniel, "The Development of Non-Directive Therapy," *Journal of Consulting Psychology*. 2, 1948, pp. 92-110.

4. Roethlisberger, F. J. and W. J. Dickson, *Management and the Worker*. Cambridge: Harvard University Press, 1939.

5. Rogers, Carl R., *Client-Centered Therapy*. New York: Houghton Mifflin Company, 1952.

6. ————, *Counseling and Psychotherapy*. New York: Houghton Mifflin Company, 1942.

7. ————, "Recent Research in Non-Directive Therapy and Its Implications," *American Journal of Orthopsychiatry*. 16, 1946.

8. ————, "The Attitude and Orientation of the Counselor in Client-Centered Therapy," *Journal of Consulting Psychology*. April, 1949, pp. 82-95.

9. Snyder, William U., "The Present Status of Psychotherapeutic Counseling," *Psychological Bulletin*. 4, 1947, pp. 297-386.

10. Stone, David R., "Teacher and Administrator Attitudes Toward Counseling," *Personnel and Guidance Journal*. January, 1955, pp. 287-288.

11. Thorne, Frederick C., "A Critique of Non-Directive Methods of Psychotherapy," *Journal of Abnormal and Social Psychology*. 39, 1944, pp. 459-470.

PERSONAL-PROBLEM COUNSELING INTERVIEW
The Case of Sarah Ann

FOREWORD

The situation

Sarah Ann was a senior student in the University. In another semester she was to receive her degree in education, and she was to start her teaching career the next September.

Although Sarah Ann was intelligent, friendly, and considerably above average in physical attractiveness, she was not engaged to be married and she had no serious suitors. A majority of her friends were engaged, and she did not wish to be different. Moreover, she had strong desires for marriage, a home, and children.

The counselor

The counselor was a member of the staff of the psychological clinic at the University. His method varies from client-centered to eclectic. He is no purist, but remains rather strongly in the client-centered framework during this interview.

To the reader and student

This is not an ideal interview to be used as an example of perfect counseling technique. It should provide learning experiences. Discussions accompanying the interview material will point out what seem to be strengths and weaknesses of this effort.

This is the second in a series of interviews with the client.

PERSONAL PROBLEM

co (1)   Well, tell us what you've been thinking about.
CL (1)   Well, let's see—didn't you say to think about reasons why I wanted to get married worse than most people?

CO (2)   I don't recall exactly. Maybe I did say something like that.

CL (2)   After we got through the other day, I thought of a couple of more reasons why I do. Mother, when she was growing up, was told, so much, that they wanted her not to and she rebelled at that and wanted to get married. She has always told me the idea of how stupid it is to give your life to something —well, like school teaching, for instance. I've just sorta always grown up thinking that's what you do. It's not quite as worthwhile as getting married and having children in the home.

CO (3)   I don't know whether I understand that fully or not. Your mother's parents talked against marriage for her?

CL (3)   At least this is the idea I get from her. She grew up here—on campus here as a girl—and was, well, had sort of an unusual upbringing; and her parents just encouraged her to study and nothing else and wanted her to be a student and all this because it was so hard for them to be. She was a good student and they were very upset when she wanted to get married; but somehow she's said the three (children) of us made the idea of getting married worthwhile.

CO (4)   In other words, she has been trying to influence you in the opposite direction from the way she was influenced.

CL (4)   Uh huh. I think so.

CO (5)   And you feel that this has caused you to want to get married more than the ordinary girl.

CL (5)   It may have an influence on it, I think.

CO (6)   And to have more of an, oh, uh, mild obsession about getting married. It sounds reasonable.

CL (6)   There's something else I thought of: that girl friend I was telling you about last time. That probably made me more conscious of it or something. In fact, I don't know how to explain that exactly. She was just sort of—I don't know how to explain it.

CO (2)   This counselor often proposes that his clients think about specific things between interviews.

CO (3)   Asking the client to go into more detail may be useful either in helping the counselor understand or in getting the client to derive deeper meanings from her own productions.

CO (6)   The counselor was obviously weighing his terms carefully. He doubtless realized that "obsession" is an emotionally-tinged term. The counselor seems to have used voice inflections, etc., here which softened this term successfully. Counselors should learn as quickly as possible just what type of language to use with each client and they may find it necessary to differentiate choice of terms at various stages with the same client.

co (7)   Review me on that girl friend just a little bit, now.

cl (7)   Well, she was a real beautiful girl that was a good friend of mine in high school and all. We were pledged the best friends and told each other everything and all that. Well, when we were first friends, she was a little different; but when we went on she just got more honors and things. It seemed to change her. At least it did to me; and she just kinda got a haughty attitude, I thought; and she would accuse me of being jealous of her and everything. I used to worry to death that I was jealous of her, but I always hoped that I wasn't jealous. I roomed with her the first year here and everything. I didn't date much then at all, so I felt kinda bad.

co (8)   You felt inferior to her, would you say.

cl (8)   Yes, I think so. I don't know whether it was her fault necessarily, but I had an awfully hard time maintaining a smooth relationship with her. And I just kept thinking about her so often; and I wished I wouldn't. I kept thinking, well, I mustn't get too interested in this boy because I'm sure he isn't as fine a boy as she would choose; and I can't let her outdo me. That sounds so silly but . . .

co (9)   That makes you more choosy about the boys you go with.

cl (9)   I think so. She'd make fun sometimes of the boys I went with.

co (10)   It must have made you quite conscious of the boy's attractiveness; and you were thinking as much in terms of how attractive this particular boy might be to her as his attractiveness to you. That's interesting.

cl (10)   I think that's probably something that has something to do —but lately, I finally woke up and realized, I don't know, I had been thinking she wouldn't like the boy when it was really me that didn't. Well, I'm just the one that feels this way. It's not her fault. And for a long time I just said I'm terrible to think that way—to not want to be around her and everything. Finally, I just started thinking that a friend doesn't make you feel good—that isn't helping you and

---

co (7)   The counselor used the "review" idea to help the client overcome a block. The block probably consisted of what the client perceived to be derogatory revelations about herself concerning her "jealous" nature.

co (8)   A good clarification of feeling.

cl (10)   In the early part of this speech, there was evidence of a desirable insight. But the client moved away from this self-criticism with a new thought. This insight seemed to be too painful at the time. The question may be raised as to whether or not the counselor should have picked up this feeling for reflection. He either failed to understand, or decided it was too dangerous to be talked out at the time. A point such as this would provide a good place for restructuring at a later time.

doesn't seem to try to—just isn't a friend. From then on, I just decided to try to get away from her because I didn't see any point in just sticking around. I've just done much better in every respect since then.

CO (11)   As long as you were with her you felt bad—jealous. It just seemed to you that she was really trying to make you feel that way.

CL (11)   Uh huh, but I don't especially care anymore. I don't know whether that has a lot—she transferred to another school, which was nice. I mean it worked into my plans pretty well. I didn't mean I wanted to get rid of her necessarily. Whenever I see her now, I don't care. She—now I recognize she's such a different type of person. Her goals in life are so different. I feel like I was kind of silly to ever let her influence me like that 'cause she—all her ideas in life are totally different from mine.

CO (12)   So at least two girls—women—have had some influence on the way you feel about marriage, on your being overly concerned about getting married, if we go so far as to say that you are overly concerned about it. That, I'm not willing to say myself.

CL (12)   Isn't everybody concerned like this, or not?

CO (13)   You wonder whether or not all girls are . . .

CL (13)   It seems they are from what I talk to them. Maybe I just think they are because I am. Isn't it pretty normal for a girl?

CO (14)   It seems to you that all girls are just as concerned about getting married as you are.

CL (14)   Well, most of us.

CO (15)   But it does appeal to you, at least as a possibility, that they are playing a sort of a role here—that they're really not as concerned as all of that.

CL (15)   Well, no, I don't know. It just seems like the girls I know that are this age and aren't married are real upset and real concerned about it—wondering why, or what's wrong with me, or why can't I find the right kind. Am I going to the wrong place, or—maybe that's not right. I know a few girls that are interested in things like going to Europe and all that.

CO (16)   Most of the ones you know are deeply concerned about . . .

CO (12)   The client was willing to accept the "mild" obsession interpretation in CO (6), so the counselor thought the "overly concerned" label would be accepted. It probably would have been had he not apologized for it in the same speech.

CO (13) (14)   The counselor is treading softly now. Such extreme nondirectiveness often agitates clients.

CO (15)   The counselor introduces a new note under the guise of clarification. He is probably trying to get away from the question in CL (12).

CL (16)   Well, most of them are engaged. Most of my friends are married.

CO (17)   Or engaged to marry.

CL (17)   They ask me every time they see me: Well, why aren't you finding somebody? And I'm just wondering, too—just trying to figure. The thing I'd really like to know is am I hunting for something that's impossible?

CO (18)   You recognize the possibility at least that the type of male you're looking for just doesn't exist.

CL (18)   Well, I don't know. I just wish I could know. How can you tell if what you're looking for is impossible?

CO (19)   That's a pretty hard question. You are pretty clear about what you're looking for.

CL (19)   I guess.

CO (20)   But you'd like to know whether that particular ideal of a man is scarce or is non-existent.

CL (20)   Uh huh. I'm sure he's scarce anyhow.

CO (21)   Well, at least, if the kind of man you're looking for is more scarce than is the type the other girls are satisfied with, it explains in part why they have succeeded and you haven't.

CL (21)   Yes, I guess that's true.

CO (22)   Obviously, the more exacting your demands, the less are your chances of finding that person and the longer it's going to take you to find him.

CL (22)   Well, I don't know. I just don't feel like I could stand it to just never get married. It's not—I don't know why necessarily but it just seems like it would be terrible to spend the rest of your life teaching school or something dreadful like that. I mean teaching school would be nice and I think I'd like it.

CO (23)   But you don't feel like it would be a good life-long objective in and of itself.

CL (23)   No. I just always liked kids a lot. I like everything about a home. I love to sew and cook. I just like to stay home so much that that's probably bad. I like to just stay at home. I like everything like that. I don't think I could stand it to be single always.

CO (18)   A good reflection. This also relates to the material in CL (10). The girl is a little more ready to examine her requirements for a man.

CO (19)   This is an invitation for the client to reveal what her requirements are. The counselor may be curious, but he probably feels that the client must examine her requirements for a mate in order to determine for herself if they are realistic.

CO (19) (20) (21) (22)   All of these counselor responses leave opportunity for the client to verbalize her requirements.

co (24)   You'd say, then, that you're the marrying kind.

cl (24)   I don't know. I guess I want to.

co (25)   As far as your personality, your basic desires—life just isn't going to be full without marriage.

cl (25)   I don't feel like it would.

co (26)   But you don't seem to feel that other girls are quite like this.

cl (26)   I don't think other girls—I don't know, but it doesn't seem like other girls are interested in things at home as much as I am. A lot of people like to run and go so much, which I enjoy, too, but I'd choose the home if I had somebody there. When it's just my parents, I don't like to stay there too much. I mean I want to be with them a lot but, you know, there is a difference.

co (27)   But you see other girls as caring more for running around, having a good time, and doing things that do not demand a marriage for happiness.

cl (27)   Well, some married people even seem to me so often—maybe it's just the age we live in. But even the married people don't seem to me so many of them want to really make a home and be interested in staying there. I'd like to find a boy that likes a home, too. So many of them couldn't stay home for anything.

co (28)   This is really one of your qualities I suppose of that ideal man. One that you figure is not easy to find.

cl (28)   I sort of think though that if a girl makes the right kind of a home, a boy is going to be inclined to want to go there. Do you think that's wrong? If a girl makes a home into what a home ought to be, then she's not going to have trouble like that. When the men aren't interested in it, it's when the woman . . .

co (29)   In other words, you think the kind of home you're prepared to make ought to be attractive to a man.

cl (29)   Yes, the right man.

co (30)   In other words if the type of home you are prepared to make is not attractive to a man, then you don't want that man.

cl (30)   I don't know. I guess.

---

co (24) (25) (26) The counselor has temporarily abandoned getting the client to describe her ideal man. He is attempting now to get her to examine her motives and feelings concerning marriage.

co (29) Here the counselor was concentrating too hard on the reflection he was hoping to make of the first part of CL (28). He interrupted the client when she was about to reveal something which may have been vital and was never picked up again.

co (30) There is implication here that the client is rigid in her requirements and will accept a man only on her own terms. This sounds too much like an accusation to her, hence, she cannot fully accept it.

co (31) Well, it sounds like that's what you want, which of course is somewhat of a requirement—a rather strenuous requirement. The requirement that you're laying down for your ideal man is . . .

CL (31) Is that a very strenuous requirement? It looks like that wouldn't be too hard.

co (32) Does it seem to you hard for a man to like the thing that you like?

CL (32) It doesn't look like it would be.

co (33) You like it and he ought to.

CL (33) Well, it just looks like the boys that I've known—that when they get married, they sort of want to settle down; and they want to have a real home and not have to go to movies three times a week, church a couple of other nights, to some kinds of civic meetings the remaining nights.

co (34) Well, then, would you say that there are many men who would fill this requirement of yours?

CL (34) Oh, yes, I don't feel like this is hard to meet.

co (35) You don't feel like this is one which keeps you from really making a decision or choice.

CL (35) No, I don't think so.

co (36) It's not one of the—while it may be one of your main requirements in a man, it is not one of those that's hardest to find. It is not the thing which causes you to reject many of the possibilities, so there must be other qualities which you desire in a man. At the same time, this is a point that could be worth following up. That this is one of your criteria for the right man—that he be willing to like the things that you like in the home situation.

CL (36) I don't think that I have hardly ever gone with a boy that I don't think met that one.

co (37) But there are others that they don't. (requirements)

CL (37) Uh huh. The boys that I seem to think that I'd like so much, they don't seem to like me. I do see some occasionally that I think would be the kind of boys I could like, but they just don't like me. It's all the boys I don't like. They just keep calling, calling, calling. I can't get rid of them.

co (38) The kind of fellows you like just don't like you.

CL (38) It has been that way for a long time anyhow. What could that be?

co (39) It's an interesting question. It seems to you like I could tell you that, doesn't it?

---

co (39) The second part of this response simply drew attention to the reluctance of the counselor to answer direct questions. There is no need for this kind of thing. If the counselor feels he should not answer a question, he should avoid it; but should not call attention to the avoidance.

CL (39)   I wish you would.

CO (40)   Well, I wish I could.

CL (40)   There is one boy on the campus that I think I'd be interested in—maybe some others mildly so—but this one I really
would be. I don't know, maybe I'm just scared or maybe I'm
just too anxious when I'm around him. I just get scared to
death when I see him. I'm just too scared to talk to him. It's
not that way—I can talk freely to boys I wouldn't be interested in dating.

CO (41)   You think perhaps you don't appeal to him because you
can't be yourself.

CL (41)   It may be.

CO (42)   At least you don't feel like he does like you.

CL (42)   No, I think he probably does. He tried to call me several
times and couldn't get me at home so he didn't call back; so
I asked him out Corrigan Week end. I didn't want to. I was
real embarrassed about it. You see, my adviser told me to do
it. I was going to plan sort of to run into him; but, no, they
told me that wasn't the thing to do. It would be better to just
be direct and honest about it; so, I asked him out. But I was
so embarrassed the whole time that I could hardly stand it.

CO (43)   Now, he did go with you.

CL (43)   Oh, he went and seemed to have a good time, I guess.

CO (44)   You were embarrassed.

CL (44)   I was just terribly afraid he'd never ask me out again and
everything, so much that I could hardly enjoy it.

CO (45)   At this Corrigan Week end, now, as everybody knows, the
girl is supposed to be forward.

CL (45)   Yeah, but the girls never are. You don't usually ask someone
unless they've dated you.

CO (46)   You asked this boy although he had never dated you at all.

CL (46)   I did, because he had tried to call me. That was the excuse
I had anyhow.

CO (47)   That was the excuse you had for yourself—for your own
benefit, or for his?

CL (47)   No, I didn't tell him that. I guess it was for me. But after I
went out with him, I was just so depressed for about two or
three days, because I was just so upset. Oh dear, what have

CO (41)   Here again the counselor uses a clarification structure (you think)
but interjects new material. Both this and CO (42) are efforts on the
counselor's part to give new direction to self-analysis for the client. Up to
this point, the client has not really examined herself very closely.

CO (47)   This is likely to be threatening. It sounds like an accusation. The
counselor was risking a loss of rapport in favor of forcing the client into
self-analysis.

I done! He will never ask me out again. She's so forward and everything. It seems like everytime I like a boy it's like that. The very few I can be interested in—it just seems like something like that.

co (48) It seems like you get off to a bad start with them, or . . .

cl (48) Well, I just can't seem to—I don't know. I'm just scared to death when I'm around them.

co (49) It seems you're actually afraid that they might like you?

cl (49) No, I'm afraid they won't.

co (50) I guess that could be either way, maybe. At least you know that you're afraid.

cl (50) Yeah, is that normal to be like that?

co (51) Well, I don't know whether it's normal or not but I do know that every girl I ever heard from is like that.

cl (51) They are afraid around the boys that they like?

co (52) I think that isn't necessarily just girls but almost anyone who approaches a goal. It's really important to them. They get the shakes when it is within their grasp. At least to some extent it's normal. Now whether it's normal to have this type of thing to the extent to which you do or not I'm not . . .

cl (52) I don't know. I guess I'm normal but . . . It just seems like sometimes I just get to feeling like I can't find anybody and it's just no use at all. Then sometimes I'll just have a date— just go somewhere and do something and I'll have a different outlook about it; but I just keep getting back. It seems like the reason I'm concerned about it is it's just more and more. I'm getting to where I get so upset about it and I feel like there's nothing I can do. My hands are just tied. Cause the world is so limited—you just have to wait and wait; and it seems like you can go places and try to meet boys and it doesn't do any good.

co (53) You're getting a sort of feeling of desperation.

cl (53) Yeah. I don't like the word though.

co (54) (both laugh) Well, it probably wasn't a very good one.

cl (54) I don't like to think of being a desperate old maid.

co (55) It's a very poor choice of words.

cl (55) I'm sure it's true, though. I guess it is.

---

co (49) This is the first serious effort the counselor has made at interpretation. The resistance was quite strong. The counselor backed away neatly in CO (50). At this point, the counselor seems to believe the girl is afraid of boys and cleverly manipulates them away from her. This is a common situation, common enough to justify opening a wedge in this direction. The client refuses to go in this direction and the counselor abandons the idea. In CL (51) the client changes the focus to being afraid *around* rather than afraid *of*.

CO (56)   Well, isn't it true that when we do get more or less desperate about something, we get even more skaky when we approach such a goal?

CL (56)   And everybody it seems like is always telling me you shouldn't be anxious about whether or not you get married —you just shouldn't give this any thought. That will take care of itself beautifully—just forget it; so, I just try to tell myself that all the time; and that doesn't work because all the time I'm trying to forget it, I'm still thinking about it.

CO (57)   But you do accept the possibility that a person can be so anxious about achieving something, that he gets in his own way in doing it—as with a basketball player when the score is tied, ten seconds remain until the end of the game, and he has one free throw. Sometimes he's so anxious to make that free throw that his very anxiety trips him up and causes him to be over tense, when he ought to be relaxed. He misses the goal purely on the basis of being overanxious about it.

CL (57)   Well, if that's true how can you keep from being overanxious about it?

CO (58)   I'm not sure that I know.

CL (58)   I don't think Peale's *Power of Positive Thinking* works too well. Mother always gives me those books to read.

CO (59)   They have their place.

CL (59)   They do. They're good up to a point.

CO (60)   But you don't feel like they work on all problems—least of all this one.

CL (60)   It's sort of like saying everything's going to be all right about everything in the world—to be optimistic. I mean that's just not true. Or at least that's the idea I get from a lot of this thing. It tells you to lie down at night, quote a scripture verse, and tell yourself that you can do anything; and that's just not reality it seems like.

CO (61)   You feel that it hasn't worked on this problem at least.

CL (61)   Well, I don't think so. (long pause)

CO (57)   This entire series of speeches on tension which begins with CO (52) should be regarded as supportive. The counselor is trying to get the client to accept her uneasiness as more or less routine. A counselor with a strong religious orientation may have utilized this situation to bring in some suggestions relative to prayer and scriptures. He would have to move against a negative set in this particular instance.

It is almost never wise for the counselor to join in criticism of a religiously oriented approach such as Peale's. In the first place, such approaches have value for some people with some problems, and that is all that may be said for any approach. In the second place, expressions of value—orientation by the counselor may interfere with the permissive atmosphere.

CO (62)   Well, let's think back over these things a little bit. You certainly recognize that you have set rather high goals or high standards for the young man that you would consider. You have the feeling that when you like one that he doesn't like you. In their presence you become sort of tongue tied, butterflies in the stomach, and everything else.

CL (62)   Yes.

CO (63)   I wonder what all that means.

CL (63)   I don't know. I think maybe it means I'm normal and that there's just nothing wrong. It just worries me that I keep getting so upset about it; and it keeps on getting worse all the time. I just seem to, well, I'm all right for awhile. I'll go along and find something different and change my routine or something and am in real good spirits then, but it doesn't take but a day or so and I'm real upset again. I don't want to stay that way. If I can't—if I can't find this kind of man, I wanta live a life that's useful anyhow and not always be this way cause I can't accomplish anything as long as I keep getting upset about things like that.

CO (64)   It seems to you that if you can't find this kind of man you want, you just ought to give it up and go ahead and plan some other kind of existence.

CL (64)   I think so, because I think it would be a whole lot better not to get married than to marry someone that you felt like wasn't what you wanted—then you'd be thinking all your life, well, I might have met that person. I have so many friends that keep saying, "Don't be satisfied with less than what you want, because I found the one." So many people and my parents say that. They say, "Well, it looked impossible in each of our cases to find the kind of person we wanted, but we did and God just has to lead you to do that."

CO (65)   So you feel pretty sure then that the type of man that you want really does exist and in practically perfect harmony with all your ideals for him.

CO (62)   This summary serves to move away from an involvement with Peale's ideas and at the same time presents three possible choices for continued emphasis.

CL (63)   It may be that this speech indicates resistance to the idea of high goals and standards. She ignored that part of the summary.
There is considerable disharmony between CL (64) and CL (65). Mother says conflicting things according to the client. The counselor has seemingly become convinced that the girl's ideal for manhood is one of the factors in her difficulty. He goes after this idea more strongly after the girl reveals how the mother feels.

CL (65)   I think so. Now, my mother's trying to convince me that I'm hunting for a knight in shining armor; but I don't think she's right because I've met some of them. I mean I've known some boys that I think would do.

CO (66)   Now you have known these boys that you feel would actually be that ideal and yet you say that they don't like you.

CL (66)   Uh huh, so does that mean that my ideal is too high if they don't like me?

CO (67)   I'm not sure what it means. You have some ideas?

CL (67)   I don't know. I just wondered if—I don't know.

CO (68)   Sometimes people run away from a situation which they themselves feel that they can't handle.

CL (68)   Yes. I don't know whether I'm doing that or not.

CO (69)   Well, I wasn't thinking about that in terms of your actions but in terms of the young man's action.

CL (69)   What do you mean?

CO (70)   Well, here's a girl who approaches a young man—put yourself in his position a minute—here's a girl who is attractive and desirable in many different ways, but who has such a terrifically high ideal for manhood that the young man is skeptical. He says to himself, "This girl expects too much out of a man. I don't know whether I can satisfy her or not; therefore, I don't think I'd better get involved any more. I don't believe I'll be able to live up to the expectations. This is a little harder job than I want to take on."

CL (70)   Yeah, I've had a couple of boys that have told me that. They haven't been the kind of boys that—I don't think that this kind of boy would think that.

CO (71)   In other words, that's part of your ideal for him that . . .

CL (71)   Well, I just don't think he'd think that way—this kind of boy . . .

CO (72)   Not only do you have a strong ideal for him, but included in that ideal is that he would be willing to really conform perfectly.

CL (72)   Oh, well, no; I don't think that's exactly it. It's just that there are some things that are important—like you want him to be the right kind of Christian boy and you want him to have high ideals of right things, to be real manly and command respect from you—things like that; but I'd be glad to do the same thing for him. I'd do anything I could, I think, if I

CL (70)   The boy she wants would not be the kind to tell her that her ideals are too high.

CO (72)   The counselor is applying a lot of pressure—trying to force this idea on her. Even if this is the key to the difficulty, she is not likely to accept it under pressure.

loved someone to try to be what they wanted. It's not exactly one of perfection. I don't think it is.

CO (73) In other words, if you loved a boy you'd be able to or be willing to conform to his ideal image of you; and so you feel that if a boy loves you he ought to be willing to conform to your ideal image of him.

CL (73) I guess. I don't exactly feel like I have such an ideal image exactly. I just feel like there are just certain basic things to have to be. I don't care about so many things that a lot of girls are so particular about—the color of the hair and eyes, where he's from and—just as long as he's nice looking.

CO (74) Then you feel like your qualifications are really not as strenuous as some other girls'.

CL (74) I imagine there are a lot of people that have more strenuous ones. Well, I think some girls have some ridiculous ones. Like the girl I know that demands that the boy not drink and not smoke and not dance and not go to movies; and conform to her ideas about everything; and be willing to do all this and still be very manly and have very independent thinking and all this. I don't think it's possible.

CO (75) In other words, you think it's possible for a girl to have an ideal that's just out of reach.

CL (75) Uh huh.

CO (76) It's just unrealistic.

CL (76) But I really don't think I do. Do you think I do?

CO (77) You feel like yours is really reasonable.

CL (77) Do you think so?

CO (78) Well, uh, I don't know, of course, exactly what they all are, and you may feel that I'm circumventing your question when I say that; but I don't think it is as important really whether I think so as whether young men think so. Possibly it would be worthwhile for you to infer from their behavior what they think. Do you follow me?

CL (78) Uh huh.

CO (79) They say that we can infer from behavior—we can infer attitudes from behavior. Perhaps over a period of time you can infer from the behavior of young men how they feel about your requirements.

CL (79) I don't think there's anything wrong with my requirements. I really don't. I have a friend, a boy that's a real good close

---

CO (78) This is a very good handling of the direct question in CL (77) except that attention is drawn to the circumvention. This client was informed about counseling methods since she had taken several courses in counseling. The counselor seems sensitive to the fact that she is aware of various aspects of the counseling process.

friend of mine that's sort of like my brother, I guess. I've always grown up with him and we've always talked about everything a lot—about our ideas. He thinks they're quite reasonable. He's a boy.

CO (80) Now this is a friend of yours but not a prospective, uh, . . .

CL (80) No. We're too close for that. He's just like a brother.

CO (81) Now do you think that your brother would think that your demands are too severe?

CL (81) No, he kids me sometimes saying they are; but I don't think he really thinks so. I'm always making him say he really thinks so. He'll say, no, I just haven't dated the kind of boy that I should and he doesn't know exactly why. That's what I don't exactly understand, why it is that so many of the boys that aren't the type I would like (or it seems aren't like the same type person) have gotten interested in me.

CO (82) It seems almost paradoxical, doesn't it?

CL (82) Yeah. It does.

CO (83) The kind that you wouldn't consider are eager to make advances.

CL (83) It seems kind of funny.

CO (84) Yet the kind that you would consider are stand-offish.

CL (84) Uh huh.

CO (85) Quite a situation. Do you suppose it's possible that young men, as they make early contact with a girl, can tell whether she's really serious or not about . . . ?

CL (85) I guess not. You mean whether she's serious about it?

CO (86) Well, yes. Whether she's inclined to be serious or whether she's maybe inclined just to have fun.

CL (86) Well, I've heard say that they can tell.

CO (87) Can you tell that about a boy?

CL (87) Not always. Some of them will fool you. You'll think that this is real casual and all, and all of a sudden it's not; or maybe I'm hoping it's real casual and all, and all of a sudden it isn't.

CO (88) Well, could it be that it is really casual and the young man knows that it is casual as far as you're concerned? So, there-

---

CO (80) The counselor is trying to raise the question as to whether this boy is giving an objective report, since he is like a brother. He returns to the same theme in CL (81), but doesn't succeed.

CL (81) The reader will be impressed (as was the counselor) that this question of high ideals has a prominent place in the client's thinking. It has been discussed with a number of people, at least. Her self-concept is that she doesn't have too high ideals. Every suggestion that she does have resulted in a further rigidifying of this self-concept.

CO (85) (86) These leading questions reveal that the counselor has moved rather far from his original nondirective framework.

fore, he can follow a rather strong romantic line without too much fear of being snapped up or taken seriously.

CL (88)   I think some of the boys that have gotten serious have recognized the way I am, the home-loving type of girl; and I think they like this and they want it. I think most boys want that and that makes them—the fact that I'm that way, I'm sure it shows, and they sort of read it to mean she's hunting for a husband now and right here; and it isn't supposed to be read that way. What they really should be reading is that she's tired of sitting at home and she wants to go somewhere.

CO (89)   Now it isn't supposed to be read that way by them.

CL (89)   Uh huh.

CO (90)   But it is supposed to be read that way by the one that you really want. Is that what you mean?

CL (90)   Well, I don't know.

CO (91)   In other words, you're reading a story to boys, and to one group it is supposed to mean that you're tired of staying at home and you want to go out and have fun; but for the other group the same story is to mean I want a husband.

CL (91)   Not exactly I want a husband. Just to interest them. They're supposed to push it. They aren't supposed to think I ever think that.

CO (92)   You're among friends. You can be honest. (laughs)

CL (92)   No, I'd feel real embarrassed if I thought any boy thought that I wanted to be serious with him.

CO (93)   Yes, I know you would. Of course you would, but between us girls, uh (both laugh)—well, this presents some real interesting sidelights; from which, after you've thought about them for a good long while, you may get some conclusions. (laugh)

CL (93)   I was talking to this boy who is like my brother. He knows you, too, and everything. I was telling him I was talking to you about this and he said he was real glad. He said that what he thinks is my trouble—and he doesn't know exactly why—is that I just have such a lack of confidence. He said that I always underestimated myself and abilities and everything.

CO (94)   You think he means underestimated your attractiveness?

CL (94)   Yeah, I think he means that in general.

CO (89) (90)   These are poor clarifications of content. The idea is admittedly hard to handle, but the counselor does better in CO (91).

CO (93) (95)   These counselor productions sound quite vague. However, communication may be good in the counseling situation even though it doesn't seem good to the reader of a record such as this.

CO (95) Does it follow then that along the line of thought you underestimated yourself, your attractiveness, physical and otherwise, with these boys for whom you have quite a feeling that
gives you an inferiority feeling and causes you to be stum-
bling and tongue-tied?

CL (95) I think it could.

CO (96) Then that in turn scares the boy away.

CL (96) It sounds like that might be possible.

CO (97) It certainly isn't impossible. It certainly might be a factor.
You see, one of the things that people do—when they are
looking for a solution to their problem—they commonly look
for a solution, just one straight answer. You probably ought
to be willing to accept the idea that there are a number of
things adding to the situation; and that (the inferiority feelings) could well be one of them. It could even be the most
important. It might even be the only one, but it isn't likely.

CL (97) Well, if so, how do you gain—I mean, how do you get over
that?

CO (98) Well, not easily. Surely you know that. You've studied psychology. People that feel inferior in any sense or feel un-
attractive or to any degree incompetent in social interchanges
—it dates back to very early childhood usually; and, since it
dates back so far and has been with us so long, it isn't reasonable to think that at the snap of a finger anything would undo
it. Whatever might help would be slow changing, so it's anybody's guess as to whether you should try hard or not to
change one's personality in terms of his inferiority feelings.
It's a question of how severe it is as to whether it's even
worthwhile.

CL (98) I don't imagine it's terribly severe. I just—a lot of times I
don't feel that way at all. I feel quite able to cope with the
situation so often.

CO (99) I doubt if it is. It's undoubtedly not a very severe thing.
Probably if you are that way over a period of years, you may
overcome it to a large extent; and, on the other hand, you
may live with it the rest of your life and either way it
wouldn't be a . . .

CL (99) Either way it wouldn't be terrible.

CO (98) One can read into this speech that the counselor has concluded that
this personality problem is not severe enough to require a psychotherapeutic approach. He transmits this to the client here and in CO (99).
Whether this is good counseling or not depends on a multitude of factors
which only the competent counselor can assess. Such assessments must be
made quickly as the interview progresses. The nondirective purist would
oppose such technique.

co (100) No, it's just one of those little things. But it could be adding to your problem. It's hard to tell whether your problem is one where there is a real central factor which is reinforced—girded by a number of minor factors, or whether it's just a conglomeration of small factors adding together. Of all the things that we have discussed, what to you seems to loom as the largest possibility?

cl (100) I really don't know.

co (101) Could you enumerate some of the ideas that we have brought out as possible causes for the problem? This inferiority feeling is one. Now, how would you enumerate some of the others?

cl (101) You mean some of the causes of inferiority?

co (102) Some of the possible causes that we perhaps have not named but worked around.

cl (102) Causes of the problem in general? Well, last time we talked about maybe in school, earlier, people said . . .

co (103) All right.

cl (103) Then Mother's attitude toward it and this girl friend's attitude toward it—and lack of confidence.

co (104) All right. (Pause) Anything else?

cl (104) We talked about so many things I'm trying to think. (long pause)

co (105) Have we talked about the possibility of your ideal being set too high?

cl (105) Oh yes. That too. I discounted that one, though. (laugh)

co (106) We talked about the possibility that young men are prone to run from what they are afraid to be too high a demand on them; which, of course, is related to this other thing.

cl (106) Well, what can I do? What is the . . .

co (107) It is always the question of what can I do. It is a big one, isn't it?

cl (107) Well, just try to forget it? Like I always try to do? It just doesn't seem to work.

co (108) Well, I think surely the thing you need to do first is to sort

---

co (101) At this point, the counselor brings the interview toward the closing phase.

cl (102) This is not clear to the reader, but seems to have been understood by both counselor and client.

co (105) cl (105) The resistance to this idea is still strong. An analytical counselor would be inclined to believe that this is the central problem because she has resisted it so much.

co (108) The counselor parried the question in CO (107), but chooses to give some answers here. The change is possibly a function of the fact that the interview is in the closing stage. This and CO (109) are the counselor's longest productions.

out all these things and put them in their proper place and to decide for yourself which is important and which isn't; and continue to think about the whole problem. Maybe there are other things we haven't stumbled on yet at all. Then if you do (in this process) decide which is the main reason or the main cause of the problem, although we don't agree Norman Vincent Peale's approach is good with everything—in self-discipline, it is possible that people can work with themselves to overcome weaknesses; and sometimes these things just work out without our knowing why they work. You relax some attitudes you have and become a little less compulsive about them maybe.

CL (108)   Uh huh.

CO (109)   I think this is probably accentuated right at this time because of the fact that you are to graduate in a little while now —in four and one-half months, is that right? And you just see this in a way as—this four-and-one-half-month stretch as being a big opportunity after which there won't be as many—as many good opportunities. You're more conscious of it. Would you say that? You did say that, I think. At times you have fluctuating feelings about this as you go along. You'll have days when you'll have a good time and this won't be uppermost in your mind at all and then have a period in which it really clobbers you—another period of dating and not being concerned—a fluctuating type of thing; but of late it has been more pressed on you. Much more on your mind lately. Didn't you say that? You seem to be concerned with it almost constantly now.

CL (109)   Especially last week.

CO (110)   Especially since our last meeting?

CL (110)   No, especially right before the last time. Just about three or four days I was just real upset all the time.

CO (111)   Now, it wasn't because of anything we had said though, because we hadn't talked about that at all. But for a period of time there before . . .

CL (111)   Yes, before.

CO (112)   Before our last meeting. Now that was between the time I told you to come back and we'd talk about anything you wanted to talk about and the time that you did come back to talk about it. Do you think there's any relationship there?

CL (112)   It may be. I don't know.

CO (113)   It's possible that you've been wanting to talk about this for a long time with somebody.

CL (113)   Uh huh. I have. I feel like I've worried everybody to death about it. Well, my parents—I've talked to them a lot about it; and I—of course, girls from the dormitory all talk to each other, but—I've sorta had a bad outlook toward it—I just seem to get into the place where I guess I have a fatalist attitude or something, feeling just like it can't work out—it's a "what's the use" attitude.

co (114) You feel almost like giving up then?

cl (114) Uh huh.

co (115) Even to the extent where you've been thinking about what sort of a life you would live if you didn't . . .

cl (115) I've thought about that a lot. I've tried to sit here at the University a lot just—I'm so upset because I can't find anybody. I'd like to have somebody now to look forward to things with and all; but, since I can't, I feel like maybe next time I'll have to take a heavy course load and just get real busy doing other things so I won't think about it.

co (116) It bothered you so much that actually you feel like it would be a relief if you could settle it—that I'm just not going to get married.

cl (116) I don't know. I sure would hate to settle it that way.

co (117) But you have been thinking about that because you said that you need to make some plans if you were not going to get married—to make some plans for a constructive life.

cl (117) Yeah. Uh huh. But I want to delay the plans just as long as I can. (laughs)

co (118) You're not really making very careful plans for it.

cl (118) Not very careful plans. I still hope I won't have to make them.

co (119) It's just once in a while that you feel like giving up—not very often.

cl (119) Yeah. I guess it's more once in a while.

co (120) But, whenever you do have that feeling, you really do feel on the floor. You just feel very low.

cl (120) Uh huh. Now is that a normal way to be to just get like that sometimes? Is that just normal that everybody has . . .

co (121) Well, we know, of course, it's normal for people to have variations of mood, for people to have their ups and downs, and have a cycle of ups and downs. Just how severe their downs may be before it's not normal just isn't very subject to guess.

cl (121) No. I think another reason I was upset right at that time was because that was right after Corrigan Week-end night.

co (122) I see.

cl (122) I asked him out and I was so upset that he'd never ask me out again and everything—which he hasn't. But he has told this girl he's going to.

co (123) It still frightens you because you acted so forward there.

cl (123) Yes. I was embarrassed.

CO (124)   You feel like if he asks you for a date you'll be embarrassed again?

CL (124)   Uh huh.

CO (125)   Your embarrassment now if he asks you for a date will stem from reminiscing back to the forwardness of your earlier venture with him?

CL (125)   Yes. I think probably a lot of it.

CO (126)   A lot of it . . .

CL (126)   Plus the fact that I'm scared of him because I like him.

CO (127)   The more you like him the more afraid you are.

CL (127)   He seems kinda unapproachable because he's—oh, well-known and a leader in everything and president of his youth fellowship and the youth council of his church. Offices in these clubs—that shouldn't bother me I guess but—I've done some of the same stuff. It just does when somebody else—it seems like it's so . . .

CO (128)   It seems like he's almost unreachable.

CL (128)   Uh huh.

CO (129)   He's really quite a bit above you?

CL (129)   I don't know. I don't usually think about people in terms of above or below very much. Maybe I do think that way more than I think I do. No, I feel like he's the same sort of person that I am. As far as our ideas about things and communication, I just feel like we're the same sort of person. I don't believe I really feel like he's above me. But I just feel like maybe it is unattainable or something.

CO (130)   That a boy as high-ranking as this, as important as this wouldn't care for you.

CL (130)   Uh huh. That's what I'm afraid of. And yet that's usually the kind that I would like. I don't think because of this high ranking—the higher ranking I don't care a flip for. But the kind that I like seems like always is, uh, . . . oh, I don't know.

CO (131)   Always is outstanding?

CL (131)   In some ways. And I don't feel like I'm very outstanding. I feel like I'm just an ordinary person.

CO (132)   You feel like you're just an ordinary person but you want a man who's outstanding?

In this section the counselor utilizes reflection techniques to bring about a rather careful summary of what has been expressed in the interview.

The pace has quickened somewhat. The client shows more emotion in CL (127) than at any other time. Her feeling is probably that the interview is about over and that she hasn't received any answers.

CL (132) I guess that's about what it boils down to, but don't you—don't you just sorta have to feel when you find somebody that—that this is the most wonderful person in the world even if rationally you know this isn't true. It's ridiculous to think so, but still you ought to feel that way.

CO (133) In other words, you recognize that this exhilarating feeling ought to be there whether or not he has high standing.

CL (133) Yes. Don't you think so?

CO (134) I am sure this is part of the picture of being in love. Now, this is perhaps a good idea to carry over to our next meeting —that is, provided you would like to come back. Actually, our time is up.

CL (134) I sure would like to come back. One more time at least.

CO (135) Well, shall we make it this same time next week?

CL (135) Okay by me. And thanks for listening to my silly raving.

CO (136) It's been fun. (at the door) See you next week, then.

CL (136) Bye.

EVALUATION

What has been accomplished in the preceding interview? Some would doubtless say little; others would possibly say much. One thing is sure; no certain evaluation is possible. The beginning counselor, whether he is religiously oriented or not, is not apt to be satisfied with counseling which does not produce demonstrable and identifiable results.

Perhaps the best source of evaluation is the client himself. If the client expresses a firm belief that much help has come to him, it may be that he has evaluated accurately. It may be, on the other hand, that he wishes to show appreciation for the counselor's efforts.

A reasonable goal in personal-problem counseling is that the client should examine the problem realistically, and himself in relationship to the problem. In the preceding interview, it appears that this has happened. Nothing at all happened which might be called magical; nothing happened which might be considered conclusive evidence of gain for the client. The client did examine herself and her problem from many points of view. She probably developed some insights—insights which may become more clearly imprinted as she thinks back on the interview. She may make some changes in her approach to young men, as a result of this effort, without knowing how the change was brought about.

Having assisted the client in self-examination and careful appraisal of the problem and at least some of its concomitants, the
counselor must accept the results on faith. There are no positive
criteria of success. The counselor who compulsively watches for
specific results may be doing so in order to bolster his own ego.

Personal problems often require extensive counseling. Sarah Ann
will come to the next session with new ideas and some refinements
of the old ones. She may never find an identifiable "answer" to
her problem.

It is entirely possible that the most basic factor in her difficulty
has not yet been touched upon. So many areas have not. Factors
so often associated with this type of difficulty include relationships
with her father, her attitudes toward sex, the tenor of the relationship between her mother and father, and a great many more.

V

*Clinical Approaches
to Personal-Problem Counseling
and Decision-Making*

The term, "clinical training for pastoral counseling," means many things to different people. Generally speaking, the term "clinical" is thought of as related to the field of medicine. Many of the present-day practices in counseling and psychological practice employ the concepts of medical approach insofar as a detailed history-taking and a full and exacting examination are concerned. The clinical method in medicine aims at developing a set of facts about the patient in order to reduce the practice of medicine from a system of guesswork and intuitive diagnosis to a scientific appraisal of all the factors involved in the patient's disability. The clinical method in counseling and psychology has aimed at a similar goal.

Whereas the clinical treatment and diagnosis in medicine involve a multitude of physical examinations, laboratory tests, and chemical analyses of body products, the clinical approach in counseling involves a detailed examination of the client in terms of his intellectual, mental, and social functioning, together with all those environmental and developmental facts that serve to make the client what he is. Such a clinical history and evaluation of the client is accomplished by the use of interviews, psychological testing, and casework techniques of environmental inquiry and evaluation.

Even as the physician does not relish the idea of working with a patient without background knowledge of his present maladies, medical case history, and laboratory information, the religious counselor finds that the possession of facts about the client aids immeasurably in his work with the client in many counseling tasks. As in medicine, the indispensability of clinical information depends upon the type of problem the individual has.

Clinical Methods in Religious Counseling

There is evidence that media of training provided for clergymen in the broad field of counseling have emphasized clinical aspects. For instance, one may observe the interdenominational Council for Clinical Training, the Department of Clinical Pastoral Training at Bellevue Hospital, and the Southern Baptist Association for Clinical Pastoral Education. It should be understood, however, that these training projects emphasize the meaning of the term "clinical" in its connection with treatment of the mentally ill and not in connection with the use of clinical information. As a matter of fact, most of these training facilities are under the auspices of the discipline of psychiatry. Psychiatry as a medical specialty is not always strongly impressed with the clinical tools developed by scientific psychology. The training the clergy receives at these centers focuses upon the understanding and recognition of mental illness through observations of behavioral factors and not through the application of psychological tests and other clinical implements.

In the field of pure psychology, the two specialties which utilize clinical tools most extensively are clinical psychologists and counseling psychologists. The clinical group specializes in "depth" problems, and the counseling group specializes in problems of the normal person. Both groups use psychological tests, inventories, case histories, and other clinical evidence extensively. Adequate preparation for the use of clinical tools, whether at the "depth" or "surface" level, requires a high degree of training not likely to be possessed by the clergyman. While some use of such tools may be made by youth workers, pastors, and others, it is the psychological specialist working either in the church or church-clinic setting who is most likely to utilize clinical tools. Wise offers valuable opinion as follows:

> The question may be raised about training in the administration, scoring and interpretation of psychological tests. In my opinion tests are the tool of the psychologist. If a pastor wants to use tests, then he had better get the training of a clinical psychologist, and openly assume the role of psychologist rather than that of pastor. The pastor should have sufficient training to be intelligent about the values and dangers of tests. If tests are desired in a given situation, the pastor should refer the person to a competent psychologist for testing. . . . (20)

There is value in the clergyman's knowing the fundamentals of clinical method, even though he may not actively engage in the administration and interpretation of tests. The clergyman usually has a supervisory function over all activities pertaining to his church. A clinical psychologist hired as a specialist in the church or who serves as consultant will be able to perform all clinical functions; all other members of the church staff having counseling functions need an orientation to the clinical method.

The following treatment of the clinical aspects of counseling are intended to orient all church-related counselors. At the same time, the material may serve as an introduction for students who aspire to positions as specialists in the religious setting. The student who intends to be a specialist either at the level of counseling psychology or clinical psychology should expect an intensive program of training, with many formal courses and supervised internship in the use of clinical methods.

As the church-sponsored clinic becomes more commonplace, the need for psychologists especially trained for religiously oriented work will increase. The counselor working in parochial and other church schools will need clinical training in dealing with educational and vocational problems. Clinical instruments may be useful to many workers even without a great amount of advanced training, provided the workers understand and abide by their own limitations. Clinical instruments useful in counseling the normal do not require as much advanced training as do those for ab-normals.

The American Psychological Association, recognizing the need for referrals by ministers and others, issues a Directory of American Psychological Services annually. A copy of the Directory is sometimes published in Pastoral Psychology (8).

Clinical Psychology and Clinical Counseling

During the earliest stages of his existence, the clinical psychologist was more concerned with the formulation of clinical evidences than in the use of them. He was closely involved with the psychiatric scene as a psychometrician, administering tests toward the evaluation of abnormal and subnormal patients. In recent years, this practitioner has sought liberation from the narrow confines of measurement and evaluation to the broader fields of *working with* the people whom he has assessed, as well as continuing his role as psychometrician and diagnostician.

The field of counseling in the schools and colleges developed rapidly following World War I, and this counseling work became identified with the effort to help the "normal person" adjust in order to handle his problems. As an expansion of this movement in counseling and guidance, a system of clinical counseling developed during the 1930's and early 1940's. This concept of counseling emphasized the utility of a systematized body of information about the client similar to that of clinical psychology and general medicine.

It is important to note that clinical counseling as defined and developed by noted authorities such as Williamson (19), Pepinski (12), Bordin (1), and Hahn and MacLean (7) among others, is not synonymous with what seems to be the most acceptable definition of clinical counseling today. Pepinski defined the early concept of clinical counseling.

> Clinical counseling is defined (*a*) as *the diagnosis and treatment of minor nonembedded, nonincapacitating, functional (nonorganic) maladjustments,* and (*b*) *as a relationship, primarily individual and face-to-face, between counselor and client.* Clinical counseling in educational institutions is further defined as professional-level counseling, to distinguish it from the lower-level activities of instructional guidance and faculty counseling (12, p. 9).

Pepinski further indicated that the clinical method was a product of two major developments, (1) the objective appraisal of the client's aptitudes, abilities, interests, and attitudes by means of a wide variety of measurements and observations, which form the basis for a more scientific guidance service, and (2) the recognition of the important part played by the client, of a need for helping him understand and accept himself so that he may be able to carry the major responsibility for whatever action is taken as the result of counseling (12).

Because of the entry of the counseling person into the field of psychotherapy and the development of the field of counseling psychology, it is probable that the term clinical counseling today connotes therapeutic counseling to most people. At any rate, the reader should keep in mind as he peruses the literature of the 1930-1940 period that clinical counseling was used in treating "nonembedded, nonincapacitating" difficulties. As a matter of fact, the largest areas of counseling served by the "clinical counselors" were vocational and educational problems.

Trait-and-Factor Approach

The principal aim of the people who developed the tools of clinical method was to make counseling more objective. For this reason, the development of tests and inventories to accomplish measurement of traits and factors was one of the major undertakings. The research of the period centered upon the idea that dimensions of human behavior can be established and that client behavior can be measured along continua defined by such dimensions (11).

A common aspect of any clinically oriented design is the schematization of classifications and descriptions so as to provide communication symbols for use between counselors and for use between counselor and client. Because of such need, the Kraepelinian system of classifying functional disorders was formulated in the early part of the century (10). Several tests, including the Minnesota Multiphasic Personality Inventory, were developed to describe personality deviations utilizing this system of classification. In addition to the necessity for syndromes of abnormal functional disorders, there arose the supposed necessity for categorizing human difficulties of less disturbed individuals. A number of categoric classifications have been devised in this area, among which are a group of six by Pepinski (12). These include (1) lack of assurance, (2) lack of information, (3) lack of skill, (4) dependence, (5) self-conflict (cultural, interpersonal, and intrapersonal), and (6) choice anxiety. Robinson (13) suggests a threefold categorization of problems; these are: (1) adjustment, (2) skills, and (3) maturity problems.

As the student examines the literature of the 1940's, he will discover a number of efforts at categorization. These efforts to categorize problems of the normal individual failed to produce a widely accepted set of syndromes, as was true of the categorization efforts for deeply disturbed individuals. It is understandable that problems of normals would not lend themselves easily to classification because of their great variability. Then, too, there was little agreement among authorities in the field of clinical counseling as to meanings of the descriptions of problem categories.

Efforts to bring about a standardized classification of normal human problems have largely failed. More recent thinking has tended to observe the individual as a unified organism possessing a great variety of interconnecting problems. The need for categorization of the normal or slightly deviant individual is not as great as for the more deeply disturbed person who is more likely to be treated by a team approach, thus necessitating communication symbols.

The fields of counseling, clinical psychology, and psychiatry have gained much by utilizing the clinical approach borrowed from medicine. However, some practitioners have been inclined to draw too close a comparison between medical problems and psychological problems. Medical problems may have definite and exclusive causes and effects. Various infectious diseases have identifiable causative factors of microorganismic nature. These microorganisms may be controlled or obliterated by drug therapy.

Psychological problems cannot be diagnosed as an inclusive and self-contained syndrome of difficulty. This is, to a large extent, true in the area of deeply disturbed individuals, and even more true of the problems of normals.

The term "clinical counseling," used in connection with treating problems of normal individuals, has brought some confusion to the understanding of the literature. The word "clinical" has not only been historically connected to the medical field; it has been used widely to connote deep psychological disturbance when applied to psychological practice. Thus, many readers have not understood the term "clinical counseling" as used to indicate a treatment of normal problems by case history and diagnostic methods. Actually, this term seems to be used less often since the development of the term "counseling psychology."

One aspect of the clinical method which makes communication possible is the development of norms of behavior. Only by developing norms could clients be intelligently discussed and compared. Effective counseling must recognize and utilize the concept of individual differences. Descriptive terms for human traits as well as norms for comparison prove valuable to the practitioner who treats these things as reasonable indicators of personality rather than as rigid and unfailing indices of evaluation.

Williamson's Work

Perhaps the earliest systematic treatment of the work of the clinical counselor was devised by Williamson. He suggests six steps for a complete counseling experience:

Analysis refers to the collection from a variety of sources of data which provide for an adequate understanding of the student. *Synthesis* refers to the summarizing and organizing of the data from analysis in such a manner as to reveal the student's assets, liabilities, adjustments, and maladjustments. A case history or cumulative record form may be used to summarize the mass of data about the student's life, and test scores are summarized on a profile or psychograph. *Diagnosis* refers to the end result of diagnosing; it is the clinician's conclusions concerning the characteristics and causes of the problems exhibited by the student. *Prognosis* refers to the clinician's statement, or prediction, of the future development of the student's problem; whether he will readjust or what will be the probable outcome of a choice of a particular course of study. Prognosis is a statement of the implications of the diagnosis. *Counseling* refers to the steps taken by the student and by the counselor to bring about adjustment and readjustment. The final step in clinical work, *follow-up*, includes what the clinician does to assist the student with new problems, with recurrences of the original problems, and what is done to determine the effectiveness of counseling (19, p. 57).

Williamson's early work and his many later works in the field of counseling have proved invaluable. It is only natural that new considerations would be given to some of the suggestions he has made. As a matter of fact, considerable criticism has been brought to bear upon some of his ideas, especially upon the concepts which he expressed concerning diagnosis and advice-giving.

Varying Concepts

The early concept of the clinical counselor was one of a highly trained person who was able to take all of the data and to make a correct diagnosis of the difficulty. The fault that has been found in the early emphasis upon diagnosis in counseling involves the question of whether or not counselors have abilities which make it possible for them to draw from any amount of data a valid diagnosis of human difficulty. No matter what level of training and what depth of understanding the counselor may have, the vastness and complex functioning of the human personality may defy adequate diagnosis. It is true that new ideas related to the trait-and-factor approach which have put greater emphasis on the feeling and thinking of the client than upon authoritative diagnosis and directing have developed in later years.

The most appropriate question concerning diagnosis in counseling is the place it occupies in the total counseling picture. Some writers have seemingly placed diagnosis at the center of the counseling process and have been willing to risk the entire process upon the ability of the counselor to make and implement the correct diagnosis. Obviously, under a system of this sort, if the diagnosis is in error, the counseling experience may be a painful and disastrous one for the client.

On the other hand, diagnosis may be quite valuable if it is used to guide the client toward the correct action. In this sense, diagnosis may be a product of a careful appraisal by a well-trained and intelligent counselor. The difference is that the diagnosis is presented for client consideration rather than for client action. In such a case, the counselor does not present the diagnosis as his carefully considered verdict. When a diagnosis is handed down as an authoritative decision, the client may feel impelled to act upon it in order not to insult the counselor. The materials of which diagnoses are made (test results, case histories, records, etc.) are not infallible; therefore any diagnosis must be tentative and exploratory.

Diagnosis in Treating the Deeply Disturbed Person

Whereas the value and use of diagnosis in counseling the basically normal individuals may be debatable, an entirely different situation may be evident in working with psychotic and neurotic people. In such cases, diagnosis may be most essential to the choice of treatment methods by the clinician.

The psychiatrist in particular must base his choice upon diagnosis. The patient in psychiatry is rarely regarded as being fully able to make wise decisions. The determination of hospitalization, drug therapy, psychotherapy, a combination of these, or other treatment media must depend upon a diagnosis. Even here, descriptive diagnoses are seldom considered conclusive. Such diagnoses are rarely translated to the patient except in terms of directions given to him.

Religious counselors make a type of diagnosis when they refer cases to medical, psychological or psychiatric personnel. Failure on the part of the religious counselor to apply diagnostic judgment could result in damage to the deeply disturbed client.

It should be evident that diagnosis of a type accompanies every involvement between religious counselor and disturbed parishioner. Just how diagnosis is utilized will depend on the depth of problems, the counselor's philosophy and training, and the setting of the counseling effort.

PSYCHOLOGICAL TESTING

As a means of providing valuable information of an objective nature for helping people to solve their problems, psychological tests have no peer. Tests are undoubtedly the most widely used of the clinical tools. They have been regarded by some as a panacea for all types of evaluation problems; but, as Darley (2) explains, the psychological test is a tool which may be either useful or harmful depending upon the manner of implementation.

Intelligence Tests

Intelligence tests are the oldest and most commonly used of all psychological tests. Their greatest utility is in the schools, but they also have broad usefulness in hospitals, clinics, and industry.

In the public and church schools, intelligence tests are given intermittently throughout the school years and are very valuable in determining placement of students and in helping them choose vocational and educational goals. The religious counselor may find considerable use for the information these tests afford in counseling with young people concerning vocations and in working with retarded children. Adult parishioners often desire intelligence tests to help them decide concerning their fitness for certain jobs and training to which they aspire.

In general, there are two types of intelligence tests, the group test and the individual test. Group tests such as the Otis Tests of Mental Ability, California Test of Mental Maturity, and the Kuhlman-Anderson Tests may be administered to many students at a time. The Weschler-Bellevue Intelligence Scales and the Stanford-Binet, administered individually, are thought to be more accurate because of the possibility of better rapport between the administrator and the testee. The Weschler test in particular has diagnostic values in determining both organic and functional mental impairment. Widely varying patterns of scores on the eleven subtests may be interpreted by highly trained people in assessing pathological difficulties (18).

Intelligence tests may be either verbal or non-verbal. Verbal tests emphasize language usage and are based upon the ability of the client either to read or to understand verbal symbols. Such tests are especially valuable as determiners of scholastic aptitudes and have more predictive value for academic success than do the non-verbal tests.

Non-verbal intelligence tests utilize stimuli designed to measure tasks performed with objects rather than with words. Some tests require the subject to arrange blocks and pictures manually. Others present pictures of objects and require the subject to discover missing parts, broken parts, or to point out similarities among pictured items.

Many of the intelligence tests have both verbal and non-verbal components. Such tests derive a verbal score, a non-verbal score, and a composite score. This allows the counselor to observe the effects of reading disabilities upon the client's performance by comparison of verbal and non-verbal scores.

Interest Tests

Occupational interest tests have been devised to furnish data about the client's likes and dislikes related to possible work situations. These are used widely in vocational guidance in schools and colleges and also in job placement in industry. Most of the tests are based upon the principle of allowing the client to make choices among several activities which may be translated into levels of interest in broad categories of work situations. The Kuder Preference Record, The Strong Vocational Interest Blanks, The Gentry Vocational Inventory, and the Cleeton Vocational Interest Test are among the best known of these tests.

In using occupational interest tests, the counselor should understand that these tests reveal activities the client favors but do not indicate that the person has ability in doing these things. However, interest in the occupation is usually counted more important than ability. Ability may be gained, but the worker will almost invariably fail at a task he dislikes.

Aptitude Test Batteries

Aptitude tests do attempt to measure native and acquired ability in various activities. These abilities range from purely motor to purely intellectual activities. Vocational guidance clinics most often resort to a test battery which evaluates a number of activities. Other tests are made to measure ability in single areas such as mechanics, art, or music.

The United States Employment Service has perfected the General Aptitude Test Battery which measures a wide variety of motor skills and performance patterns. This test may be taken at offices of the Employment Service. The Differential Aptitude Tests are widely used in junior and senior high schools.

Scholastic Achievement Tests

Achievement tests measure what the individual has achieved in academic learning areas. These tests are given routinely in schools and become a part of the students' permanent records. Such tests have utility in clinic situations occasionally. Profiles on achievement tests reveal at a glance the grade level of performance and the percentile ranking within the grade level. Achievement tests may be given for an entire school grade including all academic areas or, at more advanced levels, may be given for specific and individual courses at the high school level. They are most valuable for determining the rate of growth as the student progresses.

Personality Tests

In general, personality tests are either projective or self-report in nature. They may divulge personality traits of a surface nature or traits expressed in clinical categories.

The self-report test usually requires the subject to answer questions "true" or "false" or, in some cases, "yes" or "no." Most of these provide a third response which may indicate that the question does not apply to the subject. The Bell Adjustment Inventory, The Bernreuter Personality Inventory, and the California Test of Personality are profiled in terms of surface-level difficulties such as home adjustment, school adjustment, emotional adjustment, social adjustment, feelings of worthlessness, sense of belonging, neurotic tendencies, and so forth. Among others, the Minnesota Multiphasic Personality Inventory is profiled in terms of the clinical categories including paranoia, schizophrenia, manic-depression, hysteria, hypochondriasis, and psychopathic deviation.

The projective tests present the subject with more or less unstructured situations, and he is asked to respond to these with stories derived from the impressions or with descriptions of what is seen in the unstructured stimuli. The Rorschach Ink Blot Test is a classic example of the projective test. The subject responds to the unstructured stimuli and is evaluated on the basis of content or on the basis of quantitative scoring. The administrator and interpreter are skilled in determining the meaning implied in the responses.

The picture-story techniques such as the Thematic Apperception Test and the Make-a-Picture Story Test require the subject to make up a story about some characters seen in the pictured situation. Clients usually identify with some of the characters; and the counselor skilled in interpretation is usually able to understand the personality dynamics of the subject through the stories he tells.

Other projective techniques utilize free-hand drawings by subjects or sentence-completion techniques. Projective techniques are based upon the theory that subjects will reveal themselves in a relatively unguarded fashion. They may be inclined to defend against revelation with the self-report tests.

Methods of Test Administration

Test scores and profiles are usually thought of as a part of the systematic case study. School guidance services consider the testing program as an absolute essential to proper guidance of students. Accordingly, tests are given at scheduled times, routinely, before time for their use arrives. There is usually no loss in testing because it is firmly believed that every student will enter into a counseling situation in which his scores will be utilized or his teachers will be able to make valuable use of the test scores in various ways.

In clinic situations, the question of test administration becomes a more definite problem. Case history may be taken by the intake interviewer or by the counselor. The question of giving a battery of tests prior to a counseling experience, and of just which tests to include is one which is settled individually for each client or in some cases by broad clinic policies. Another problem in such settings is who shall administer the tests.

In some clinics, each counselee is administered a battery of tests before he sees the counselor and these test scores are woven into the case study to comprise a part of the clinical data on the counselee. Where this is done, it is most typical to have a psychometrician whose main function is the testing of the entering client or patient. Clinics which follow this procedure are most likely to be those of a somewhat singular function such as vocational guidance clinics; or on the other hand, they may be clinics such as child guidance clinics, which deal almost exclusively with disturbed children. In such clinics, the information most likely to be needed can easily be predicted, and time waste in unnecessary tests may be held at a minimum. For instance, the vocational guidance clinic likely would administer an intelligence test, an occupational interest test, an aptitude test battery, and possibly a personality projective test such as the Thematic Apperception Test. The child guidance clinic would desire an intelligence test, a figure-drawing test, and a projective test such as the Make-a-Picture Story Test.

Most neuropsychiatric hospitals, including the veterans hospitals, utilize admissions centers where diagnostic clinical tests are administered by clinical psychologists. Where the clinical psychologist is used as specialist in the church setting, it is common for the psychologist to administer tests and send the results along with the client to the privately practicing psychiatrist when such referral is made. Tests utilized in a clinical diagnosis of the deeply disturbed person may include the Rorschach Ink Blot Test, The Bender-Gestalt, and the Draw-a-Person Test. These tests provide a basis for diagnosis as neurotic or psychotic personality types and differentiate between those with organic brain damage and those who are functionally disturbed. These tests also identify homosexuals and suicidal patients.

Counseling centers such as those found on most university campuses and church-related clinics are most likely to utilize a method of test administration more tailored to the pattern of maladjustment which the individual displays during the initial intake and exploratory interviews. In some cases, the counselor becomes the psychometrician and administers the tests to the clients he is to counsel later. Test administration by the counselor may provide rapport-building possibilities; and the client does not have to be passed from one to another of the staff members.

Other clinics that do not administer a battery of tests before counseling do utilize a psychometrician to administer tests on demand. The advantage in this is that the counselor's time may be utilized in more productive pursuits. Psychometricians do not need to be as highly trained as the counselor in the broad psychological area, but, with experience, they may become very adept in test administration. The counselor may know test administration, but may be less adept than the person who administers tests continuously. The clergyman may depend upon the specialist for test administration and may confer with him on interpretation of test results.

Test Results and Diagnosis of Mental Illness

Much of the work done in religious counseling is with deeply disturbed psychotic or neurotic individuals. As explained earlier, this work may be in support of the efforts of psychotherapists or may be an aspect of pastoral care. Although the clergy and religious workers rarely utilize psychological tests of the kinds used in psychiatric assessment, some familiarity with the types used is in order.

As reported earlier, a large number of counselors, including clinical psychologists and medical psychotherapists, depend largely upon diagnosis as an aid to therapy. Such diagnosis has particular meaning in working with the deeply disturbed. Incorrect handling of a depressive patient might precipitate him into stress which would end in suicide. Unfortunately, one cannot determine his dynamics by talking to a depressive individual. The cyclic nature of depression would prevent such an observational diagnosis from being made unless the patient were in depression at the time. Gurvitz (5) indicates that although an individual reveals his personality in everything he does, psychological tests "give us the maximum amount of information in the minimum of time and with a lessened degree of subjectivity." He says of tests:

> Conflicts are aroused in miniature to see how they are handled or mishandled, anxiety is provoked, basic relationships to figures in the environment are encountered, phantasy is forced upon the patient— all to duplicate the world in miniature. The process of interpreting psychologic procedures is based upon the assumption that the person handles the microcosm of the testing situations in the same manner as he handles life. In the very large majority of cases this hypothesis is sustained (5, p. 7).*

In the area of diagnosing the dynamics of the deeply disturbed patient, projective tests become by far the most common psychological device used. Such tests tap the unconscious dynamics

---

* From Milton S. Gurvitz, *Dynamics of Psychological Testing* (1951). Reproduced by permission of the publishers, Grune & Stratton, Inc.

of the individual and, of course, demand a high level of specialized training for meaningful interpretation.

The development and use of tests has been closely related to the field of psychological research and practice. Psychiatrists, in comparison with psychologists, do not use tests widely. Some privately practicing psychiatrists depend upon a behavioral situation and an evaluation of verbal responses by the patient more so than upon tests. Actually, the training of psychiatrists does not usually emphasize the use of psychological tests.

On the other hand, some psychiatrists do recognize the value of diagnostic tests and have studied the field of testing. Others rely upon test evaluation by clinical psychologists who work with them. Since the emphasis upon drug treatment of the mentally ill has become so strong, it is quite probable that psychiatrists will not have the time nor the inclination to study and practice extensively in the area of psychological testing. At the same time, it is probable that psychiatrists will become more accepting toward psychologists and will enlist their aid in diagnosis through psychological tests.

It is unavoidably true that many mental pathologies which cannot be diagnosed through behavioral observations or by verbal contact between psychiatrist and patient can be ascertained through psychological tests. The patient often covers his anomalies very cleverly and makes himself appear normal. Projective tests will reveal dynamics which may be reasonably predictive of incipient mental illness and may bring about a treatment aimed at prevention rather than cure. Since mental breakdown usually results in irreversible damage, it is only reasonable that psychological testing should become a strong emphasis in church-related counseling as soon as adequately trained people become available.

THE CASE HISTORY

Nature and Purpose

One of the most useful aspects of clinical methodology is the case history. The term is somewhat self-explanatory. The formal case history finds little utility in a church setting where most of the counseling is done by the clergyman whose dealings with his troubled parishioners come about through hurried unplanned conferences. Case history is part of a systematized clinical approach typical of a painstaking effort to aid the parishioner. In the religious setting, it is likely to be used extensively in the church clinic and by the psychological specialist.

The clergyman needs to understand the basic purposes of the case history so that he may communicate with all who have counseling functions both in the church and in the community. The student of religious counseling needs an introduction to case history, since he may become part of a counseling program which could make profitable use of case history methods.

The case history is not an attempt at gathering all of the possible material about the client. It is an attempt to synthesize materials related to him and, more specifically, to his problem. Thus, case histories utilize selected material about the client. To compile detailed records and to incorporate all known material about the client into the case history would be uneconomical. Neither is it reasonable to suppose that all needed material relevant to the problem under consideration may be found in a record about the client that is already available. Invariably, the synthesizing of a valid case history requires a bringing together of materials already in possession and the acquisition of new materials which are not a part of any existing record.

In this connection, the case history is the purposeful organization of all materials perceived to be related to the individual and his problem. Earlier concepts of the case history were inclined toward a very comprehensive treatment of early childhood events and environmental factors which conceivably could touch upon the problem. More recent case history methods have tended to emphasize factors of present reality rather than background and early childhood factors. Naturally, a case history developed on a given client will reflect, by its content, the nature of the problem, which will require emphasis on certain areas of development. Thus, a case history developed for use in working with a known neurotic anxiety state would be likely to place more emphasis upon early traumatic events of childhood. Again, the specific nature and order of the case history would reflect the counselor's basic philosophy. For instance, a counselor who was basically nondirective would be more inclined toward a concentrated study of recent events than an analytically oriented counselor.

The use of the terms case history, case study, and case work may present some difficulty to the reader. Ruth Strang performs a valuable service in differentiating these:

> The case study goes beyond the case history, which systematically traces the individual's development, ideally beginning with direct observation at an early age. The case study leads to case work, which carries out the treatment indicated by the interpretation of case-history data. Thus the cycle of case history, case study, and case work is completed (15, p. 207).

Case work in this sense does not necessarily imply social case-work. The implication is rather that case study should lead to some type of activity. Although case study may be used as a pedagogical method in the training of counselors, it should be followed by activities designed to help the client. These may be psychotherapy, vocational counseling, social casework, or any number and combination of other activities to benefit the client.

DERIVING THE CASE HISTORY

The Intake Interview

Many clinic situations utilize the intake interview as a device for deriving the case history in addition to other values. Drasgow (4) has emphasized the undeveloped state of the intake interview as well as the great potential it has for counseling implementation. Usually, the intake interview serves to identify the problem area initially, at least to the extent that assignment of the client to a specific counselor may be made. The choice of a counselor will be in terms of the abilities of the counselor and his experience with the type of problem being presented. For instance, a young woman will reveal in the intake interview that her problem revolves around her marriage difficulties; and, perhaps, one of the clinic staff has more training and experience in marriage counseling than any other.

However, some counselors object to the entire process of the intake interview on the grounds that each counselor should carry on the interviewing, from the beginning, with the client he is to serve (16). In this case, the individual counselor would take the case history of his own clients and could take it in terms of the problem as he sees it and within the framework of his own theoretical background and approach.

When the intake interviews are done by a single worker for a number of counselors, it is necessary that this worker be much better trained than the average clerical worker. This intake person actually needs a high degree of training, inasmuch as the intake interview can be as significant to the process of counseling as any other single meeting between the client and a member of the clinical staff. Some intake interviewers are assigned only the task of taking case history, others serve also in structuring the counseling method of the clinic staff. Most counselors consider structuring of method to be such a valuable means of entering the counseling interview and of gaining rapport that the most common arrangement is for the intake interviewer to take case history, to present this to the clinic director, and possibly to suggest which staff member should see the client.

When the intake interview is used for case history purposes, it is common that the interview questions are highly structured. Structuring is usually done to the extent of providing questionnaires to be filled out by the interviewer in the process of the intake. It is not unusual to have clients fill out questionnaires without benefit of direction or quizzing by anyone. This method of obtaining case history is not very desirable, inasmuch as entries on the questionnaire may not be completely understood by the client. When skilled interviewers take the case history on prepared blanks by questioning the client, it is possible that valuable information that is not covered by the structured questions may be divulged. In such cases, these entries may be made in specially provided spaces or on separate paper.

Case History During the First Interview

Many counselors prefer to take the client's case history, themselves, during the initial interview. There are advantages and disadvantages in this procedure. Case history development requires probing, and such probing may produce negative effects on the psychological atmosphere. It is likely that case history which involves many revelations of a nature considered derogatory by the client will result in a loss of rapport. On the other hand, case-history taking, if handled diplomatically, may be used as an "ice-breaker" for the counseling process.

Counselors who operate in a nondirective fashion typically do not care to take their clients' case histories. As a matter of fact, such counselors may not feel that the case history drawn from the client is advantageous to counseling. Opinion is that the client may have difficulty relating to the counselor who knows many somewhat derogatory things about him. Generally, the nondirective counselor feels that the client will reveal his own case history at the time it is most meaningful to him, and at a time when it is least threatening. It is also considered likely that foreknowledge of case history would cause the counselor to form evaluations of the client and thus hinder the development of the "internal frame of reference" considered so necessary to the client-centered counselor. In this connection, Rogers says:

> Instead of elaborate case histories full of information about the person as an object, we would endeavor to develop ways of seeing his situation, his past, and himself, as these objects appear to him. We would try to see with him, rather than to evaluate him (14, p. 367).

AREAS COVERED BY CASE HISTORY

It has already been pointed out that the content of case history depends upon the nature of the problem and upon the philosophy of the person taking it. At the same time, there are common areas of coverage in the case history. Variations in case histories are most likely to indicate differences in emphasis on certain areas rather than the omission of the common areas entirely. Broad areas of case history are listed below, together with sub-areas usually covered:

I. Family History
   A. Marital status of parents (present status and past events)
   B. Information about parents (ages, occupations, education)
   C. Siblings (ages, education, sex)
   D. General socio-economic level both present and past

II. School History
   A. Grade completed and scholastic summary
   B. Preferences in academic fields
   C. Pattern of grades (significant variations over period of time)
   D. Participation in extra-curricular activities
   E. Behavioral record (punctuality, disciplinary, sociability)

III. Health Record
   A. History of childhood diseases
   B. Record of surgical operations
   C. Record of physical disabilities

IV. Vocational Experiences
   A. History of jobs held and locations
   B. Preferences
   C. Present job situation
   D. Special data on job difficulties

V. Social and Recreational Interests
   A. Hobbies and sports
   B. Preference in social activities

VI. Psychological Test Results

VII. Miscellaneous Information
   A. Unusual events in past life
   B. Unusual complaints (physical or psychological)
   C. Previous counseling experience
   D. Observable abnormalities

A most comprehensive system of case-history taking, utilizing five questionnaires filled out by interviewers, has been developed by the Purdue University Psychological Clinics (6). These questionnaires are entitled (1) Registration, (2) Educational History, (3) Family History, (4) Developmental History, and (5) Sociological History. The student is urged to study these forms in order to understand the comprehensiveness of some case history efforts.

Case history formulation sometimes becomes the job of the social worker. This is most often true in the treatment of children. The most pertinent facts in many cases involving children may be derived from a visit to the home. Valid material may be gleaned from parents, grandparents, and neighbors. Broad investigation of environmental conditions and influences becomes most useful for probation workers who work with delinquent children as well as emotionally disturbed children.

THE USE OF CASE STUDY

If clinical case studies of the client are useful only in diagnosis, it is questionable whether or not the value of such efforts could be sustained. Fortunately, there are many other uses for the case study in counseling. It has already been pointed out that information about clients is useful in communicating various aspects of the case. Such communication is valuable in consultation, in interviews with the client, and in referral to other specialists.

Even so, the greatest utility for case information is undoubtedly as a means through which the client may come to know himself. It may be suggested that the client already knows himself, that he knows all the facts of his case history better than anyone else could. It is true that he may know all the individual facts of his own case history; even so, a review of experiences may open up new vistas for the client. He may achieve a high degree of self-understanding; and test scores, in particular, may bring fresh insights to the client.

Justification of detailed clinical materials about the client is most easily accomplished in educational institutions, but such information may be useful in many ways other than in the pure counseling situation. Case material may serve to convey important information to staff members which could not logically be conveyed in any other manner. Should communication of information concerning students depend upon verbal exchange between staff members, guidance and counseling activities in the schools would be seriously hampered.

The Case Conference

Case studies utilize case histories in an effort to determine causes of difficulties and to formulate directions for case work. The case conference often becomes a valuable method, utilizing the combined efforts of a number of staff members of the school, clinic, or hospital. It is often true that valid evaluations will be reached when several staff members confer on a case; and it is the unusual counselor who does not welcome suggestions in handling counseling problems of any kind.

The Ministerial Counseling Center in St. Louis makes excellent use of the case conference. After the intake process is completed, a staff conference, attended by a psychiatrist, at least one minister, a staff conference director, and the Administration Director, is called for each client. From a study of case materials, a decision is made concerning the need for psychiatric care; and if it is indicated, the client is referred for treatment. If the problem falls within the scope of the religious counselors who staff the clinic, the client is assigned to the counselor chosen by the Administration Director (3).

The case conference is often used in the church when clergyman and staff members meet together to discuss problems. Such conferences may prove valuable in the counseling sphere where specialists, the clergyman, and perhaps the youth worker meet to discuss a case.

Counseling by Utilizing the Case Study

The nondirective revolt has undoubtedly turned the attention of many counselors away from the case study. Many problems which were handled by the clinical approach before the advent of nondirective methods are handled effectively without case study of any kind. Students who prepare themselves for counseling without emphasis on clinical methods may expect to be handicapped.

The ways in which counselors use case study to promote the aims of counseling are as varied as the philosophies of the counselors. Some counselors who pose as authoritative figures utilize the case study approach in order to give direction to the client. There is no denying that many counselors are authoritative in their approach to counseling. Neither can it be denied that some clients receive outstanding benefits from authoritative approaches to counseling. Clinical practitioners, medically oriented or otherwise, who work with deeply disturbed persons may have little choice of being other than authoritative and directive. The question of what is best for the client in terms of permissiveness involves many questions which can be settled only on the basis of the specific client and his problem.

This much is certain: If the counselor is inclined to be directive, either by virtue of his basic philosophy and training or of a perceived necessity for the benefit of the client, he will be more likely to function for the betterment of his client if he has accurate information upon which to base his interpretations, diagnoses, and directions. Clergymen and religious counselors are not exceptions to this rule. Information which the clergyman uses may not be highly organized and systematized, as it will be in the psychological clinic. Without denying the values inherent in careful organization, such is not always a reasonable aim in some religious settings. However, all counselors must guard against utilizing faulty information.

DECISION-ORIENTED COUNSELING

Decision-making represents such a large proportion of the work of the religious counselor that it becomes necessary to devote special consideration to these problems. The youth worker, in particular, is called upon to aid in making decisions; and the clergyman who is sensitive to the needs of his young people will often be called upon.

A principal area of decision problems brought to the religious counselor is that of religious vocations. The question of whether or not to enter a religious vocation is a weighty one with many young people and a difficult one to deal with in counseling. It is a problem often referred to the religious counselor by counselors in schools and colleges.

The task of the clergyman or youth worker here is to assist the young person in evaluating his motives. There are many reasons why religious vocations are chosen, some of which are highly questionable. Religious vocations are often chosen because of guilt reactions, for instance.

The clergyman usually is very interested in having some of his young parishioners choose religious vocations, and he often attempts to motivate them through his pulpit messages. He seldom expects that a sermon will serve to answer all questions, and he should be prepared for considerable individual counseling following any such emphasis from the pulpit.

Not only do young people need help in determining whether or not they shall enter a religious vocation; decisions must be made also concerning the specific area of service. The religious counselor should not neglect to acquire a very specialized knowledge of religious vocations and of training institutions where young people may be prepared for them (9).

Many religious counselors view the "call" to a religious vocation as distinctively different from a decision relative to other vocational pursuits. Even if such a decision is different, there are many common aspects about all types of decision problems. Then, too, the religious counselor faces parishioners having many other types of decision problems.

Because decisions are so varied and indecisiveness has so many causes, it is true that to develop counseling methods specifically for this area has been difficult. Workers have been inclined to view implementation of this type of counseling as involving an intuitive approach. On the other hand, our best authorities have viewed therapeutic and other types of counseling as being more of a challenge to their genius.

It is true that as one approaches the field of adolescent problems, in particular, he is subject to the impression that order can never be brought out of the confusion which obviously exists in the minds of this highly energetic mass of humanity. These young people, in particular, become a challenge to the counselor in terms of dealing with decisions. As one attempts to visualize the breadth and depth of decision-oriented problems among young and old, he may conclude that there can be no method in decision-oriented counseling, and that each case must be taken as a separate and unrelated entity.

Specifics in Decision-Oriented Counseling

Among the few who have endeavored to set forth specifics for the decision-oriented counseling interview, is Leona Tyler:

The first thing the client needs to achieve is a sense of the general direction he wishes to go, the purposes that the decision he makes must serve for him. Until this general sense of what one wants exists, there is little likelihood that specific choices will be satisfying. After this or along with it, the person must consider the limits within which his free choice operates. These may consist of university requirements, . . . or one's own talents and disabilities. . . . A multitude of other factors operate in this way—age, financial condition, past record, physical appearance, family commitments, draft status. Knowing what he wants and understanding the limitations that are placed upon him, the individual can narrow down the range of possibilities open to him, thus cutting down on the amount of confusion. Thinking in these terms he can usually identify more precisely than at the beginning just what is the factor that holds him back from each of these possible courses of action. . . . Once this stage is reached a decision comes fairly easily (17, p. 232).

Regarding the atmosphere most conducive to decision-oriented counseling, Tyler says:

There should be a general atmosphere completely free from any sort of threat to one's self-esteem, an atmosphere of genuine respect and liking. Attitudes should be given the same status as facts. They should be recognized, clarified, accepted, and understood. Dependable information should be readily available and freely used. It should be clear from the beginning that the decision is in the client's hands. The counselor will help him put things together but will not attempt to decide for him (17, p. 233).

In addition to the general skills any good counselor has, the counselor needs special skills in decision-oriented counseling:

The first and most important of these is perceptual sensitivity as to whether or not a real decision has actually occurred. Another way of putting this is to say that a counselor needs to be able to distinguish between a genuine decision and a pseudo-decision. This, like so many other special skills, requires the picking up of small cues through which the attitude behind the words can be sensed. Pseudo-decisions are fairly common in counseling, as it is natural that they should be in a situation where there is some pressure to decide. . . .

The second kind of contribution he can make is to help the client with the task of identifying the reasons for his inability to decide. . . . More often than not the attitudes and expectations of other persons in the client's immediate circle are involved (17, p. 234).

A chief function of the counselor in decision-making is to help the client identify the factors which cause him to be indecisive.

Tyler (17) lists five common causes of indecision. These are (1) attitudes and expectations of the client's immediate circle, (2) distasteful roles believed by the client to accompany the decision to be made, (3) an equipotentiality among several alternate choices, (4) limitations imposed by circumstances, and (5) personality problems.

It is obvious that a sufficient amount of time must be spent in choice counseling to allow the client to work through each factor which inhibits his decision. If family and friends are hampering the client's decision by their expectations, the client must be helped to evaluate realistically the effects of going against these expectations. In some cases, conferences with parents or others become desirable in order to effect a relaxing of their demands upon the client.

It is often true that the client has falsely concluded that certain situations are in effect concerning job situations and other aspects of decision-making. He may have been impressed with the idea that *all* missionary workers are ministers, for example. Sometimes, the client needs to be given more materials for reading, so that he may receive correct impressions and valid information.

As reasons for indecision are identified, each must be followed to a conclusion. In case of equipotentiality among several possible choices, it is usually true that the client does not yet have all the related information. Upon further study, he will be able to choose one job or one direction from among the several which seem equally desirable.

When personality problems seem to be hampering decision, the choice of direction for the counselor becomes especially difficult. The counselor must decide either to deal with the personality problem or to ignore it in favor of moving toward a choice by the client which circumvents the damaging effects of the personality problem. This decision is usually made by the counselor through a careful consideration of the time available, the nature of the personality difficulties, and the perceived motivation which the client has toward pursuing the personality problem.

The youth counselor and other religious counselors look to educational research for leadership. School counseling has always emphasized decision-making. It may be noted here that a great deal of change has occurred in this field in the past few years. Earliest efforts in counseling emphasized the use of test and background data as a means of arriving at choices for individuals without consideration of their attitudes and personality factors. In general, counselors have come to recognize that factors may operate in the lives of people which sometimes make questionable the choice most indicated by test scores and other data. In some cases, a choice based solely upon tests scores turns out to be extremely unwise. Decision-making counseling may no longer be thought of as an area for mechanical approaches. Good decisions will always be founded upon a consideration of the complete personality structure of the individual.

Special Problems of Youth Workers

Such a large proportion of decision problems arises in working with youth that some special remarks may be worthwhile. In the first place, decision problems of young people should be treated with great seriousness. The counselor may think that the decision has little importance one way or another; nevertheless, he should approach counseling from the point of view of the young person.

A major area of youth decisions relates to their efforts to decide whether to do what they know is proper or what they selfishly desire to do, even if it is improper. The clever counselor will recognize immediately if the youth is struggling with himself rather than with the decision. For instance, the high school student may realize that he needs to take trigonometry but that he is tempted to take an easier course. This is more than a decision problem; it becomes an opportunity for the exercise of the will and for building maturity. In cases like these, where perhaps the counselor may feel that the young person really knows what course of action he should take but is struggling with himself, the best thing the counselor may do is to emphasize the powers and privileges of choice the young person has. Usually the struggle involves an experience with a parent or teacher who has been somewhat authoritative in suggesting that the youngster should do this or that.

If the counselor is able to make the young person feel that he really has the choice, and if the counselor refuses to be drawn into an advisory role, it is almost certain that the young person eventually will make the decision in terms of what he really should do. Upon having the right of choice emphasized, the young person usually makes his decision at first to do what he wishes rather than what he feels he should. If the counselor then reiterates that the privilege of choice resides in the individual, he may expect after further pursuance of the problem that the young person will decide in favor of what he knows he should have done in the first place. If he has the prerogative of changing his mind, having made it up by exercising his own powers of choice, then he is still exercising his autonomy in changing his mind again, back to what the parent or teacher had originally told him he should do. Only, now, the decision is his and not that of the power figure.

Decision-making is an area in which the counselor must wear his best "armor" of resistance to advice-giving. One may be sure that the person seeking to make a decision will ask for advice in some manner or other. He will say, "What do you think I should do about this?" Or he will say, "What would you do if you were in my place?" After he has made a tentative decision, he may say, "Don't you think I have made the right decision?" The counselor should be fully aware that clients make tentative decisions in order to gain his evaluation.

School workers, church related counselors, and others who work with youth often have some unusual conflicts because of divided loyalties. So often a young person seeks help with a decision that has great importance, perhaps to an entire family. For instance, a high school senior may have decided to drop out of school and join the Navy. The counselor comes to know through one source or another that the parents are frantic about this decision. They often use some means of letting the counselor know that they are depending upon him to get John to change his mind.

The greatest difficulty experienced by the counselor in such cases is to get the young person to face the realities of the situation. Many young people make up their minds about things through emotional involvements. They are not receptive to facts and figures which might otherwise be meaningful. One avenue of help in such cases is to bring about procrastination in making the decision. Young people are often headstrong in making decisions and would be better able to decide wisely if they would allow emotional involvement to subside.

Philosophically, the reins of decision should always be left in the hands of the client; and he should not be driven or directed toward one course or another. This is the essence of professional counseling.

References

1. Bordin, Edward S., "Diagnosis in Counseling and Psychotherapy," *Educational and Psychological Measurements.* Vol. 6, 1946, pp. 169-184.

2. Darley, John G., *Testing and Counseling in the High School Guidance Program.* Chicago: Science Research Associates, 1943.

3. Deitchman, Robert B., "The Evolution of a Ministerial Counseling Center," *Journal of Pastoral Care.* Winter, 1957, pp. 207-215.

4. Drasgow, James, "Intake Interviewing in Counseling," *Personnel and Guidance Journal.* October, 1956, pp. 100-102.

5. Gurvitz, Milton S., *The Dynamics of Psychological Testing.* New York: Grune and Stratton, Inc., 1951.

6. Hadley, John M., *Clinical and Counseling Psychology.* New York: Alfred A. Knopf, 1958.

7. Hahn, Milton E. and Malcolm S. Maclean, *General Clinical Counseling in Educational Institutions.* New York: McGraw-Hill Book Company, 1950.

8. Heiser, Karl F., "Specialist Services in Psychology," *Pastoral Psychology.* January, 1960, pp. 37-48.

9. Kemp, Charles F., "Occupational Information for Church Vocation," *Pastoral Psychology.* March, 1961, pp. 54-58.

10. Kraepelin, E., *Clinical Psychiatry.* New York: The Macmillan Company, 1902.

11. Pepinsky, Harold B., and Pauline Nichols Pepinsky, *Counseling Theory and Practice.* New York: The Ronald Press Company, 1954.

12. Pepinsky, Harold B., *The Selection and Use of Diagnostic Categories in Clinical Counseling.* Applied Psychological Monograph, No. 15. Stanford: Stanford University Press, 1948.

13. Robinson, Francis P., *Principles and Procedures in Student Counseling.* New York: Harper and Brothers, 1950.

14. Rogers, Carl R., "Some Observations on the Organization of Personality," *American Psychologist.* September, 1947, pp. 358-368.

15. Strang, Ruth, *Counseling Technics in College and Secondary School.* New York: Harper and Brothers, 1949.

16. Tyler, Leona, "Comment on Drasgow's Article, 'Intake Interviewing in Counseling'," *Personnel and Guidance Journal.* October, 1956, p. 102.

17. ———, *The Work of the Counselor*. New York: Appleton-Century-Crofts, 1953.

18. Wechsler, David, *The Measurement of Adult Intelligence*. Baltimore: The Williams and Wilkins Company, 1944.

19. Williamson, E. G., *How to Counsel Students*. New York: McGraw-Hill Book Company, 1939.

20. Wise, Carroll A., "Education of the Pastor for Marriage Counseling," *Pastoral Psychology*. December, 1959, pp. 45-48.

VI

Marriage and Family Counseling

Studies concerning the incidence of marriage problems as compared to other types indicate that marriage problems comprise approximately one-half the counseling cases in the religious setting. A study of the first 200 cases handled at the Ministerial Counseling Center in St. Louis revealed that, of these, 112 were marital problems (5). In 1100 interviews held in the Pastoral Counseling Service at Boston University, marriage and family difficulties were among the leading problems (15).

Dealing with marriage problems requires the same professional understanding as do other types of problems. Troubled marriage partners are people in quandaries having basically the types of difficulties described earlier as personal problems. Hence, the reader should refer to Chapters IV and V for techniques of counseling in this area.

As Wise (32) indicates, "Marriage counseling is like any other kind of counseling in that it deals with persons rather than problems." This statement is made in reference to the training required of pastors who do marriage counseling. While this is true, there are some specifics to be considered relative to marriage and family problems (21).

In general, the specifics of marriage counseling revolve around the consideration that there are at least two persons involved in any marriage and family problem. As Gomberg (11) says, the traditional view of treating the individual as an individual does not take into consideration the interaction between the two parties or the use that one partner makes of the other. In this relation, Stroup and Glasser (26) postulate a sociological dimension in marriage counseling. "Personal counseling emphasizes the psychological, marriage counseling emphasizes the sociological or sociopsychological."

It is possible, of course, that marriage counseling may be nothing more than personal counseling, inasmuch as much of it is done with only one of the partners. A strong emphasis is developing, however, on the solution of marriage problems through joint interviews, separate interviews with the same counselor, and close collaboration between counselors working with the two individuals separately (11). Marriage problems usually focus on specific problems such as sex, money, or in-laws; but, most likely, the problem involves the totality of the relationship (13).

THE DEVELOPMENT OF MARRIAGE AND FAMILY COUNSELING

Before the development of a professional counseling discipline, the clergy was called upon almost exclusively for help. Aside from parents and friends of the marriage partners there was little place to turn except to the clergy. Today, even with other resources available, the clergyman receives more requests for help than others because he is by far the most logical source of help. Marriage ceremonies are performed by the clergyman; and because of his trusted position, he is consulted when some difficulty threatens the relationship. He has a correspondingly strategic position for shaping attitudes of young people relative to wise mate selection and for premarital counseling.

Marriage counseling found little place in educational and vocational counseling fields which developed in the early part of the century. Since little attention was given to it, marriage difficulty remained an area which was kept under cover. People lived with their marriage difficulties and were, for the most part, ashamed to admit they were having problems.

The greatest impetus for marriage counseling seems to have evolved from the mental health movement. This movement was inaugurated in 1909 with the formation of the National Committee of Mental Hygiene and had as its chief concern educating the public about mental health and improving treatment of mental illness. It is natural that this group should foster the study of marriage and family problems seen as chief causative factors of the poor mental health of many people. Thus, the realities of marriage maladjustments were accentuated, with the result that the demand for such help increased enormously.

The Family Welfare Association of America was established in 1911 to promote family agencies and services. Although the principal function of this group at this early time was financial aid to needy families, a developing interest in marriage and family counseling was maintained throughout the depression years. This organization changed its name in 1946 to Family Service Association of America and has been very instrumental in founding present-day marriage clinics around the nation. Marriage counseling as a specific entity has been more constantly dealt with by those in the social work field than by those in psychology or education. A majority of the agencies engaged in marriage counseling today are under the auspices of the Family Service Association. Some of the most noted agencies have been sponsored privately; for example, the American Institute of Family Relations in Los Angeles, under the direction of Dr. Paul Popenoe, was established as a private institution and has received wide publicity and acclaim.

In recent years, a number of organizations and clinics have been set up by church groups, domestic courts, and social work departments of colleges and universities, among others. These installations utilize the service of clergymen, psychiatrists, social workers, and psychologists. Medical personnel are usually utilized on a consultant basis, and the clergymen of the community may alternate in voluntary service to the clinics. Marriage counseling in the clinics has usually been developed as a community service offered to clients at very nominal cost or at no cost at all.

Today there is an expanding marriage and family counseling

interest among privately practicing psychologists, social workers, and professional counselors; but the major portion of the work still rests upon the clergy and upon the community clinic (4).

There is no doubt that the favorite source of help is the clergy, but the man of God is in more constant demand by those who belong to religious congregations. Although most non-church members are reluctant to approach a religious leader, it is almost certain that they would receive help regardless of their lack of affiliation with a church.

Early marriages are bringing more requests for marriage counseling to school and college counselors. College students make constant use of the premarital counseling facilities on college campuses. In addition, the demand for college courses on marriage continues to increase.

Marriage problems become family problems when children are born. Because all difficulties within the home affect all people therein, the concept of marriage counseling has been enlarged to that of family counseling. However, this does not mean that all family problems stem from difficulties between husband and wife. Any unhappy interpersonal relationship within the family group may be considered as a problem in the broad field of marriage and family counseling, since all family members will be affected.

PREMARITAL COUNSELING

The original point of attack upon the problem of unhappy marriage was the elimination of divorce by legislation (10). The second attack was upon marriage problems per se. Now it has been demonstrated beyond question that success in marriage depends upon proper planning for marriage and upon proper selection of a marriage partner. Accordingly, emphasis has been extended to the area of premarital counseling.

Instructional Measures

Young people are being made aware of the seriousness of marriage through courses at both high school and college levels.

These courses bring into the minds of young people the factors which go to make up compatibility in marriage. The content of these courses in courtship, marriage, and family living emphasizes personality, religious, and cultural factors as matters to be considered in the choice of a mate. Undoubtedly, such courses have done immeasurable good.

Similar courses are often taught in the religious setting in the form of study courses for which a number of books have been developed, including Burton's *Tomorrow You Marry* (3). In the church setting, also, the pastor may occasionally speak directly to young people from the pulpit on matters pertaining to establishing a happy home. A popular theme for student retreats is courtship, dating, and marriage. The youth worker in particular may aid in the instructional aspect of the courtship and marriage program by promoting group discussions among young people.

As Elia (7) points out, young peoples' groups may be organized in the churches, utilizing the services of the "professional personnel in the church—the doctors, lawyers, nurses, social workers, and men and women of the business world." He says, "The church must be prepared to accept the challenge. It will grow because young people are hungry for correct information; and they find what they get interesting and helpful."

Premarital Counseling and the Church

Information accumulated by Wiser (33) shows that of 179 Methodist Churches surveyed in the Baltimore Conference, 98 per cent of the ministers who replied felt the Church had a definite responsibility in preparing people for marriage, and 92 per cent reported either one or two interviews were held before the marriage ceremony.

It has been established that marriage counseling is the area most often touched upon in the minister's counseling work. It may well be that premarital counseling is the most important phase of the marriage counseling program in terms of numbers of people who come for counseling. When the aspect of instruction toward formulating happy homes and preventive aspects are considered, it may be that premarital counseling is the most worthwhile of all marriage counseling.

Counseling the Undecided

It is difficult to pinpoint the time when premarital counseling begins. The church instructional program may be considered premarital; but young people are reluctant to use the term "premarital" until they have committed themselves to an engagement. Even though it is recognized that the engagement in modern times is often little more than an agreement to consider marriage seriously, the engagement should represent a point of serious contemplation.

Among the serious questions which will come to young people and will be brought to the religious counselor is whether they have made the right choice. Actually, only about two out of three engagements result in marriage.

The counseling of the unsure person may involve one or both partners. When it involves only one, the other may not be aware of the counseling. In this case, the task is similar to any personal-problem involvement. When both partners are being counseled, the typical procedure is to see the parties separately either once or a number of times and, perhaps, to meet jointly with the prospective partners another time. As a rule, young people are unwilling to admit to each other that they are unsure but they are able to make this admission in the joint interview with a third party present. These are soul-searching experiences for young people and should not be regarded lightly.

Indecision about marriage either before or after formal engagement revolves about the broad question of compatibilities. The most important points of compatibility concern religion, background, personality, and socio-economic status.

The problem of different religious backgrounds is most likely to be brought to the minister (20) (23). Sometimes, unfortunately, the young person is coerced into consulting him.

Many religious workers feel strongly about mixed marriage. Several studies have shown that there is a high incidence of divorce arising from mixed marriages (30) (17). The religious worker owes it to the counselees to present such statistical information, but he will make a mistake if he incites their hostility. Usually, young people react negatively to what they consider radical thinking. They often insist that what has happened to others will not happen to them. It must be admitted that much has been said about failures in mixed marriages and little about the successes.

The religious counselor should not overlook the possibility that the mixed engagement may be motivated by hostility, especially that involving parents. Young people are taught constantly that the mixed marriage is dangerous. The opportunities for finding a mate among members of one's own religious group are legion. Why then should one choose a prospective marriage partner from another religious group?

There is little doubt that the partners are really in love, at least in the sense that love is understood by them; and there is no easy way for them to relinquish their avowed claims on one another. Where hostility has been the motivating factor, one or the other of the young people may bring an end to the situation, if it is possible to promote insight concerning the real motive for the affair. This cannot usually be accomplished by directing attention to the hostility; it can be accomplished by nondirectively leading the young person toward self-understanding.

All that has been said concerning mixed marriages relative to religion is pertinent also to marriage between young people of widely divergent cultures and ethnic groups. In some sections, there is much opposition to marriages between Caucasians and Latin Americans; and, of course, marriages between Caucasians and Negroes meet disapproval almost everywhere. Young people choose prospective mates from divergent ethnic groups for many reasons. Some are seeking escape from various frustrating circumstances. Motives for mixed marriages are seldom altogether conscious.

It is possible for young people, under optimum conditions, to overcome great obstacles, including massive incompatibilities, and to make successes in marriage against terrific odds. The duty of the counselor in this sphere is clearly one of pointing out the difficulties which accrue from wide divergencies between prospective marriage partners. Where possible, he should have statistical evidence to use in pointing out the probabilities of success and failure with certain types of incompatibilities.

The clergyman does have an advantage over other counselors in that he can afford, at least in some cases, to be more persuasive and personal as he counsels a young person whom he has known intimately for a long time. It is true, also, that his knowledge of the family of his parishioner will help him judge the probabilities which may grow out of a given union between members of families who are incompatible on one or more of the bases discussed above.

Some of the most serious incompatibilities are cultural ones. Marriages between those having great differences in socio-economic backgrounds are bad risks, but young people in love are seldom eager to consider these things with open minds. The counselor should be careful not to create defensiveness and rebellion in young people by a strong elaboration of the dangers involved in such marriages.

A special danger lies in the situation in which the young woman has been reared in luxury and the young man grew up in semi-poverty. The young woman typically feels she can adjust to lower standards; she feels that love will overcome this obstacle. It is often true that young people could overcome the economic and cultural obstacles, if the parents of the bride would leave them to their own resources. This difficulty is a common theme in counseling during the first years of marriage.

Using Tests and Inventories

Working with young people to make them aware of salient factors in mate selection is one of the most desirable means of insuring future happiness in marriage. Along with the dispensation of printed matter, much good can be accomplished by utilizing the many inventories, self-rating scales, and personality assessment devices. Typical of these is the SRA Youth Inventory, published by Science Research Associates of Chicago. Some of these have been developed specifically for helping teenagers evaluate their long-range aspirations in mate selection. These seldom probe deeply and may be useful as "starters" in group or individual sessions.

It must be recognized that when young people have already committed themselves to marriage, it is usually too late to bring about a more intelligent selection by determining compatibility. Most of them simply wish to be assured that they are suited for each other and would not take seriously any suggestion to the contrary. However, some advantage may come from tests and inventories at this stage, since young people may endeavor to correct glaring deficiencies before marriage takes place and may have direction in a continued attack upon their incompatibilities after marriage.

It must be admitted that it is difficult to diagnose marriage success from any given amount of information regarding compatibilities. It has long been assumed that good marriages could be expected if the parties had common interests and not too uncommon backgrounds. It has also been thought that personality needs of the parties should be complementary, but recent research has questioned the reasonableness of earlier theories of complementary needs (24). It is clear that no mechanical approach to mate selection can ever be highly successful, and that tests, while useful, may be second in importance to the judgments of a trained counselor (28) (29).

Weigert (31) believes that interpersonal factors are of greatest importance in determining premarital diagnosis and prognosis. She suggests that information is needed on at least the following four subjects:

(1) The relationship of the marital partners to their parental families.
(2) The preparation for sex adjustment.
(3) Acceptance of sexual roles and competition in marriage.
(4) The attitudes of both partners toward their offspring.

It is perhaps true that the area of sex knowledge is more amenable to exploration by inventories than any other. *The Sex Knowledge Inventory,* Forms X and Y are widely used in pastoral counseling. This inventory is published by Family Life Publications, of Durham, North Carolina.

Although sex education is more complete today than previously, it is often advantageous that young people have some counseling concerning factors related to sexual activity and matters pertaining to the intimacies of married life. In times past, young people have sought advice and suggestions from many sources, including parents, friends, and older brothers and sisters. These sources are still prevalent and for the most part desirable. Landis (16) points out that a trained marriage counselor is usually in a better position to give professional attention to these matters than are the untrained. While the average pastor is in a strategic position and probably is sufficiently well-trained to counsel on sex matters, his position may inhibit young people from bringing the subject forward. On the other hand, a recent survey of 1000 ministers revealed that only 44 per cent thought sex attitudes and information appropriate topics in premarital interviews (8).

Proper handling of premarital counseling often makes necessary the use of various anatomical charts concerning sexual functions and printed material concerning the physiological and psychological differences of the two sexes. It is easy to believe that the untrained person does not know a great deal about many of the matters pertaining to the physical aspects of mating, conception, and birth. Adequate counseling in this area does not require the technical knowledge of a physician. Printed materials and logical planning have opened this area to the religious counselor.

Religious Meanings in Marriage

A survey of 179 Methodist ministers places "spiritual basis for marriage" at the top of the list of most representative topics covered in premarital interviews (33). A survey of 1000 Presbyterian ministers shows that the topic considered most appropriate is "religious responsibilities of the new family" (8). This is not at all surprising and is completely as it should be. The value of the minister as premarital counselor is predicated in large part upon his concern for the religious life of his parishioners. No other counselor could be in as strategic a position in order to implant religious meanings into the new unions, destined to procreate and formulate the homes of the future.

EARLY ADJUSTMENT PROBLEMS

Duvall and Hill (6) emphasize that conflict in marriage is both normal and desirable. This is undoubtedly true of the early stages. Were there no interpersonal conflicts, one would be justified in believing that at least one party was being browbeaten.

Mace (19) suggests that there are five major adjustment areas: sex, money, work, in-laws, and parenthood. If these are to be problems, this is likely to happen in the early years of marriage.

Sex Adjustment

The difficulties which young people experience in the early stages of their marriage are often related to sexual adjustment and to problems that come naturally as two people engage in close relationships on a continuing basis for the first time. Young people have to get used to one another. That is why the first year of marriage is said to be the most difficult.

Early difficulties related to sex adjustments may be solved by means of instruction in matters of sexual adaptability. Even though modern young people have been taught about sex far more than their parents were, experiences of marriage counselors indicate that the information young people have is still far from complete. Even so, it is not reasonable to expect that marriage partners could become sufficiently informed about sex before marriage to insure trouble-free adjustment.

A word of caution is advisable on the general subject of sex adjustment problems. In the early stages of marriage and in marriages of long standing, apparent sexual adjustment problems may represent broader patterns of difficulty. Bowman states:

> Satisfactory adjustment sexually and in other ways (if they may be separated for purposes of discussion) go hand in hand, reacting one upon the other. Where there is failure, either may be cause or effect, depending upon circumstances. If the couple's adjustment in general is unsatisfactory, there may be a sexual element at the root of the difficulty. On the other hand, unsatisfactory sexual adjustment may be the result of nonsexual factors. Success in either increases the probability of success in the other; but neither guarantees the other. Often sexual maladjustment is blamed for marital failure when it may be only one among several causes or may be the result of the factors that are working together to make the marriage fail. Under such circumstances sex becomes the hook on which the couple hang their marriage wraps.
>
> Sexual adjustment and personality adjustment are aspects of a single complex process. There is not one problem of adjusting per-

> sonalities in marriage and another separate one of sex. Sex in marriage is not a simple physical act, distinct in itself. It is one component of a complicated whole, ramifying through other elements, which in their turn ramify through it, a thread of changing hue inextricably woven into the warp and woof of life (1, p. 365).

Problems of sex adjustment may be very simple and easy to work out; on the other hand, they may be deep-rooted and difficult to deal with. For some couples the difficulty is largely physical or may be a combination of physical and temperamental factors.

In other cases, sexual maladjustment may spring from faulty attitudes and may be outgrowths of what Johnson (14) has called the unconscious motives in marriage. The unconscious motives in marriage usually come into focus during the first year or so. The counselor may be able to see that one or both partners' motives for marrying were not only unconscious but unhealthy. For instance, the man may have chosen a partner who reminded him of his mother, and he may find sexual activity inhibited with this mother figure.

When sexual maladjustment stems from deep motives such as these, the religious counselor may feel that referral is the best answer. If he decides to deal with the problem, he will likely expect a rather long-term counseling experience.

Divergent Interests and Backgrounds

Young married people often have difficulty adjusting to each other because they have divergent interests. Counseling with such problems often includes the admonition that the young people be tolerant and understanding toward each other. Where there is a strong basis for love, the religious counselor may be able to encourage Christian principles of tolerance and understanding and consideration of the rights of the separate individuals.

It is often true in this respect that young married people need to be reminded that each of them is an individual and each has a right to some interests and pursuits separate and apart from the partner. In other matters there may be complete unity of purpose and activity.

It is unavoidably true that some young couples recognize very soon and very clearly that they are so different that to continue the relationship would be to make each other continuingly unhappy. If this realization comes before there are children to be considered, then there may be times when the counselor feels that separation is best.

Undoubtedly, the framework of religious viewpoints about separation and divorce will enter the situation here. The viewpoints of the partners are more important than those of the counselor. Even so, the counselor may have strong feelings which he may not and should not avoid in the religious setting.

Unless strong conviction motivates the counselor in other directions, he should allow the partners to work out their own decisions. It would seem that if nondirectiveness is a virtue anywhere, it must be doubly so in marriage counseling. The ordinary couple can work out their own solutions; but they do need a counselor to aid them in being objective and to help them communicate with one another. The counselor serves here as a catalyst and as an objective helper who aids the partners in seeing issues clearly.

Problems of Home Management

Many problems of the early years of marriage relate to the management of the home, handling of finances, and child training. It is difficult to generalize procedures for working with these problems since they are so varied.

The clergyman and his co-workers need to keep the possibility of dependency relationships constantly before them. Most of the problems listed above must eventually be worked out by the marriage partners. Constant seeking for help should not be encouraged, although the values of help where self-sufficiencies may be developed through counseling should be accented.

The clergyman has a valuable counseling function, of course, in the religious and moral training of children. His function in working with the wayward child and the juvenile is unique and valuable. The clergyman is truly a family counselor in most cases, and his concern reaches out to the fullest development of every member of his congregation.

DIFFICULTIES IN MARRIAGES
OF LONG STANDING

Goldstein lists five specific types of problems in marriage. Most of these seem to relate to the marriage of long standing—not to the adjustment phase of the first year or so. These types of problems are: (1) legal problems, (2) economic problems, (3) biological problems, (4) psychological problems, and (5) ethical problems (10).

Of these problem types, the economic problem seems to be the most common. Many misunderstandings arise over the handling of funds. Quite often the two partners have come from varying socio-economic backgrounds, and one or the other has to give up a higher standard of living. In other cases, there is disagreement over how the money should be spent and by whom. Perhaps the husband is a spendthrift and the wife is inclined to be thrifty. There is no end to the difficulties which may evolve over money matters.

Ethical problems involve religious conflicts. Much has been said about the mixed marriage, and there is little question that some types of mixed marriages result in marital conflict. These conflicts may center upon religious aspects of child training, upon differing standards of conduct, and upon intolerance related to religious practices.

Many marriage difficulties occur over personality conflicts. Ideally, man and wife should have personalities which complement each other. Where there are drastic differences in temperament, interests or social desires, difficulty often becomes unavoidable.

Biological problems may be regarded in part as sexual adjustment problems. Beyond this, however, there are problems related to the health of the marriage partners. Marriage difficulty may develop because of ill health which incapacitates one or the other of the partners in a manner particularly objectionable to the other. For instance, the husband may desire a wife who can be active in sports; and the wife may not be physically able to conform to his wishes. The counselor should be aware of the fact that many people do use health factors as a means of playing out hostilities in marriage. Invalidism in which a person becomes ill in order to frustrate the marriage partner is not uncommon. It is also true that illness may represent a result of marriage difficulty rather than a cause of it. Many psychosomatic illnesses may be traced to marital discord.

Re-establishing Communication

There are no positive answers either to what is wrong with a marriage of long standing or to methods for dealing with the problems. It is obvious in counseling with such marriage partners that at least a part of the trouble is the lack of communication. Hey and Mudd (13) say, "The thread that runs through most recurring marital problems is that of the breakdown of meaningful communication between the two parties, or among family members."

It is true that the breakdown of communications may be a result of the problems rather than a cause. On the other hand, it seems certain that problems cannot be worked out without re-establishing communication (12). The counselor's function often becomes one of breaking down barriers which have been erected over the years. It is often true that two marriage partners wish very much to return to a former level of closeness and neither has the courage to take the first step. Feelings have been hurt and each feels the other should make the first move.

The chief contribution of the counselor may be that he becomes a subject for conversation between the marriage partners. As he meets with first one and then the other, they may feel constrained to discuss their opinions of their counselor and what he says or does. The joint interview may be productive in getting the two lonely people to find and understand each other. Many couples, having lost their power of communication, really do not know what it was that caused the breach in the first place.

Divorce or Reconciliation

Many marriage counselors have philosophies which cause them to urge efforts at reconciliation in the face of great diversity. This is especially true where children are involved. At the same time, most counselors recognize that some marriages should be abandoned. The clergyman is likely to work for reconciliation against unusually difficult obstacles, and his tenacity in this relation will depend at least in part upon his religious feelings about divorce. Some clergymen recognize the logic of divorce in some cases, but because of their convictions concerning scriptural teachings about remarriage, they stress reconciliation.

There is good evidence that most marriage partners strive very hard to remain together. The domestic relations court in Toledo employs seven trained counselors who endeavor to circumvent divorces and to provide other types of marriage counseling. Judge Paul W. Alexander has reported that 8000 persons come to the marriage clinic annually, seeking to avoid divorce. Approximately one-fourth of these ultimately file for divorce.

Even if the religious counselor is committed philosophically to a non-interfering role, he will find it difficult to give assent to self-determined action by adults which do unavoidable harm to children. Here, as in other situations, the religious leader may forsake counseling philosophy and seek divine leadership in determining a course of action.

PROCESSES IN MARRIAGE COUNSELING

The general procedure in marriage counseling is to get the story of first one and then the other of the partners. This is desirable in order to make it possible for each to express freely his grievances and his interpretation of the difficulties. It is also desirable in order that the counselor may hear both sides of the story, not necessarily as a means of placing fault, but so that he may be instrumental in helping the counselees to adjust and to mediate their differences.

It is too often true that counseling must proceed without benefit of a second partner. Such counseling effort is not promising. It is possible that the partner who is counseled may be helped to adjust to the situation; but it is unlikely that any real change in the relationship will take place.

The Joint Interview

The final sessions of counseling effort are often held jointly with husband and wife, and during this period they attempt to settle differences or to move into a more understanding relationship. Although the joint interview has advantages in many cases, it is also a difficult type of interview for the counselor. He may find that he is in a cross fire between two irate people. However, it is possible that the marriage partners may see each other objectively for the first time in the joint interview (25). The presence of the counselor sometimes facilitates conversation and often is a depressant to emotional expressions which have made conversations unproductive beforehand.

It is a generally accepted rule that the counselor will see the partners individually at least once. During these initial interviews, he will apply some criteria in deciding if joint interviews would be helpful. Geist and Gerber have provided the following criteria for joint interviewing which deal with at least three factors: (1) mental interaction, (2) the degree of concern of each partner, and (3) the degree of involvement of each partner. There are six conditions, any one of which may indicate the need for joint interviewing.

1. When there is a breakdown in verbal communication between marital partners.
2. When there is distrust of the other partner's actions.
3. When the degree of security of one or both marital partners is too slight for them to work individually with the same worker.
4. When there is lack of focus in individual interviews.
5. When the client himself asks for joint interviews and the caseworker senses the client's intuitive knowledge that this is the best method of solving a particular problem.
6. When the caseworker senses intuitively that the use of joint interviews would be the treatment method of choice (9, p. 77).

Skidmore, Garrett, and Skidmore offer a list of safeguards for the joint interview:

1. The joint interview should be conducted only by skilled counselors, since it is always difficult and is packed with emotional explosiveness.
2. The counselor should be one who is equally comfortable in working with either sex.

3. The counselor should have good rapport with both partners before such a conference is held.
4. The joint interview should be on a permissive basis, agreeable to both partners.
5. The counselor should guard against over-identification with either partner.
6. The counselor must be skilled in guiding the discussion and in introducing relevant material without betraying confidences.
7. Effort should be made to avoid either counselee's feeling pressured or rejected.
8. The counselor must be responsible for guiding the interview in such a way that it does not become just a "telling-off" session; otherwise the whole experience may be destructive and increase hostility.
9. If the counselor plans to work with both spouses and use the joint interview in the course of therapy, spouses should ordinarily be counseled individually at first. Where there is considerable tension, hostility, and conflict in the marriage, seeing one spouse only for a relatively long period of time before seeing the other makes it difficult to work equally well with both spouses.
10. If the counselor feels that he is strongly identifying with one of the spouses, he should not attempt to counsel both partners. The joint conference, however, may in this case be successfully used if both counselors are present (25, p. 314).

Group Processes in Marriage and Family Counseling

Group meetings have been utilized to some extent in working out marriage and family difficulties (18) (22). As a general rule, group attack is not recommended for problems which are in an agitated state. The principal utility is as a study group aimed at correction of minor difficulties and at developing broad understandings concerning family problems.

An exception to this was the group therapy attempted in a mental hygiene clinic setting which dealt not only with couples but with people who were rather deeply disturbed. Boyer reports on this experience and lists three reasons why group meetings may hold marriages together:

1. The couple is sharing a common experience.
2. Separation or divorce means separation from the group since

    one criterion for membership is that each couple is married and
    living together.
 3. Most important of all, through group interaction communica-
    tion between spouses is reestablished which tends to reduce
    long-standing tensions and to speed up treatment (2).

Marriage and family counseling in groups has been developed
more for women than men. As the women come together under the
guidance of the counselor, who usually functions nondirectively,
they bring up the difficulties of their households; and each woman
has an opportunity to seek help from the entire group. Such activity
helps some mothers and wives to solve problems; in other cases
women gain help in socialization. Through discussing common
problems, some real help may come as one person describes a
successful means of handling a problem in her home.

Other group experiments have brought widows together to
discuss common problems, and have promoted meetings of groups
of men with invalid wives. The best criterion for choosing group
members has proved to be a common situation rather than a common specific problem.

MARRIAGE COUNSELING
AND PSYCHOTHERAPY

Since most eligible Americans do get married, it is
only reasonable to suppose that some of those who present themselves for marriage counseling will be emotionally maladjusted to
the extent that they need psychotherapy. It has been suggested that
as many as one in ten persons in the general population could
benefit from psychotherapy. Actually, there may be more than the
ten to one probability among distressed spouses, since the same
difficulties which render one in need of psychotherapy also set off
many marriage difficulties not necessarily related to the personality
deviation.

When the counselor is faced with a client whom he perceives as
needing psychotherapy, he has at least three alternatives. First, he
may embark on a combined treatment of the personality disorder
and the marriage difficulty. Second, he may decide to ignore the
need for therapy and attempt to work on the adjustment problem

with the hope that helping the adjustment may have beneficial effects upon the personality difficulty. Third, he may refer the client for psychologic or psychiatric treatment, either postponing other types of counseling or moving forward with surface treatment in conjunction with therapeutic treatment.

The decision of the counselor in this regard will depend on several factors including the accessibility of practitioners and the perceived depth of disorder. Some marriage counselors look on psychiatric consultation as an emergency measure; but there is good reason to believe that consultation with psychiatric personnel should be used consistently where available (27). The religious counselor should make every effort to establish liaison with psychiatrists and psychologists whom he confidently feels to be sympathetic with the religious convictions which he and the majority of his parishioners hold.

INSTRUCTIONAL AND PREVENTIVE ASPECTS OF MARRIAGE COUNSELING

Many marriages fail because the husband and wife do not know how to work for a good relationship. There is no denying that a happy marriage is the result of intelligent striving on the part of husband and wife. Some counselors approach marriage counseling from the instructional point of view. Much time is spent in pointing out to husbands the things required to keep a woman happy. The wife is counseled concerning the needs of the husband that are not commonly understood.

If husband and wife continue in ignorance as to means of keeping the marriage relationship vibrant, it stands to reason that such instruction would be helpful. Instruction may be offered in the promotion of mutual respect, the need for status and selfhood in both partners, the desires of wives to have interests outside the home, and even the art of lovemaking.

These types of instructional approaches to the prevention and cure of marriage difficulties may be promoted best by group meetings. The clergyman may consider sermon materials that emphasize means of getting along in marriage. Study courses and short-term clinics may be planned utilizing people from community clinics as resource persons.

There are many psychologists who feel that this approach is a waste of time. The claim is that people are not able to change their ways just because they have been told they should. Religious counselors should not expect the instructional approach to be a panacea for all marriage troubles. On the other hand, marriage partners cannot be expected to adjust without having information. Information may be helpful; it is possible that marriage partners may also receive inspiration from the instructional counsel causing them to make a stronger effort at adjustment.

In a speech to a group of ministers, Lloyd H. Jones, Director of Family Life Foundation in Dallas, listed the following essentials to happy marriage and urged the ministers to counsel their parishioners on these matters: good behavior, in the home as well as away from it; a respect for the partner who, like everyone else, needs status and self respect; the study and practice of love-making in the full range of all its possibilities; good communication by both work and action; talking things out before the little things pile up into a barricade; working toward the emotional maturity that even the best adjusted never quite reach; a desire to serve not shine; an ability to laugh at oneself; and a determination to find harmony.

The many columns on marriage counseling found in magazines and newspapers serve a need. Most columnists write about broad aspects of marriage adjustments which have value as instruction and possibilities as inspiration. The psychologist does not strongly favor these, but he feels they may be helpful as long as the columnist counselor does not endeavor to solve specific problems, through the column, concerning people whom he has never seen.

References

1. Bowman, Henry A., *Marriage for Moderns*. New York: McGraw-Hill Book Company, Inc., 1954.
2. Boyer, Clayton L., "Group Therapy with Married Couples," *Marriage and Family Living*. February, 1960, pp. 21-24.
3. Burton, Joe W., *Tomorrow You Marry*. Nashville: Broadman Press, 1950.

4. Chikes, Tibor, Richard N. Hey, Lynn H. Corson, and Emily H. Mudd, "An Experiment in Marriage Counseling by Three New Jersey Churches," *Pastoral Psychology*. February, 1961, pp. 29-34.

5. Deitchman, Robert B., "The Evolution of a Ministerial Counseling Center," *Journal of Pastoral Care*. Winter, 1957, pp. 207-215.

6. Duvall, Evelyn M. and Reuben Hill, *When You Marry*. Boston: Heath and Company, 1945.

7. Elia, Andrew D., "Teamwork in Premarital Counseling," *Pastoral Psychology*. December, 1959, pp. 33-38.

8. Fairchild, Roy W., "Variety in Premarital Interviewing," *Pastoral Psychology*. December, 1959, pp. 9-13.

9. Geist, Joanne and Norman M. Gerber, "Joint Interviewing: A Treatment Technique with Marital Partners," *Social Casework*. February, 1960, pp. 76-83.

10. Goldstein, Sidney E., *Marriage and Family Counseling*. New York: McGraw-Hill Book Company Inc., 1945.

11. Gomberg, M. Robert, "Family-Oriented Treatment of Marital Problems," *Social Casework*. January, 1956, pp. 3-10.

12. Harper, Robert A., "Communication Problems in Marriage and Marriage Counseling," *Marriage and Family Living*. May, 1958, pp. 107-113.

13. Hey, Richard N. and Emily H. Mudd, "Recurring Problems in Marriage Counseling," *Marriage and Family Living*. May, 1959, pp. 127-130.

14. Johnson, Paul E., "Emotional Problems in Premarital Counseling," *Pastoral Psychology*. December, 1959, pp. 18-24.

15. ————, "The Pastor as Counselor," *Pastoral Psychology*. February, 1956, pp. 25-28.

16. Landis, Paul H., *Making the Most of Marriage*. New York: Appleton-Century-Crofts, 1955.

17. Landis, Judson T., "Marriages of Mixed and Non-Mixed Religions," *American Sociological Review*. June, 1949, pp. 401-407.

18. Levine, Lena and Irving Brodsky, "Taking Stock of Marriage: An Illustration in Group Counseling," *Marriage and Family Living*. May, 1956, pp. 162-168.

19. Mace, David R., *Success in Marriage*. Nashville: Abingdon Press, 1958.

20. Morris, J. Kenneth, *Premarital Counseling: A Manual For Ministers*. Englewood Cliffs: Prentice-Hall, Inc., 1960.

21. Mudd, Emily H., *The Practice of Marriage Counseling*. New York: Association Press, 1951.

22. Neubeck, Gerhard, "Factors Affecting Group Psychotherapy with

Married Couples," *Marriage and Family Living*. August, 1954, pp. 216-220.

23. Pike, James A., *If You Marry Outside Your Faith*. New York: Harper and Brothers, 1954.

24. Schellenberg, James A. and Lawrence S. Bee, "A Re-examination of the Theory of Complementary Needs in Mate Selection," *Marriage and Family Living*. August, 1960, pp. 227-232.

25. Skidmore, Rex A., Hulds Van Streeter Garrett, and C. Jay Skidmore, *Marriage Consulting*. New York: Harper and Brothers, 1956.

26. Stroup, Atlee L. and Paul Glasser, "The Orientation and Focus of Marriage Counseling," *Marriage and Family Living*. February, 1959, pp. 20-25.

27. Taylor, Joseph L., "Psychiatric Consultation in Family Counseling," *Marriage and Family Living*. August, 1956, pp. 250-263.

28. Terman, Lewis M., "Predicting Marriage Failure from Test Scores," *Marriage and Family Living*. Spring, 1950, pp. 51-54.

29. ———— and Paul Wallin, "The Validity of Marriage Prediction and Marital Adjustment Tests," *American Sociological Review*. August, 1949, pp. 497-504.

30. Weeks, H. Ashley, "Differential Divorce Rates by Occupations," *Social Forces*. March, 1943, pp. 334-337.

31. Weigert, Edith, "Interpersonal Factors in Marital Adjustment," *Journal of Pastoral Care*. Winter, 1954, pp. 195-202.

32. Wise, Carroll A., "Education of the Pastor For Marriage Counseling," *Pastoral Psychology*. December, 1959, pp. 45-48.

33. Wiser, Waller B., "Launching a Program of Premarital Counseling," *Pastoral Psychology*. December, 1959, pp. 14-17.

VII

Psychoanalytically Oriented Therapy and the Religious Worker

Few workers in the religious setting will expect to become fully trained and competent as psychoanalytical therapists. It is true that there are a few clergymen who are also psychiatrists or clinical psychologists, but these are the exceptions and will always be. Such training as that required for competency as psychiatrists or clinical and counseling psychologists is lengthy, as is the theological training of the clergyman.

It is true, however, that the specialist in the church setting may be a clinical or counseling psychologist. Many of the persons who study this book may be pointing toward such church-related positions. For such people, this chapter should be considered an orientation study to precede several years of intensified study of psychology together with a supervised internship.

There are several other reasons for including a discussion of psychoanalytical theories and techniques in this book. There is logic in making the clergyman, as well as other counselors in the religious setting, aware of the fundamental tenets and practices in this general area.

A considerable part of the counseling experience of the religious counselor will occur with those who have undergone or are undergoing psychoanalytically oriented psychotherapy. A general understanding of this area will enable the clergyman to cooperate with the psychologist or psychiatrist in the treatment of the disturbed person. He will better understand his parishioners in the various stages of treatment and will be able to do and say things that are appropriate and helpful.

It is generally concluded that to separate a mentally ill person from his clergyman is hurtful. It is possible, however, that most therapists have misgivings concerning the values which may come from having the uninformed religious worker talk with the mentally ill. Psychiatrists would welcome a clergy informed concerning the basic understandings of theory and technique.

Wiesbauer (19) points out that the clergyman has a definite task to perform with the mentally ill; he must "minister helpfully and cooperate effectively." It is completely possible that religious workers may gain a basic understanding of analytical techniques sufficient to aid them in ministering helpfully, without gaining complete competency in treatment of depth problems. There seems little logic in maintaining a veil of secrecy around analytical concepts.

If one faces facts squarely, he must admit that analytical concepts have become community property. Through the women's magazines, through mass media, and through courses in psychological concepts available to the general public in colleges and universities, psychoanalytical terms are on every tongue. The trouble is that understandings thus achieved are vague, out of focus, and at times absolutely erroneous.

It must be understood that many psychological concepts useful to counselors at all levels have their origins in psychoanalysis. Every counselor may benefit from exposure to analytical thought. Properly understood and utilized, these concepts aid immeasurably in understanding and in helping people. There are definite dangers of improper usage, and the person who studies this book should understand that such elementary study does not qualify him to engage in planned psychotherapy. The author believes that what follows will be helpful to the religious counselor in understanding both normal and disturbed people.

It is likely that no single stream of thought has had a greater influence on the broad development of counseling theory and method than has the psychoanalytic system. It seems safe to say that the majority of psychiatrists, clinical psychologists, psychoanalysts, and psychiatric social workers are applying analytical methods as the principal base of psychological operations, and that every counselor has been influenced by psychoanalysis. Many counselors, including a great number of clinical psychologists, do not claim a first allegiance to analytical doctrine, but even these are influenced by it to a degree.

Few practitioners follow a plan of counseling along puristic lines of one theoretical framework or another. Most are anxious to be known as eclecticists. Yet there seems to be at this time a rather well-defined differentiation between analytically oriented theories and client-centered theories of counseling used in treating deep-seated emotional problems necessitating psychotherapy. These two theoretical concepts are not mutually exclusive, but there does seem to be merit in discussing counseling theory under first one then the other of these two labels. That some analytical concepts have entered into the formulation of nondirective theory has been acknowledged (16). That some influences of the warm and permissive atmosphere championed by nondirectivists has permeated analytical practice is denied only by the radical antagonists of nondirective thought.

This chapter will deal with theories and methods which have come into being and into usage chiefly through the efforts of persons who themselves have chosen to be counted among the analytical group of theorists and practitioners. The reader is reminded that the validity of method depends upon the situation in which it is applied. There are some situations in which analytical methods have particular relevance; the same is true for client-centered methods.

A SHORT HISTORY
OF PSYCHOANALYSIS

The Orthodox Freudians

Historically, psychoanalysis began with Sigmund Freud. That Freud was influenced in his formulations of theory by those who lived contemporarily with him and before his time is freely acknowledged by him, his critics, and his biographers (12). His expressions of theoretical concepts were so definite and crystallized as to make it appear that he formulated his theories "on the spot" from personal experience.

Although all analytical groups look upon Freud as the primary inspiration of the theory which they support, there have been many splits from the original or orthodox group. And even among those who wish to be known as orthodox Freudians, there is evidence of new trends of thought, some of which modify the basic postulates. For instance, a trend has developed in the directions of treating the "ego" as having greater importance in the total personality than Freud assigned to it. The "ego psychologists" are among the most energetic groups today in terms of theoretical developments.

The term "psychoanalyst" originated with the orthodox Freudians. The term is broadly applied today, however, although not without resistance from the orthodox psychoanalytical societies who lay down very strict requirements for inclusion in the "orthodox group." These include medical training, a personal psychoanalysis by an acknowledged orthodox analyst, and confinement of practice to a long-term process continuing for at least a year on an hour-per-day basis (8).

The Neo-Freudians

Splits from the orthodox group came about principally because of variance of opinions concerning the role of sex in personality dynamics. Early splits included those by Carl G. Jung, who termed his system analytical psychology, and Alfred Adler, who founded individual psychology.

An important event was the formation in New York City of the Association for the Advancement of Psychoanalysis under the leadership of Karen Horney in the late 1930's. Although this organization was not originally intended as a definitive split from the orthodox group, developing divergent theories have set the two groups at a wide variance. A further splitting from this group has resulted in the Washington School of Psychiatry, under the leadership of Harry Stack Sullivan (8).

Perhaps the most "unorthodox" of all psychoanalytical groups has been the Chicago Institute for Psychoanalysis, which has been under the leadership of Franz Alexander and Thomas M. French. Although holding to the basic tenets of analytical theory, the workers at Chicago have raised questions about the necessity for long-term treatment as in standard psychoanalysis and have experimented with newer methods of shorter psychoanalysis. Not only has the Chicago group participated in grossly "unorthodox" studies, but they have also made the greatest contributions of theory and method, which have modified the analytical method for usefulness by the rank and file of psychological practitioners.

ANALYTICAL CONCEPTS OF PERSONALITY STRUCTURE AND FORMATION

The Unconscious Mind

The name of Sigmund Freud is little less revered today than it was thirty years ago. Almost all practitioners acknowledge belief in his fundamental premises and acknowledge a debt to him for the methods which they utilize, usually in greatly modified form. Few practicing psychiatrists, clinical psychologists, or social workers care to present themselves to the public as psychoanalysts; but when asked if they are psychoanalysts, they might well say, "No, I am a psychoanalytically-oriented psychotherapist."

Freud's most important concept and contribution was the "unconscious mind." Although others had hinted at such an entity, Freud made definite pronouncements concerning this most important construct. Stated simply, the unconscious mind is that depository for motivations which may propel man to action without his conscious understanding of his motives in acting. It has been suggested that only a small portion of our motivations arise out of a conscious desire to act. The major portion of our activity stems from drives within us which lie in this reservoir of unrealized reasons for doing, thinking, and feeling.

The Libido Theory

Another psychological construct postulated by Freud was the libido. The libido is largely synonymous with sexual drive or desire. Freud thought of the sex drive as operating from infancy and as a chief arbiter of the behavior of the human individual. He believed that the adult personality constellation is the result of original libido and of the results of frustrating and satisfying events in terms of the satisfaction of the sexual urge. Sexuality is thought of in a very broad sense, referring to all pleasurable body sensations. Thus, the sucking of the infant, elimination of feces, as well as fondling and caressing are sexual expressions. Sexual behavior motivated by the libido, and fulfilling as well as thwarting of desire are thought to produce marked effects upon attitudes and upon modes of behavior (5).

Personality Divisions

Sexual energies were termed instinctive by the Freudians; a second instinct was said to be aggression. The best-known Freudian construct is probably the concept of personality as composed of the id, the ego, and the superego. The id is said to represent all that is instinctive; thus, it is the expression of sexuality and aggression, the drive to satisfy the basic urges. This means that part of the human personality is "animalistic." Without restraint the human animal would kill, destroy, and exploit others in an effort to satisfy his own biological demands. Freud postulated that the id is the source of psychic energy, that behavior becomes a modification of this surging energy system.

A second system of personality is described as superego. This is the conscience of man that has been formulated out of moralistic restraint. Superego forces in the human are related to parents, codes of conduct, laws, and religious training. These forces are at war with the id and endeavor to keep this "monster" under control.

> The main functions of the superego are (1) to inhibit the impulses of the id, particularly those of a sexual or aggressive nature, since these are the impulses whose expression is most highly condemned by society, (2) to persuade the ego to substitute moralistic goals for realistic ones, and (3) to strive for perfection. That is, the

superego is inclined to oppose both the id and the ego, and to make the world over into its own image. However, it is like the id in being non-rational and like the ego in attempting to exercise control over the instincts. Unlike the ego, the superego does not merely postpone instinctual gratification; it tries to block it permanently (7, p. 35).*

The ego or self is thought of as the system of personality which endeavors to mediate the conflicts between id forces and the demands of society. Under analytical theory, the individuality of man is determined by the strength of his inherited and biological drives and the power of restraint residing in the forces of society which would deny him the privilege of making the world subject to this biological urge. The ego is the self, the operant personality which logically is the resultant of the innate characteristics and the events of life. Freud assigned the powers of arbitration, of reason, and of decision to this "executive" of the total personality, the ego.

In concluding this brief description of the three systems of the personality, it should be pointed out that the id, ego, and superego are not to be thought of as manikins which operate the personality. They are merely names for various psychological processes which obey different system principles. Under ordinary circumstances these different principles do not collide with one another nor do they work at cross purposes. On the contrary, they work together as a team under the administrative leadership of the ego. The personality normally functions as a whole rather than as three separate segments. In a very general way, the id may be thought of as the biological component of personality, the ego as the psychological component, and the superego as the social component (7, pp. 35-36).**

Munroe (15) offers an excellent treatment of the trichotomy of Freudian systems of personality.

The Relationship of Past and Present

Perhaps the most basic premise of analytical theory as related to psychotherapy and personality structure is that present

---

* Reprinted with permission from Calvin S. Hall and Gardner Lindsey, *Theories of Personality,* John Wiley & Sons, Inc., 1957.

** Reprinted with permission from Calvin S. Hall and Gardner Lindsey, *Theories of Personality,* John Wiley & Sons, Inc., 1957.

tensions and difficulties are related to past events. This means in effect that all neuroses, maladjustments, and psychological distresses have bases in the past. This premise is a psychological one and pertains, of course, to difficulties based upon emotional reactions to life. Situational difficulties such as poverty or bad health may be related to past events, but not in the same sense as psychological distresses. Neurotic anxiety has been identified as free-floating fear which disturbs the individual without his being aware of the source of it. Analytical psychotherapy deals primarily with the relief of present psychological distress through recognition of the influence of the past.

It is typical that people are able to deal with those things which they can understand. Fears which have no known origin cannot be successfully dealt with except through therapeutic help. For instance, if a person is driving down the highway and has a flat tire, he may be temporarily upset and frustrated. However, the source of his distress is evident to him; he can do something about it. A neurotic anxiety which has its origin in a childhood event cannot be handled with such ease because the reason for the distress is not known.

Neurotic Anxiety and Repression

Psychoanalytic theory proposes that the presence of those components in the unconscious mind which have ability to cause neurotic anxiety arises from a process of repression. When a person represses something, it is driven from consciousness. Repression, thus, is a deep process of forgetting an event to the extent that the memory cannot be recovered. Ironically, the event which is repressed cannot be remembered but does have the power to bring about neurotic anxiety. The unconscious materials are "ghosts" from the past which are able to bring about a state of tension without being consciously experienced by the individual.

For instance, this writer worked with a teenage boy who was filled with fear at the sound of a buzz saw operating in the shop-work building at the high school he was attending. Since the sound of the saw permeated, at a reduced volume, the entire school building, this student was in a constant state of agitation; he could not study or concentrate on anything. Strangely enough this sound of the saw did not bother him until he had occasion to see the saw operating in the shop one day. After that he was terrified whenever the sound came to him in even the smallest volume.

Under extended counseling, this boy was able to recover the memory of having been run down by a road grader which had the same whining sound and the type of belt and pulley system which this particular saw in the shop had. This illustrates how a "ghost" from the past may bring about anxiety. Experience which is internalized may at some later time be externalized.

The theory of repression holds that any event in life which is unbearable to the person will be repressed into the unconscious areas of the mind. Residing there, it is able to bring about much distress in the individual. Analytical theories emphasize that the more traumatic an event is the more deeply repressed it is likely to be. It is also indicated that the events of early childhood are likely to be more deeply repressed than others because the child in his helpless state is so much more apt to be terrified by events.

A discussion of repressed traumatic events is useful in indicating the nature of repression and unconscious motivations that have the power to engender neurotic anxiety. It is true, however, that a large part of those elements of the unconscious mind which have power to disturb are related not to traumatic events of short duration and of terrifying nature, but are related to long-term situations which are able to deposit feelings of inadequacy, hostile attitudes toward people, and emotional reactions to events over an extended period of time.

As an example, consider the student who is able to perform well for women teachers but is blocked with men teachers, especially men teachers of a certain age. It is possible that a long-continued hostility toward a father who has been domineering, demanding, harsh, or rejecting can account for this attitude. Unfortunately, the feeling of anxiety in the presence of certain types of men may not end with elementary school or even with high school. The anxiety and loss of competency may persist throughout college and into adulthood as the man continues to be anxiety ridden on the job where he has a male foreman.

Psychosexual Development

As mentioned earlier, the analytical theories place much emphasis upon the psychosexual development of the individual. It is believed that the child in growing up passes through several sexual stages. These are consecutively the oral stage, the anal stage, the urethral, phallic, latency, prepuberty, adolescent or puberty, and adult sexual stages. Much of the difficulty of the adult human being is thought to be related to interrupted growth within a given stage. A child who has a difficult time during a given stage or the person who is held in a given stage too long and not allowed to leave it for the next is said to have fixated at that point. For example, many people are described as oral characters, having failed to mature properly through the first psychosexual stage. These people have personality traits in adulthood characterized by overeating and over-attention to oral desires. Much of the difficulty encountered by such individuals is attributable to faulty learnings at the fixated stage level. Thus, the person who has been held too long at the oral stage usually does not learn to emancipate himself from the mother figure. He may become alcoholic in adulthood or he may be unable to relate to female figures except in dependency relationships. Thus, the person's entire adult life would be warped by faulty growth at an early stage of development.

Human personality is undoubtedly dependent upon experience. Whether or not that experience is interpreted with emphasis on sexual components of life, it is understood that certain experiences will deposit traits in the personality that may have power to make one a most unhappy and poorly adjusted individual. Other traits deposited may only serve to make the individual a distinctly different and interesting individual. Thus, while some elements of child treatment during the oral stage may result in deep-seated difficulty such as alcoholism, sexual perversion, and psychoneurosis, other elements may only serve to make the person happy or cautious in his over-all personality pattern. For instance, it is hypothesized that the person who is well fed and affectionately nurtured during the oral stage will be an "oral optimist." This type of person will see the world as a friendly place, a place that is conducive to a happy existence. On the other hand the person who was grudgingly fed and not affectionately treated (the oral pessimist) will likely be a disconsolate, easily discouraged, gloomy-dispositioned individual.

The oral character is used here as an example of how improper growth through psychosexual stages may affect the adult personality and how psychoanalytical theories regard personality formation as being related to psychosexual development. It will not be within the limits of this book to give detailed discussion to the particular personality characteristics said to be deposited by frustrated development at the various stages of psychosexual development. The reader is directed to a detailed treatment of these ideas by Blum (2). It should be pointed out that interruption of psychosexual growth usually carries with it failure to grow out of childlike relationships with one or both of the parent figures. Actually, much of the analytical theory of adult maladjustment is related to faulty attitudes toward people in the past, particularly toward immediate family members.

Fixation and Regression

It is interesting to note that in addition to determining broad personality traits, events involving the stages of child psychosexual development seem to have power to determine adult behavior at all levels. It is believed that the choice of psychosomatic illnesses is based upon a desire of the adult to return (regress) to an earlier stage of development where he was comparatively free from frustration. Thus, the person who was held comfortably in a mother-child relationship for an over-extended period during the oral stage would be apt to develop an oral type of psychosomatic illness, a peptic ulcer for instance. Regressive behavior is usually related to a fixation at one or the other of the psychosexual levels (4).

THE NATURE OF NEUROSIS

Psychoanalysis as a system of treatment is generally understood to be a method for treatment of neuroses. Although psychoanalytical principles are used in working with psychotics on the one hand and with slightly disturbed individuals on the other, the theories were developed with emphasis on the neurotic personality. Because of this, it seems necessary to preface a review of the methods common to the analytical field with a discussion of the principal concepts of neurosis held by those who have propounded not only theory but methods of practice.

An attempt to describe neurosis or the origin and etiology of it must always fall short of perfection due to the abstract nature of the task. Neurosis, basically, is a method of approach to life. More than this, it is a faulty approach to life, a method that produces unhappiness. Alexander and French (1) define neurosis as "a failure of the individual to deal successfully with a given situation, a failure to find socially acceptable gratification for subjective needs under given circumstances."

Obviously, this is a broad concept of neurosis and under this definition, a person for whom circumstances interrupted his gratification of needs might be a neurotic temporarily or until he had found a new way of satisfying his needs in a socially accepted manner. The reader needs to understand, then, that a neurosis may be temporary and situational or it may be chronic and related to childhood events. Broadly speaking, any person who is unable to cope with life's situations to the successful fulfillment of his needs is neurotic. However, the clinical classification of neurosis is related to situations which produce anxiety and which do not yield to manipulation of environmental factors, to simple revamping of goals, or to an improvement of socio-economic status. In the main, neurosis is thought of as a condition over which the individual has not been able to exercise control and which involves factors related to personality structure, attitudes, impulses, and feelings. From the point of view most commonly held by psychotherapists, a neurosis represents a situation which defies an understanding by the client and which places him under unidentifiable threat.

In the broad sense, a person who has lost his means of support and must resort to begging for food would be a neurotic. This might be termed a situational neurosis. On the other hand, a person who, although he has high intelligence and scholastic ability, is unable to pass his school work and who has no idea why he cannot do so, would likely be suffering from a neurotic involvement rooted in personality structure. Neurotic involvement then, occurs along a continuum from the simple, frustrating but easily solved situational conflict to the deeply embedded neurosis arising from traumatic childhood events and defying analysis or correction.

THEORIES CONCERNING DEVELOPMENT OF NEUROSIS

Common Bases

If neurosis be a faulty way of approaching need fulfillment, the question must arise as to what causes the individual to adopt such a faulty method. If one individual adopts a workable and reasonable approach to his problems, but another adopts a faulty method, it must follow that something has happened to one that did not happen to the other or else there were differences in hereditary make-up. As varied as are the events which may precipitate neurosis, there are common factors.

This writer feels that all neuroses have five common aspects. These are: (1) a threat to the physiological and psychological securities of the individual, (2) a repression of feelings and of impulses (hostilities) arising out of the threatening situation, (3) an interruption of learning processes plus faulty learnings, (4) development of a protective organization (defenses) to ward off the anxieties arising from the repressions, and (5) a failure of the protective organization.

The Role of Defenses

The student should realize that the final development of a neurosis depends upon the failure of defenses. Should neurosis depend upon threat, repression, faulty learning, or defense, every human being would have one. Some of us are threatened but do not repress events or feelings. We feel neurotic anxiety, formulate defenses, and our defense system works. We have no neurosis. However, it is important to understand that where anxiety is great and where defenses must be massive, it is probable that a breakthrough is imminent.

The severely neurotic person has some qualities not found in the person who has a lesser neurosis. For instance, his defenses become rigid; he must defend himself in a certain habitual manner; and he cannot discard an unworkable defense and choose another. Rigidity is a trait almost always observable in the severe neurotic. He can behave in only one manner because he is fighting panic so desperately that he dare not relax and try to find another defense. Then, too, the neurotic becomes habituated to trying to solve a problem in adulthood by a method that he learned to use (although without outstanding success) in childhood. The neurotic typically fights adult battles with the weapons of childhood.

> . . . Because they are staving off unbearable anxiety these defenses cannot be relaxed, but they prevent reappraisal of the threat and new action in regard to it. The conditions that are just right to freeze defenses probably bear a close relation to the severity of threat and the intensity or anticipated intensity of anxiety (21, p. 234).†

Sequence of Events

The typical sequence of events in development of a neurotic process is, first, that a threatening situation forces a repression of feelings or of traumatic events and interrupts the normal learning process. Then follows an effort to defend against the anxiety which wells up from the repressions.

Let us consider the man who attempts to solve his need for affection from the opposite sex by becoming dependent upon the female figure and who gives evidence of neurosis by many nervous tendencies. He feels anxious in the presence of females and can still his anxiety only by a dependency relationship; failing to establish the type of relationship he desires in a woman, he may turn to alcohol.

The original threat probably arose from experiences with the mother. As a child, the man probably endeavored to become self-sustaining but was repeatedly thwarted by a possessive mother who offered her love only to the child who would submit to the self-destroying domination. Threatened by loss of love, the child

---

† Robert W. White, *The Abnormal Personality*. Copyright 1948, The Ronald Press Company.

invariably submitted to domination and repressed not only his desires for self-sufficiency but his hostilities toward his mother as well. Although he probably feels extreme hostility toward females in adulthood, he did not learn to approach his need fulfillment in a relationship conducive to feelings of self-worth and independent activities. He did not learn correctly that some women are domineering and others submissive. He learned (incorrectly) that the only way to satisfy a woman is to submit and let her direct.

Unless set free by therapeutic means from his faulty approach to need fulfillment, this man will live a life of submission and dependency upon females that will put him in constant conflict because he feels hostility toward females for making him dependent. Thus, the last basis of neurosis will be fulfilled in that his defense (dependency) fails to hold up. The threat of loss of love by his mother has thwarted his growth and has set up components in his unconscious mind capable of bringing about anxiety in the adult life.

An Example of Threat, Repression, and Anxiety

Threat, repression, and anxiety may be exemplified clearly in the neurosis that stems from a traumatic event. Let us suppose that a three-year-old child becomes separated from his mother in a crowded bus. A terrifying panic seizes the child when he believes that he has been deserted. Although the separation lasts only a few moments, and although he is comforted and cuddled by his mother when she finds him, this moment of panic is too great to bear in consciousness. All memory of the event may be repressed, but the event may bring about an anxiety in adulthood any time a vaguely similar situation may develop. The adult man may be afraid of buses without knowing why; and he may experience acute panic each time his wife leaves home for a few days for a visit with her parents, leaving him in somewhat the same manner as the mother deserted him in the traumatic experience.

An example of a traumatic event provides the best means of illustrating neurotic processes. It should be understood, however, that neurosis may develop from chronic situations in childhood where continuous threat is present. As a matter of fact, these chronic threats have power to deposit a nucleus for a neurosis that will be more difficult to eradicate than will be that deposited by a traumatic event.

> . . . It is not incorrect, therefore, to say that the adult neurotic patient is *basically* afraid of the danger situations of his childhood, even though he is more *immediately* afraid that his well-practiced protective organization will be cracked open and that he will have to change his way of life. It takes high-powered anxiety to make a neurosis. Acute combat stress or similar traumatic situations can do it in adults. Otherwise only the panics and apprehensions that occur in the helpless years of childhood are sufficiently high-powered (21, pp. 257-258).††

The Neurotic Nuclear Theory

In some contrast to the orthodox view of threat origin, is the viewpoint championed by Karen Horney. Freud hypothesized a sexual basis for all of the threatening situations of childhood. The Horney school of thought emphasizes the helplessness of the child as a point of departure for theories of the genesis of neurosis (10). Because of his extreme helplessness, the child regards the experiences which threaten his need fulfillment as being fraught with danger. Thus, the importance of relationships with parents and family circle are accentuated but not in the context of sexual strivings.

Horney visualizes the human infant as being a creature who has definite needs over and beyond those of tissue maintenance. These needs are psychological and for the most part are interpersonal and social. Thus among other needs we find that every person needs affection, every person has a need to submit to someone, and every person has a need to dominate (9).

Basically, the nuclear theory embraces the idea that for every need the child has there is the possibility of the deposit of a neurotic nucleus in the personality structure if the need is not met. Thus, the child who does not gain enough affection to fulfill the need for it would have a neurotic nucleus deposited in this

---

†† Robert W. White, *The Abnormal Personality*. Copyright 1948, The Ronald Press Company.

area. Supposedly this nucleus may remain inactive throughout life or it may be activated, depending upon whether or not life's situations supply a required measure of affection for the individual. A person may have a very meager fulfillment of the need for affection in his childhood and a large neurotic nucleus deposited in the personality structure, but he still may have a life of freedom from neurosis because of having an affectionate wife and children. On the other hand, a child who may have had deposited a nucleus of smaller size may encounter a life of little affection and may suffer the agitation of a nucleus which under ordinary circumstances would not result in neurosis at all. Thus, the concept is that every person has a number of neurotic nuclei which may or may not spring into activity.

Neurotic Trends

When situations in real life bring about an activity of the neurotic nucleus, a person is said to develop a neurotic trend in an effort to escape the anxiety of the agitated nucleus. Horney has indicated that all such trends have to do with attitudes toward people. She proposes that every person who develops a scheme of activity to aid him in escaping from the dangers in adult life which resemble those he has repressed in childhood either develops the trend of moving against people, moving toward people, or moving away from people (9). Thus, a person who has experienced a neurotic nucleus based upon unfulfilled needs for affection may enter a trend of trying desperately to make friends, he may strike out aggressively against people, or he may withdraw into a seclusive type of existence.

Let us suppose that Mr. A has experienced an unfulfilled need for affection and that the nucleus is driving him into a neurotic trend. It is possible that Mr. A might seek relentlessly to get people to like him. In his office situation, he likely would be ingratiating toward everyone. With a neurotic anxiety welling up each time someone should reject or even seem to reject him, Mr. A would seek to please everyone in every way. He would be apt to be extremely sensitive toward others, but his neurotic trend would be toward others, because his movement toward them would be a defense against his fear of rejection.

However, Mr. A's neurotic nucleus is based upon having had a cold and unloving mother. Interlaced with his attempt to move toward people would likely be a repressed hostility which would cause him to "fly off the handle at people around him," and then to be ingratiatingly sorry for having done so.

Mr. A's defense against anxiety is an overcompensation in being oversolicitious. He realizes that it does not always work very well, but is rigidified in his behavior because he is too insecure to try anything else. He not only feels driven to make people like him, but is afraid to have people like him since this will make rejection possible.

The most difficult part of Mr. A's dilemma is that his over-reacting makes people dislike him rather than like him. Since his co-workers find this fawning type of person a bore and a bother, they begin to reject him in reality. He really is not the type person most people like for a friend. Thus Mr. A's defenses have not only crumbled, they have reinforced his original anxiety and he shall have to strive all the more to make people like and appreciate him. This illustrates that the severe neurosis is really a system of cyclic nature and becomes a pattern of self-perpetuating conflict.

METHODS AND TECHNIQUES IN ANALYTICAL PSYCHOTHERAPY

The Aims of Therapy

People come to the religious counselor and to the privately practicing psychotherapist because they are unable to solve or face their problems, because they are unhappy, and because they are disillusioned with life. Some come to the medical psychotherapist because they suffer from psychosomatic illness.

As pointed out in Chapter I, a large portion of those who come to the clergyman are definitely in need of depth psychotherapy. The parishioner does not usually express his difficulties in terms of the common psychological syndromes of difficulty. He may say he cannot get along with his spouse, he may say he cannot quit drinking, that he is frightened, upset, or nervous. As Wallen (18) says, "He is likely to think of therapy as a way of getting rid of these handicaps without affecting the rest of his life."

Just as there are many ways for the individual to express difficulty, so there are many ways in which the clinicians may express what is wrong with people. Some may say that the person is suffering neurotic anxiety and that the purpose of therapy is to allay anxiety. Another, speaking from a different framework, might say that the person needs to learn how to handle his feelings and his tensions. Still another would say that the person needs to find himself, to set realistic goals, and to move toward them.

One of the most common ways of expressing the aims of analytical therapy is in terms of the self or "ego." In a very broad sense, the same thing is wrong with all of the people who come for psychotherapy, they are lacking in a unified, integrated ego. This is another way of saying that there is inner conflict. The person who needs therapy is a divided person, and the divisions within are pulling so hard against one another that the person is being "pulled apart." Examples are men who love their wives and yet have hostilities toward them and bring about marital conflict by playing out these hostilities. A woman may have a great desire for children and then suffer conflict over having to stay at home to care for them. She doesn't understand why she treats the children cruelly when she loves them so much.

The person who suffers neurotic anxiety has dissociated many areas of his life by repression. An example of this is the frigid wife who has denied her sexual urges. She suffers anxiety because her physical impulses drive her in one way and her psychological inhibitions another. She may regard her nervous tensions and anxieties as completely mysterious and incomprehensible; but they are plainly related to an "ego" which is torn asunder by conflicting desires and impulses.

In a broad sense, psychotherapy aims to unify the personality, to help the person to formulate goals and a style of life which makes it possible for him to receive gratification for all his needs. Psychotherapy aims to bring about an awareness of the nature of the conflicts and a decision on the part of the client as to which of several conflicting desires must be subjugated to the others. In some cases the conflicts may subside with an understanding of the nature and origin of them. Other conflicts yield only to a lengthy and painstaking re-education. Conflicts which cannot be obliterated may be accepted and relief may follow.

Mikesell offers a valuable statement concerning a criterion for adjustment:

> If this is the case, then the proper standard to adopt is the integral functioning of the mind where needs are met and friction is absent. Adjustment would then mean a lack of conflict. All vital, mental drives, such as desires for love, companionship, recognition, etc., would be equally satisfied. Obviously adjustment in the sense of a mental integration would call for tension-reducers. The adjusted person is thus one who is getting what he wants out of life, although, as we have said, some people want little and are apparently contented merely to go along with their narrow and restricted way of living. They have few wants, but if their few are satiated then there is some sort of a balance of their minds even though it lacks the quality of those whose aspirations are higher and recreative. The best sort of mental integration is, therefore, that achieved by those who strive to fulfill the highest needs of mankind without friction. This high level of mental integration entails a social reference; though some psychotics, shut within themselves, think that their isolated minds are all right. A person adjusted, as we define the term, would automatically serve others and be a credit to the community. His own happiness leads him to seek the happiness of others. But there would be not only the reflection upon society of his own mind, but it would also work in reverse. His happiness would be increased through the well-being of others. As others were adjusted, so he would be adjusted. There would thus be a double reflection; society would reflect his own mind and he would reflect the welfare of those about him . . . (14, pp. 10-11).

Techniques Summarized

Efforts will be made in this writing to present the techniques of analytically oriented therapy under four headings: (1) emotional discharge, (2) insight development, (3) relationship technique, and (4) re-education. The student should understand that the treatment of the individual in therapy will depend upon the nature of the problem. In some cases all four categories of technique may be employed. In other cases, one is sufficient. It is usually true, however, that all four do come into incidental usage even when the therapy is not planned around this event.

It will be understood that although the following discussion may present these sets of techniques separately, they are not mutually exclusive nor does one wait upon the other for implementation. Usually, they are all utilized simultaneously. Although it is assumed that the therapist maintains control of the movement in therapy, some events may transpire without his planning for them or without his consent.

CATHARSIS AND EMOTIONAL DISCHARGE

Catharsis refers to the expulsion of emotional tension by the process of verbal expression. It is not unusual that a person may receive a demonstrable benefit simply by "unloading" his troubles. To be sure, this type of thing is not one of the identifying characteristics of all analytical therapy. As a matter of fact, valid support could not logically be given to catharsis as a technique of therapy at all. It is a method utilized by therapists in helping people either as an entering wedge in therapy proper or as a method of helping a person who wishes to receive help with a situational problem which actually does not involve a therapeutic necessity.

Whether the cathartic release is related to future therapeutic undertaking, or whether it is a matter of emotional discharge related to a situational condition such as loss of a loved one or a disappointment of financial, romantic, or other involvement, catharsis usually is followed by some type of supportive gesture. Supportive measures may or may not deserve the title of supportive therapy depending upon the nature of the problem and of the support. Support is usually aimed at helping the individual regain equilibrium and giving a reasonable boost to his morale.

Supportive therapy usually refers to the practice of carrying a person along over a period of time by bolstering his courage. It is used sometimes to the exclusion of other methods when it is surmised by the therapist that the person may regain his own balance with the passing of time without help of a more distinctly therapeutic nature. Supportive therapy may be used, for instance, with a remissed schizophrenic individual who has lost job or loved one and who needs some support for a period of time and who would not be benefited by a re-entry into his deviational patterns. There are times and cases when reassurances may be not only beneficial but therapeutic, but the therapist must evaluate each situation carefully or he may engender a dependency relationship with its many concomitant dangers.

Although emotional release of tension is thought of as providing only a temporary benefit, there are times when such a temporary improvement may make possible the entry into the problem area at a level considered impossible before the release took place. For this and other reasons, several techniques have been worked out to provide for emotional release. Some special methods utilized by psychiatrists in particular include forms of drug administration in which the person is narcotized to a certain level at which he is able to gain emotional release and expression. Hypnosis has been used in a similar manner. Other methods of achieving release of expression from a blocked person are role-playing and psychodrama.

Most analytical therapists regard the ability of the client to utilize emotional discharge as a desirable adjunct to therapy. Accordingly, most therapists encourage the client to express himself freely. Inability on the client's part to express emotion is a therapeutic liability. It is often true that unexpressed emotion whether repressed or suppressed is the chief deterrent to dramatic improvement of the client.

THE DEVELOPMENT OF INSIGHT

All neurotics and psychotics and many people who are simply maladjusted have repressed events or feelings which have become externalized as anxiety, hostility, aggressiveness, or withdrawal tendencies. It is only reasonable that a treatment of these people would entail a development of insight. To gain insight means to understand oneself, to understand the reason one does things or feels as one does. Since the reason for things in the present lies largely in the past, insight development involves techniques for uncovering past experiences.

Undoubtedly, psychoanalysis has gained more notoriety for its uncovering methods than for any other category of techniques. It is assumed that repression, denial, and dissociation are involved in the dynamics of any person who is suffering neurotic anxiety. If this assumption is correct, special methods for uncovering or recovering the repression must be utilized in order to bring about insight by the client and understanding of the complete problem by the therapist.

Self-understanding becomes a very important aspect of psychotherapy. As Ingham and Love say:

> One of the most important effects of self-understanding is the increased capacity to adjust to present reality. It serves to remove rigidities that have hampered adaptive efforts in the past. When an individual has covered up emotional reactions, pushed them down, as it were, out of his conscious life, he has lost the possibility of changing or influencing them. This means that earlier concepts removed from consideration during childhood, for example, still exist in childish form, though the individual has grown to an adult. With them go attitudes, sentiments, and reactions. When repressed, they cannot be altered or in any way adapted to fit changing situations. The unavailability of the repressed material means that it has been untouched by the maturation and development that has occurred in other, more conscious areas of the person's life. Though unchanged, they are still present and serve as absolute barriers against which the individual stumbles time after time. We can illustrate this with an incidental finding in the case of a man who went to a psychotherapist for help. He had a number of complaints, one of which was this fear of going down into his own cellar. He did not understand it and had never been able to overcome it. In the course of treatment, he discovered that his emotional reaction to cellars harked back to the time when that was the place he received whippings from his father. He had repressed the memory of the incidents but still lived with the apprehension. As he was now an adult, there was no longer any need for realistic fear of his father. This he came to appreciate and his reaction to the cellar disappeared when the connection between it and his childhood experiences was understood (11, pp. 42-43).

It should be thoroughly understood that insight per se does not usually result in a disappearance of symptoms or a cure for the neurosis. Insight does have many values in therapy, including the motivation of the client to move further into the therapeutic situation. Insights are usually encouraging to the client, but they may be accompanied with attendant anxiety if they come too fast.

Association Techniques

Among the earliest of the Freudian methods to be developed was free association. Although usually greatly modified from the early form, associative methods are still used widely today. In the early days, association was done by means of the couch and through a training in free association on the part of the client. The gist of the method was to have the patient recline on a couch facing away from the therapist and to verbalize every thought. This meant that the patient would usually verbalize at a rapid rate for an hour (4).

The use of associative methods in analytic therapy gives assent to the theory that the therapist must devise a diagnosis of the difficulty and that the therapist must seek and find an explanation for patient difficulties. The analyst listens to the patient's expressions and is able from these to reconstruct the neurotic nuclear dynamics of his past and to interpret them for the patient toward insight development.

By and large, the role of the analyst in modern analytical treatment is still to derive meaning from the anamnestic associations of the patient. Modifications have come about chiefly in the manners in which client expressions are derived. Few analysts, even among the orthodox group, use the couch any more. Free association as such seems to be leaving the therapeutic scene in favor of other types of expressions which are not so time-consuming. In the orthodox analysis, free associations take many hours. The major portion of treatment consists of free associations for an hour per day for weeks on end.

Modern, analytically oriented therapists use other methods of obtaining material for their diagnostic minds. The particular methods vary with the general field of practice. The clinical psychologists are inclined to emphasize testing materials as data for analysis and diagnosis. Psychiatrists are more inclined to favor an open discussion and directed conversation with the patient in an effort to gain from his expressions the dynamics of his difficulties. Some psychiatrists use dream analysis and hypnosis somewhat extensively as means of deriving material for analysis. Patient expressions are usually interpreted in the context of the perceived transference relationship.

All association techniques emphasize the belief that the patient may be led to express ideas which have meanings beyond his recognition, but which may be understood by the analyst in terms of past motivations for present verbalism. The feeling among most therapists is that if the patient may be motivated to talk, the astute analyst will find material to aid in an analysis and diagnosis. In general, the therapist is sensitive to such things as slips of the tongue, identification with certain individuals, recurrent themes, and above all, avoidances and resistances.

Interpretation

Most counselors who utilize analytical tools are apt to use interpretation of the patient's actions and statements. In doing this, the therapist reveals to the patient the state of affairs or the meaning of expression as perceived by the therapist. It is perhaps true that the matter of interpretation draws more heavily upon the skills and artistry of the counselor than does any other technique. The question of timing, of accuracy, of client anxiety, and of possible motivational repercussions is involved in every interpretation. The feeling is that if the interpretation must wait until the counselor is absolutely sure about it, the interpretation will come too late to insure constant movement and client cooperation (1). Actually, the therapist can never be absolutely sure of the accuracy of an interpretation and he must put it to the test sooner or later.

If the interpretation is done in the spirit of raising legitimate questions as to the possibility of this or that meaning, the client may become more cooperative. However, it is true that there are times when the therapist may wish to agitate the client into an emotional denial of a certain meaning. Some clients may be motivated well by making them angry through the use of an interpretation which has derogatory implications. The therapist must move with caution in this area and of course must base decisions on the merits of the individual case.

Resistance

Oddly enough, resistance to an interpretation may be regarded as an evidence of accuracy almost as often as may acquiescence. The therapist must study his client carefully over a period of time in order to be able to judge whether or not an interpretation has struck "pay dirt." Many times the client will deny a given interpretation at first, and perhaps on several subsequent occasions, only to admit its truth ultimately.

Resistance to the therapist and to his interpretations may be regarded neither as all good nor all bad. Strong resistance does have the power to interrupt progress in therapy. On the other hand, a degree of resistance may not only be meaningful in revealing certain characteristics and information about the client, it may actually serve to stimulate client participation and ultimately to accelerate progress of therapy. The therapist must be very alert to the possible meanings of resistance in the client. These resistances have implications for the counselor in terms of the transference also, and such resistances will be discussed more fully in a later section.

Resistance is a tool used unconsciously by the client which may be useful provided the therapist is able to appraise and direct it correctly. Ingham and Love say:

> In a particular instance the interference with progress caused by resistance may be desirable or not. But in general the patient certainly needs a way to avoid discoveries about himself that would be excessively disturbing. The function of resistance is to slow down the progress of psychotherapy to the speed that can be tolerated by the patient. It is valuable, even necessary, and is something to be worked with rather than simply an interference to be eliminated. It can certainly be excessive. It is far more frequent that the therapist wishes to decrease resistance than he needs to augment it. However, it is fairly often true that he prefers to leave it alone and let it serve its own function without interference, at least temporarily. We might consider some instances from the standpoint of the effect of the resistance.
>
> The patient may be avoiding an insight quite appropriately. Usually he is able to escape ideas and feelings that are too disrupting for him. This is a valuable capacity on which both participants may well rely. At a given moment, then, his persistent evasion may be a sign that he cannot face the subject under consideration. Then the

therapist would be wise to presume that the patient is right in maintaining his resistance to the topic (11, pp. 95-96).

The Relation of Uncovering and Insight

Uncovering actions and techniques have both a cause and effect relationship with insight development. The original idea as developed by Freud was that the client went through various activities designed to uncover repressed material; and he believed that upon the laying bare of repressed facts, events and impulses, a stirring insight sometimes developed.

Alexander and French have questioned this sequence and have hypothesized a reverse order of events:

> This exaggerated emphasis has long hampered both the understanding of why patients remember repressed events and the correct evaluation of their therapeutic significance. It was not until 1930 that the recovery of memories was demonstrated to be not the *cause* of therapeutic progress but its *result*, and that recollection of repressed childhood memories occurs, as a rule, only after the same type of emotional constellation has been experienced and mastered in the transference situation (1, p. 20).‡

---

‡ Alexander Franz and Thomas Morton French. *Psychoanalytic Therapy: Principles and Application.* Copyright 1946, The Ronald Press Company.

It seems quite logical that the sequence of insight and uncovering activity including transference utilization is not always the same. In some instances it may be that uncovering precedes insight and that the initial insight provides more uncovering which in turn provides still more insights.

Dream Interpretation

Dream analysis is popularly associated with analytical theories and techniques. It is true that dream analysis was a major emphasis of Freud's method; and present-day therapists continue to utilize dream material, but the usage seems to be declining to some extent.

There is no question as to the potency and meaningfulness of dream material. There is considerable question as to what the meanings of dream material really are. It is generally conceded that dreams represent the mental functioning of the individual with considerable inhibitory depression. Thus, dreams represent ideation which cannot be logically tolerable in waking states. The main difficulty is that there is still inhibition enough to prevent a coming through of clearly conceived images. Most of the material of dreams obviously is so fraught with dangers that it must be expressed symbolically and mysteriously. The situations being acted out are much too dangerous and threatening to admit to dream consciousness except in camouflaged form.

Although many people regard their dream material as proceeding from some external source, as being magical and supernatural, it is impossible to escape the conviction that what occurs in dreams is really an extension of experience or at least is based on experience. All that is required in an analysis of dreams is to relate dream experience correctly with actual experience. This is either very difficult to do or is impossible. Freud states:

> All the material making up the content of a dream is in some way derived from experience, that is to say, has been reproduced or remembered in the dream—so much at least we may regard as an undisputed fact. But it would be a mistake to suppose that a connection of this kind between the content of a dream and reality is bound to come to light easily, as an immediate result of comparing them. The connection requires, on the contrary, to be looked for diligently, and in a whole quantity of cases it may long remain hidden. The reason for this lies in a number of peculiarities which are exhibited by the faculty of memory in dreams and which, though generally remarked upon, have hitherto resisted explanation . . . (6, p. 11).

Freud's theories on dream analysis interpose that every wish is generated by the motive force of unfulfilled wishes and that all dreams represent fulfillment of wishes. This theory is very useful in interpretation of dreams, although the inclusiveness of all dreams as wish-fulfillments has been attacked by some other students of dream work. Principal among the criticisms of the wish-fulfillment hypothesis has been that such an hypothesis does not take proper cognizance of the anxiety-laden dream so common to mankind. Freud seemed to believe that the anxiety-laden dream is the expression of a wish that is not symbolized well enough to reduce the anxiety. The defense of symbolization is insufficient (4).

In general, Freud's early theories on dream analysis are considered tenable. Chief objections arise in his insistence on analyzing every dream on the basis of repressed material. It seems more likely that some dreams arise from more immediate stimuli such as events of the day or physical stimuli while sleeping.

The most general technique utilized in dream evaluation is to search for the wish being fulfilled and then to endeavor to work through the symbolism. An example may be beneficial here. A woman who was in her fifties asked for the interpretation of the following dream:

> I dreamed that I went to put on my new shoes to go to town and found that they had been stolen. I started walking down the highway, barefoot, walking right down the center stripe. I got so tired, I thought I would drop. Finally, I got to Mrs. Downey's house and, lo and behold, there were my shoes on her doorstep. But they were not new any longer; they were all scratched up and old looking.

The analysis of this dream seems quite simple. We must accept that the woman had wished for something that was being expressed in the dream material. The central fact in the dream was that her shoes had been stolen. Must we assume that she wished to have her shoes stolen? No; we must remember that the pair of shoes is more apt to be a symbol. Then what is the symbolization?

Questioning revealed that Mrs. Downey was a widow who had some reputation as a flirt. So the shoes may be understood to be a symbol of the woman's husband who was stolen in the dream by the widow. And, then, we understand that the reason for having the husband stolen in the dream is that he had become old, like the scratched and shabby shoes.

As reported previously, dream analysis in modern psychotherapy is not a major medium of revelation. Dreams are utilized by some therapists as a point of departure for free discussion. Many patients are anxious to participate in dream telling; they feel that there is definite advantage in it. The therapist may or may not believe strongly in the usefulness of dream material. He is likely to agree that as a means of motivating discussion, dreams have no peer. Good revelations may come from having the client attempt an interpretation of his own dreams. There is more, usually, for the therapist to think about in the patient's interpretation than there is in the dream material; and the interpretation is much more understandable.

Narcosis and Hypnosis

Narcosis and hypnosis provide specialized methods for altering the state of the client and causing an expression of repressed subjects. Narcosis is useful to the counselor who is also a medical doctor, but hypnosis may be useful either to psychiatrists or psychologists. Under the effects of drugs or hypnosis the patient may bring out repressed memories that will have advantage in giving impressions to the therapist. They may be interpreted to the client with some success, but of course will not be a part of his conscious reaction at the time they are divulged.

Hypnosis has the added advantage of providing means of benefiting the client through post-hypnotic suggestion. Although this type of activity by the client does not have lasting effects, it may provide benefits of learning for the client. For instance, a person who suffers from stage fright may have suggested to him that he has no fear of audiences. Under post-hypnosis, the client may participate in a stage production or make a speech without fear; and, having learned that he can do so, he may gain the ability to continue without fear.

Although these specialized methods have come into prominence as dramatic methods often supported through motion pictures and television, their utility is not general. It should be understood that neither hypnosis nor narcosis should be used without a high degree of training by the therapist.

Insufficiency of Insight Alone

Insight development is a part of most techniques of therapy, but it is an error to believe that insight alone supplies the need for personality change. It should be remembered that neurotic behavior itself is a defense against anxiety. When a person has insight into his neurotic symptoms, he does not necessarily give them up. As a matter of fact, the giving up of his symptoms is synonymous with giving up his defense against anxiety. He will do this only if a means of doing so is provided which reduces the anxiety he feels. Such a course of action requires considerable planning and implementation beyond the insight stage.

Then, too, most neuroses provide the patient with a pattern of secondary gains. By means of the neurosis, the patient often becomes the object of attention, which is desirable for him. He may exercise power over someone because of his neurotic symptoms. Secondary gains often deter improvement. It should be clear that the patient must have a powerful motivation for improvement if he is to be able to give up primary and secondary gains.

RELATIONSHIP AS A THERAPEUTIC TECHNIQUE

The Nature of the Transference Relationship

People who suffer from neurotic anxiety are reacting to the externalization of repressed events and feelings which occurred in the past. Most chronic neurotics are reacting to repressed feelings which have connection with the people in the past life who were able to bring threat upon the neurotic individual. Most of the times these are parent figures.

In the therapeutic situation, it is more often than not the case that the client begins to react to the therapist as though he were a figure of the past. Thus, he has transferred the personality of the power figure who was involved with his repressions into the physical body of the therapist. The patient is reacting to the therapist as though he were someone else. This is called transference.

Transference is actually a very common occurrence, not only in therapy but in everyday life as well. People constantly transfer other personalities into their friends and acquaintances. It should be understood that transference in therapy may be utilized to benefit the client or it may be a detriment to him, but transference at one level or the other is almost inevitable in therapy. The counselor may choose to ignore it altogether, to use it and plan therapy around it, or even to induce it to a more than normal degree in the client. As a methodology, analytic therapy has made broad usage of the transference phenomenon.

Transference may operate at a surface level or at a deeper level. Freud made reference to the transference neurosis, which is the deepest type of transference. The therapist is reacted to with strong affect as the authority figure who precipitated the neurotic nucleus. Most modern therapists make use of the relationship but do not think of it in as deep a sense as Freud did.

When transference is utilized in the deep sense, it is possible for the relationship to take place across sex lines. That is, the male therapist may be reacted to as the mother figure and vice versa. However at the level in which transference is utilized in most modern therapies, transference rarely crosses sex lines. Certain efforts are made in some clinics to utilize the desirable effects of transference by allowing a male alcoholic, for instance, to be counseled by a woman. Some problem areas indicate in advance that the transference may best be made to a woman than a man or vice versa.

Most transferences are not at a depth which demands that they persist at every moment during the counseling session. There may be times when the counselor is perceived as a counselor and as nothing else. Then intermittently he may become the father figure for the client, particularly as the client moves into the troubled areas of his life. It is even possible for the identity of the transference figure to change during the interview. The transference may fluctuate from the father figure to the figure of the husband, for instance.

It should be understood that the client is scarcely aware of the transferences which are in effect. The typical client expresses himself and moves into the transference realm without complete or even fragmentary knowledge of it. It may be that the client is aware that the counselor reminds him of "father," but he will not understand that he is reacting as he did toward his father during the time of difficulty in earlier life.

The Values of Transference

There are several distinct values of transference relationships. In the first place, these relationships give an incomparable opportunity to the counselor for studying the dynamics of the client. If the counselor is aware that the client is reacting as if he (the counselor) were the father, then he can study the reactions, hostilities, and blockings toward himself, making possible a real understanding of the early relationships of the client. Thus, he may add to his understandings of the client and bring about worthwhile interpretations.

The fundamental value of the transference is that it provides a relearning situation. This is the emphasis in analytical therapy. As a matter of fact, it is possible that the relearning in the transference relationship is the most important technique residing in the ortho-dox analytical framework of methodology.

If the difficulties being encountered in adult life are related to faulty learnings in relation to the father, it is reasonable to believe that relearning must take place with a father figure. The transfer-ence relationship provides a means for the playing out of re-pressed feelings and impulses in a favorable, non-threatening at-mosphere. It supplies a laboratory for experimenting with new types of behavior toward this figure who has created so much difficulty in the past. As we have said, the typical neurotic reacts toward people as he did when he was a child. The reason for this is that his growth was thwarted in childhood by a faulty relation-ship in the family setting. In order to obtain relief, this person will have to return symbolically to the scene of childhood and work out the problems which tied him to the past. The client is a victim of childhood threats and fears; he must learn to conquer these fears in a relationship similar to the one in which they first arose and were repressed.

For an example let us consider the case of the neurotic man who has unfulfilled sex needs but who cannot relate to women without great anxiety. Such a person is apt to be driven to some sexual perversion and may have latent homosexual trends. In early life his mother probably reacted to him in a coldly hostile manner; she rejected him and treated him cruelly because she did not wish to be bothered by a young child in the home.

The child learned correctly perhaps that his mother was hostile toward him. But, he learned incorrectly that all women are hostile and dangerous. If this man is to receive help, he must experience relearning. He must learn in a transference situation that some women are warm and accepting, that contrary to early experience all females are not cold and hostile. This relearning must furthermore take place in a therapeutic situation where the trained therapist can handle the relationship objectively; it cannot be accomplished in a real-life situation very well. Should the man become interested in a warm and affectionate woman in real life, he would be sure to "blow" his chances because of the feelings of hostility he has toward women. He would quickly alienate the affections of any women who should show him regard.

It should be obvious that transference may be either positive or negative in tone. That is, the client may react toward the therapist with warmth, or with hostility depending upon how he reacted basically to the transference figure. As a matter of fact, transference feeling tone fluctuates greatly because of ambivalent feelings in the client. Herein lies the great demand on the therapist. He must be able to fathom what level of hostility and affection to allow in the transference situation. It is possible for the able therapist to build the level of feeling in the patient as he might determine the need. He may react to the patient in such a way as to enlarge the hostility or to effect a warmer relationship. Realistically, some patients require a beginning situation consisting of an enragement toward the therapist. Only by beginning thus may some clients work up through their hostilities and bring about the needed relearning.

On the other hand, some clients are rendered incommunicative when the negative transference is great. There is also the danger that the client may terminate counseling with negative transference in force and be more disturbed than when he began therapy. Negative transference always increases the anxiety level in the patient and the therapist must be on guard against bringing about more anxiety than the client can bear.

It is true that some therapists work with analytical tools generally but do not wish to exploit the possibilities of the transference. Unless the therapist has adequate training, he should be cautious in dealing with transference; he should recognize it but not exploit it. The more basically analytically oriented therapists would deny that any therapy can take place without utilizing the transference. There is little doubt that the transference is a most valuable means of facilitating relearning. Transference values do accrue even with those counselors who make no particular effort to induce or manipulate it.

Inducing and Evaluating Transference

Transference at some level is almost always operative in a counseling session. Should a counselor desire to induce a deeper transference, he may do so by handling the interview in such a manner as to create an atmosphere similar to that in operation in the early family scene of the client. Deutsch and Murphy (3) suggest that repetition of the language patterns of the client comprises a means of inducing and accentuating the transference.

It is possible, by observing and reflecting the language mannerisms and peculiarities of the client, to create an atmosphere conducive to transference. Basically, this is accomplished by repeating phrases and words that seem to be features of the family language habits. Each family does develop peculiarities of speech and also of general conduct such as posturing and so forth. Depth of transference may not only be implemented by counselor attention to atmosphere determiners, but the counselor may in turn be able to judge the level of transference by evaluating the tendencies of the client to emulate language and postural nuances that are characteristic of the counselor.

The Over-All Aspects of Transference-Handling in Therapy

In general, therapists who place great emphasis on transference therapy think of a threefold process. The first stage is that in which transference is induced or accentuated, studied by the therapist, and allowed to become clearly defined. The second stage is that in which relearning takes place through interaction between the symbolic parent and the patient who dynamically has regressed to an earlier stage of existence. This may be called the core stage and is the most meaningful stage in terms of the client's growth. The third stage involves the ending stage of therapy, and may be classed as a dissolution of the transference state. In this last stage, the adult who became a child becomes an adult again. The neurotic processes will have been broken in the core stage; and the patient needs a period for return to the self-sufficient state where the transference dependency is no longer needed. There is a danger in terminating therapy without having resolved the transference relationship.

It is clear that the movement into the transference relationship will be accompanied by an irrational component and an excursion into a land of fantasy. This is true for both client and therapist. The therapist will be reacting to the client in a manner not completely devoid of irrational aspects. Naturally the therapist will maintain a firmer hold on reality than will the client; and although he may experience some emotional involvement in the past world of the client, he will be able to maintain an objective directiveness of the treatment.

There are dangers of a countertransference, an identification of the client by the therapist as a figure from his past or present. The able therapist will be on guard against this because it usually results in a loss of objectivity and a possibility of real damage to the client. If the therapist mingles his own problems with those of the client, nothing constructive may be expected to evolve.

Nowhere has a more graphic description been made of the process of transference therapy than by Whitaker and Malone:

> Now, however, this same patient-person relates to another human being, the therapist, in such a deep way that the latter replaces his symbolic family. The same internal, repetitious frustrations once more develop initially. The patient relives with the therapist his transference experiences in much the same way in which he lived them initially, and has been living them since, i.e., his repetition compulsions. This relationship, however, differs significantly. By virtue of greater therapist potential, this other person is a more adequate parent. This makes possible a different outcome to the transference experience resulting from better and deeper gratification. This new parent responds more adequately to the patient's transference needs, adding the maturity of his person as a significant factor over and above the transference factor. The therapist, at first, serves simply as a symbolic screen for a projective repetition of the earlier parental experience. However, the therapist is also a real person and therefore more than, and different from, the sum of the patient's projections. The wholeness of him relates to the patient. Out of the therapist's maturity the patient constructs a more adequate and, finally, a truly satisfying internal parent. The patient

certainly experiences the discrepancy between his projection and the maturity of the real person of the therapist and this may well constitute the most important disequilibrium dynamic. The transference repetition-compulsion is thus continually projected and altered until, either in massive or in splintered movement, the circular neurotic process breaks. Once the repetition-compulsion alters, the relationship can become totally fantastic bilaterally, i.e., achieve a pre-transference level. This affords the patient a chance to regress to the pattern unconsciously directed toward the ultimate and complete satisfaction of those infantile needs which underlie self love (narcissism) and antecede the love of others (transference). In this relationship, the patient achieves the gratification of certain infantile needs. This gratification leads toward a gradual dissolution of the patient's symbolic and neurotic processes. The patient's understanding of the character of his therapeutic transference relationships has little to do with the value of the experience. The actual child-parent gratification on a deep and meaningful level may or may not be understood. Growth, however, is always experience. No matter how this ensues, this gratification constitutes the effective force which shatters the neurotic process in the patient (20, p. 93).

Special Dangers for the Clergyman

The clergyman should be aware that special dangers prevail in transference relationships which he may willfully induce or unwittingly encourage. The fact that he has been cast by many as a father figure makes the likelihood of transferences greater. Transferences which may develop with a minister, priest, or rabbi are apt to be deeper also.

Many cases are on record in which the female parishioner has been caught in a transference web with her clergyman to the extent that her marriage has been endangered. The transference relation between female parishioner and male clergyman may produce romantic entanglements, inasmuch as the woman may be seeking security she can receive only from someone who becomes unconsciously a father substitute for her. If the clergyman also unconsciously seeks escape from a marital situation not altogether satisfying for him, a type of relationship may develop which can only bring trouble.

The psychological and medical psychotherapist can handle these relationships with greater success and less danger because he can avoid close and constant contact. The clergyman cannot regulate contact nearly so easily. Then, too, the clergyman is in a precarious position as regards the possible hurt that may come from misapprehensions among his congregation.

For all these reasons, many clergymen have come to prefer methods of counseling which play down the transference possibility. As will be seen in Chapter VIII, the client-centered approach does not encourage transference.

Regardless of the basic orientation of the clergyman, the clergyman will not be able to avoid the fact that he has a relationship with the parishioner that is unique and one that may be utilized to the benefit of the parishioner by recognizing and building upon it. Lehrman (13) suggests that the sexual content of counseling sessions between clergyman and female parishioner is inevitable and should not be looked upon guiltily. Rather, it should become a factor through which the counselor may understand both present conditions of the relationship and concomitant personality dynamics of the parishioner.

Stewart (17) emphasizes the relationship aspects of the counseling effort as being of great importance. "Therapy is a conversation and a relationship." In therapeutic counseling it is probable that the relationship is more important than the conversation in both pastoral and secular situations.

RE-EDUCATION AND WORKING THROUGH

A large measure of the values found in utilizing the transference relationship in therapy resides in the ability of transference relations to produce relearning. However, the relearning acquired in transference therapy is of an elementary although basic type. These learnings must be developed, expanded, and put to the test in the everyday experiences of the client. Together with the insights that have been developed in therapy, the learning acquired in reliving childhood events comprises a basis for movement toward a fully integrated existence in the world of adult human beings. Unless the client is able to put his insights to work, they will avail little and will be nothing more than intellectual insights.

Insight that has an emotional impact will ultimately force the client to be dissatisfied with his narrow and rigid involvement with life; and such insights will not allow the client to gain previous benefits from his neurotic behavior, but will make neurotic behavior a source of anxiety rather than a defense against it.

When a person has reached the stage of primary relearning of childhood errors in relationship, when the client has gained insight into the reasons for his neurotic activity, when the neurotic process begins to break up, the crucial time is at hand in therapy. The client is like a helpless baby who must be nurtured for a time until he can gain control of his reactions and can test his new learnings and insights. The counselor should be prepared to assist the client for as long as he needs a type of sustenance. To be sure, the counselor must allow the client to build and rely upon his own strength in time; but he must be sure that too much is not entrusted to the inexperienced new self of the client.

Clients who have been released from neurotic activity are apt to follow one of two possible extreme patterns. Either the client will be insecure in his new roles or he will suddenly go "wild" with activity in the opposite extreme from his restricted behavior before therapy. For instance, a person who has had great conflict with the opposite sex is not usually an accomplished heterosexual mixer by virtue of his new insights. He may be inclined to try out his new activities very gingerly and may need some continued help from the therapist. In an effort to demonstrate to the client how friendly people can be the therapist may have overdone his acting. Leaving the protected therapeutic relationship, the client may be badly hurt by coming in contact with a person who has the same personality traits as did the power figure of his past.

On the other hand, some clients feel such a great surge of relief upon their emancipation from neurotic conflict that they may get into difficulty by their overreactions to this freedom. A person who has been living under crippling inhibitions may actually commit acts which are explosive and which hurt someone else. As the client experiences distressing reversals in his approach to life outside the therapy session, he needs the privilege of return to the counselor for corrective chartings of his course. Eventually, of course, he will gain complete independence and autonomy of control; he will perceive life as being fraught with frustrations, but will learn to survive. Ingham and Love say:

> As working through is the final stage in a series of activities, a stage that can be achieved only when the other steps have been successfully completed, it results in a feeling of gratification and sometimes of completion. It converts the theoretical considerations and abstractions from the therapist's office into practical application in the rest of the patient's life. It is more forceful than almost anything else which can occur in psychotherapy. It makes people feel good. It is likely to create enthusiasm and is a good part of the reason that some of those who are successful in treatment become oversold with the whole process and believe it to be a panacea (11, p. 129).

Although there are definite antagonisms between religious thought and psychoanalytical theories and although Freud has openly derided religion, it is probable that analytical therapy and religious concern reside on common ground. Zilboorg (22) points out the common acceptance of religion and psychoanalysis by stating "that among the members of the American Psychoanalytic Association there are God-fearing Protestants and devout Catholics who are also Freudian psychoanalysts."

References

1. Alexander, Franz and Thomas French, *Psychoanalytic Therapy*. New York: Ronald Press Company, 1946.
2. Blum, Gerald S., *Psychoanalytic Theories of Personality*. New York: McGraw-Hill Book Company, Inc., 1953.
3. Deutsch, Felix and William F. Murphy, *The Clinical Interview*, Vol. II. New York: International University Press, Inc., 1955.
4. Freud, Sigmund, *A General Introduction to Psychoanalysis*, trans. Joan Riviere. Garden City: Garden City Publishing Company, Inc., 1943.
5. ————, *An Outline of Psychoanalysis*, trans. James Strachey. New York: W. W. Norton and Company, Inc., 1949.
6. ————, *The Interpretation of Dreams*, trans. and ed. by James Strachey. New York: Basic Books Inc., 1955.

7. Hall, Calvin S. and Gardner Lindsey, *Theories of Personality*. New York: John Wiley and Sons, Inc., 1957.

8. Hiltner, Seward, *Pastoral Counseling*. New York: Abingdon-Cokesbury Press, 1949.

9. Horney, Karen, *Our Inner Conflicts, A Constructive Theory of Neuroses*. New York: W. W. Norton, 1945.

10. ————, *The Neurotic Personality of Our Times*. New York: W. W. Norton, 1942.

11. Ingham, Harrington V. and Leonore R. Love, *The Process of Psychotherapy*. New York: McGraw-Hill Book Company, Inc., 1954.

12. Jones, Ernest, *The Life and Work of Sigmund Freud*. New York: Basic Books Inc., Vol. I, 1953, Vol. II, 1955.

13. Lehrman, Nathaniel S., "The Normality of Sexual Feelings in Pastoral Counseling," *Pastoral Psychology*. June, 1960, pp. 49-52.

14. Mikesell, William H., *Techniques of Living*. Harrisburg: The Stackpole Company, 1953.

15. Munroe, Ruth L., *Schools of Psychoanalytic Thought*. New York: The Dryden Press, 1955.

16. Raskin, Nathaniel, "The Development of Non-Directive Therapy," *Journal of Consulting Psychology*. 2, 1948, pp. 92-110.

17. Stewart, Charles W., "Relationship Counseling," *Journal of Pastoral Care*, Winter, 1959, pp. 209-220.

18. Wallen, Richard W., *Clinical Psychology—The Study of Persons*. New York: McGraw-Hill Book Company, Inc., 1956.

19. Wiesbauer, Henry H., *Pastoral Help in Serious Mental Illness*. New York: National Association for Mental Health, n.d.

20. Whitaker, Carl A. and Thomas P. Malone, *The Roots of Psychotherapy*. New York: The Blakiston Company, 1953.

21. White, Robert W., *The Abnormal Personality*. New York: Ronald Press Company, 1948.

22. Zilboorg, Gregory, "Psychoanalysis and Religion," *Pastoral Psychology*. November, 1959, pp. 41-48.

VIII

Client-Centered
Therapy

Among counselors who practice psychotherapy, there
are those who hold tenaciously to one or the other of several basic
systems of theory and practice. These people probably feel that
it is best to learn one system thoroughly, and that trying to learn
a number of systems makes one inept in all of them. Others feel
that the counselor should learn as much as he can about personality theories, techniques of therapy, and personality assessment, and that he then may choose theory, techniques, and
methods to fit the individual and the problem at hand. Still other
therapists remain within one single framework throughout all their
practice because they sincerely believe in the exclusive excellence
of the system which they have embraced.

This writing attempts to present two points of view, of basically
different premises, that are currently the most popular systems.
These are the psychoanalytical and client-centered theories of
counseling. The psychoanalytically oriented methods have been
presented in Chapter VII, and this chapter is concerned with
client-centered theories and methods. These are presented separately and distinctively, without attempt to evaluate whether one

is better in some cases or in all cases. It has been pointed out that counselors generally have concluded that the directive-nondirective controversy has been largely resolved in terms of choosing the method to fit the requirement in counseling. While this is true for the most part in the realm of counseling with the problems of normal individuals, it is not nearly so absolute concerning counseling with personality disturbances in a psychotherapeutic sense. Client-centered therapy is an extension of nondirective counseling. The two are stems from the same root. Yet, in the realms of psychotherapy proper, the reluctance to mingle theory and technique is maintained; whereas inter-acceptance of ideas in the areas of nonembedded, non-therapeutic difficulties has become much more commonplace.

There are those practitioners who use both client-centered methods and psychoanalytically oriented methods; but each practitioner is aware of a distinction in the methods being used. That is to say, there has not yet developed a hybrid method in therapy as is true in lower-level counseling. Perhaps a hybridizing will become evident later; but it is not quite apparent, even as a trend to this writer, at the present time.

Client-Centered Therapy
and the Religiously Oriented Counselor

It was suggested in Chapter II that nondirective or client-centered methods in counseling spring from psychological systems that are compatible with the Christian understanding of personality. Several writers in the field of pastoral counseling have strongly commended the client-centered method and philosophy as being most consonant with the requirements of church-related counseling. Speaking of the client-centered approach, Clymer states, "Christian ministers were not only quick to seize upon this approach as a means for effective pastoral care, but have also sought to show its affinity to the Christian faith" (2).

In addition to the fact that the basic theories of personality underlying the client-centered approach are compatible with Christian belief, there are several other reasons why this method is of primary importance to religious counselors. In the first place, the period of training required for this type of therapy is not as long as that required for psychoanalytical types. This is not to say that the client-centered counselor needs little training. The more training and experience one has in client-centered methods, the more effective he will be. However, the method is of such nature that the dangers of hurting the client are not as great. It is conceivable that a minister with a short, intensive training in these techniques would be able to engage in psychotherapy to assist his church-members by use of these techniques. With the same amount of training in psychoanalytically oriented methods, the minister would be treading dangerous ground if he opened therapy.

Many people believe that counselors who enter into the therapeutic area should have training equivalent to the Ph.D. degree in counseling or clinical psychology. This conviction wavers somewhat when attention is brought to bear upon the multitudes of people needing some type of psychotherapy and the meager supply of counselors who have advanced training.

Perhaps a part of the answer lies in providing intensive but short-term training for many counselors who are not able to pursue the Ph.D. degree. In this sense, we are most fortunate in having the client-centered method, which lends itself to training either by intensive short-term approaches or by extensive long-term approaches. If the counselor learns the basic tenets and methods and adheres strictly to these, the possibility of accomplishing gain for the client is considerable, with a negligible danger of inflicting damage. The highly trained counselor has a much greater chance of helping while his risk of hurting remains negligible.

In order for the student to have basis for understanding client-centered techniques, it will be necessary to review thoroughly and tediously the theories of personality that underlie these. Through this review, the reader will also come to understand how it is possible to give aid with a small risk. One should observe most carefully how the client-centered method avoids the transference relationship, which has been pointed out as the most dangerous aspect of the psychoanalytical method.

THEORIES OF PERSONALITY

The Effect of Individual Differences
on the Phenomenal Field of the Individual

No one denies the fact that all people are different. Most people who have given assent to this fact have failed to comprehend the full meaning of the phrase, "individual differences." When the term is used, most people think of the physical differences in people, but some think of the personality variations; and few fully appreciate the tremendous range of differences in the way people perceive the world, in the way they think, feel, and react to the environment. Yet, these variations in perception and in reaction to the stimuli which the individual faces are more meaningful psychologically than physical or personality differences.

Snygg and Combs (23), among other writers, have emphasized the "phenomenal field" which is the entire universe as perceived by the individual at an instant of action. We can only speculate concerning the vast differences in the way the world appears to two individuals standing in the same place at the same time. Experiments have been made, to be sure, in the area of structural perceptions to indicate that different individuals observing the same accident, for instance, report entirely different impressions. These visual and sensory differences in perception are important, but the more important aspects of individual differences are the feelings, the emotional reactions, the fears, and the excitements that race through the consciousness of individuals, as well as the deep-lying churnings of the inner person that defy adequate description.

This private world of the individual becomes very important in counseling and psychotherapy (10). Generally speaking, it is thought that the ability of a therapist to effect change in his client is a function of his being able to understand his client. Many people naively suppose that they have the ability to understand their fellow man. It is undeniable that some people do have unusual powers of discernment, of analysis and diagnosis, and of reading the feelings of others into their actions; but to say that any man has ever completely understood another is absurd.

The Internal Frame of Reference

To understand another person we should have to dwell in his private world with him (11). We would have to see the world as he sees and feels it physically, emotionally, and unconsciously. Since the private world of the individual depends upon every physical cell in his organism, upon every attitude, upon every neural pathway that has been blazed upon the nervous system, and upon every learning which has occurred in his lifetime, one person could never really understand another unless he were that other person.

But as impossible as it is to become another person, this line of thought leads us to a consideration of the means by which we may, in a measure at least, move into the internal framework of the individual whom we are counseling. Counselors, having become convinced of the foolishness of trying to understand the individual from their own or the external framework, have endeavored to find a means of making at least a partial entry into the private world of the individual. In large part, the theories and methods of client-centered therapy are devised to make this possible.

It will be worth our while to consider further that the individual's private world has great meaning for him; it is the only reality he knows (10). The matter of facing reality has had great importance for all psychotherapists; yet, we cannot be sure just what reality is. That there is an objective reality for the physical elements is true, but reality factors for the world of attitude and feeling exist only in the minds of people. If one man sees women as warm and affectionate and another sees them as threatening, then reality is neither warmth nor threat, but is warmth and threat to the two men involved.

Differentiation in the Phenomenal Field

Turning again to Snygg and Combs (23) as pioneer authorities in this field, we understand that the phenomenal field of the individual is composed of things important and those not so important to the perceiver. These elements of perception and differentiation are called "figure" and "ground" of the phenomenal field. As a person perceives his world, some objects and impressions stay in the background; they are not perceived with clarity; they do not draw attention or focus the awareness of the perceiver upon themselves. These are "ground." Other impressions of the phenomenal field spring into "figure"; they are sharply placed in awareness because they have much importance. Of course, there are impressions in the field that are more in "figure" than others. Some impressions dwell in the transition zone; they almost spring into "figure" but never do.

It is natural for us to suppose that some of the things that are in "figure" at one instant of action may recede into "ground" at other times, and that the relative values of various stimuli vary from moment to moment. Some impressions are differentiated from ground to figure by an assault upon the physical sense organs, as a bird becomes "figure" when he sings a shrill note. However, most impressions maintain their positions of importance in the phenomenal field not on the basis of physical stimulation by energy waves but, rather, by the attitudes which the individual has toward them.

Psychotherapy and Theories of the Self

Client-centered therapy has become firmly established upon the broad base of a system of thought usually referred to as self-theory. This theory is concerned with the entity of the self, which is the unique totality of a personality. Self theorists believe that a human being gradually draws from the environment and from his many phenomenal fields many aspects which he conceives to be related to himself. The self consists of all those aspects of the universe that are related to "Me." As James (4) has indicated, these objects and impressions in the universe spread out from the center of the "self," the inner person, the individuality known to theologians as the soul of man, in ever-widening, concentric circles to include those things that are far removed from the seat of the "self," the physical body. For instance, the aspects of self spread out from the inner entity of the self to parts of the body, then to wearing apparel, to possessions, to friends and family, to fellow Americans, to public properties, and to every feature of the universe that is thought by the "I" as being related to the

"Me." All of these things have a relationship to the "Me." And all things that make up the self have great importance to the individual.

The reader may begin to wonder what all this has to do with client-centered therapy. It should be apparent that therapy is largely concerned with a person's feelings about things and especially with feelings about himself. It is also within the province of therapy to seek an understanding of why people feel the way they do about everything. It is important to the development of client-centered theories of counseling for the student to think of all a person's perceptions and feelings as having a relationship to the self. This is so reasonable that few will deny it; but there is some resistance, perhaps, because of the common conviction that being self-centered is undesirable. Our concern is not whether it is proper to base every feeling, attitude, and perception upon self-values, but we must conclude that nothing is as important to an individual as self.

The sharpness of configuration of environmental impressions is determined by the amount of felt relationship to the self. Sharp differentiations from ground to figure in the phenomenal field occur as impressions are perceived to be either enhancing or threatening to the self. This is the cause of tension. Tension rises as the individual perceives either enhancing or threatening meanings in the things around him (23).

Formation of the Self-Concept

As has already been indicated, a part of the phenomenal field of the individual becomes differentiated as the self. Beyond that, another formation is the self-concept, which consists of all the attitudes that a person has about himself in the many areas of his functioning. In every area of life all men have a concept of self. A man believes himself to be handsome, friendly, attractive to women; or perhaps he conceives himself as being unfriendly, unworthy, and ugly. The self-concept involves all facets of one's social, religious, physical, moral, and intellectual beings, to mention only a few of the multiple aspects of life. The structure of self has been described by Rogers (10) as an organized, fluid, but consistent pattern of perceptions.

Raimy (9) says, "The self-concept is the more or less organized perceptual object resulting from present and past self-observation." What one thinks of himself is determined by the events of the past life. A person may believe himself to be handsome because of the introjections of statements made by his mother. Many of the concepts of self are based on attitudes taken from others. These concepts result from the processes of life. The young child, according to Allport (1), does not have well-defined and immutable impressions about himself; but people make up their minds about themselves as they mature, and beliefs about oneself become quite stable in adulthood. However, it is possible for a person to change his attitude toward self somewhat over a period of time; thus, there is some fluidity to the self-concept even in adulthood.

Not only do all people conceive of themselves in various ways but they also attach values to these attitudes about themselves. For instance, a person who thinks of himself as dishonest may put a positive or negative value upon his dishonesty. He may feel that being dishonest is an advantage to him and he may be glad that he is dishonest; or, on the other hand, he may suffer much guilt from such attitudes about himself.

We can imagine that if a person's feeling that he is dishonest came from accusations of his parents concerning childhood thefts, and if these were severely punished, there would be a concept of dishonesty with negative evaluations. If the person felt himself to be dishonest because his father had taught him to be dishonest and always praised his dishonest acts, then the dishonesty concept would be a positive one. In this way all of us have ideas about ourselves and have attached values to the concepts.

Enhancement or Threat of Experiences

One of the things most difficult to understand about the self-concept is that, usually, we are not completely aware of what we think about ourselves. If a person is asked to describe the way he thinks of himself, most likely he will not be able to divulge this. Immediately, one begins to answer questions about self-concept in terms of what he feels to be desirable features. A young lady who sees herself as beautiful seldom will admit that she thinks herself beautiful. Yet, the self-concept can be brought into awareness if a person, either with or without help, examines himself carefully. A recent study by Taylor (24) indicates that changes may occur in self-concept by repeated self-description.

Another thing of puzzling nature about the self-concept is that the person struggles to maintain and enhance the self-concept regardless of what it is or how he feels about it. A person who believes that he must give up feeling the way he does about himself is beset with the severest type of anxiety; and the concept becomes more rigidly fixed than before. This is more than simple resistance to change. To give up the self-concept that one has built over a period of years is more terrifying than facing a firing squad. It is psychological death.

As one examines history, he is impressed by example after example of men who have accounted physical danger and loss of life as nothing in order to preserve their concepts of self. Early Christian history is filled with examples of those who underwent torture and death without giving up their values.

If an experience in life is in keeping with the self-concept, then that experience is said to enhance the self-structure; if the experience is inconsistent with the concept of self, then such experience creates a threat. Thus, a college student who conceives himself as a top-ranking student is severely threatened by a failing or low grade, but the student who thinks of himself as a student of little ability is not threatened by low grades because low grades substantiate his self-concept.

These things are perhaps easy enough to understand; but it becomes more difficult when we postulate that the student who thinks of himself as a low-grade student would be severely threatened by making a high grade. The ordinary belief is that a person who experiences things that place him above his own concept of self would be elated at being rated higher than he expected.

According to self-concept theories, an experience inconsistent with self-concept threatens an individual whether such experience is at a higher or lower level than the conception. As a matter of fact, it is believed that a person, upon being made aware that his experiences do not conform to his concept of self, will deny the experiences or defend against them. A student who conceives himself as low-grade will be likely to think that the teacher who gives him a high grade is being partial to him; he is unlikely to think that he really deserves the grade.

The effect of experiences that do not conform to concept of self is so important to the practice of client-centered therapy that it is necessary to dwell on the subject for some time. The psychological threat to the self-organization that is felt by the person whose experiences indicate a higher-than-conceived rating cannot logically be the same as the threat that faces the person who experiences events in life that are below his concept of self. While both types of experiences do bring threat, the activation of the threat is different. Typically, the person who faces experiences that deny his high level of intelligence, friendliness, or other traits will be agitated by his experiences. He reacts with a great deal of anxiety and is usually driven to more and more effort in order to disprove experiences. He must prove at any cost that his concept is correct. He will be driven into more and more compulsive and relentless pursuits of his life goals.

On the other hand, the person who achieves above his conceived level may become despondent; he is likely to be morose and depressed because a supreme effort is not required of him. Actually, he has overperformed already. Typically, the person who is hard to motivate has a concept of self that is easy to reach and may be attained without a great deal of effort. Actually, this person is afraid to try hard for success because, if he does, he may disprove his concept of self as a person of low ability.

It is true that our culture develops more of the type of person who conceives of himself too highly. This is especially true of college students, most of whom have a rather high concept of themselves not only in the intellectual realm but in social realms as well. A person's reaction to experience is a good indicator of his concept of self. A person who is agitated by experiences that are below his concept of self is most likely to have a high concept of self. This illustrates, also, how difficult it is for the average person to evaluate correctly his self-concept. The person who suffers greatly because of failure in any field would interpret his emotions as feelings of inferiority. He does feel inferior, but his concept of self is likely to be just the opposite. If he did not conceive of himself as superior, he would not be threatened by experiences that showed him to be inferior by society's standards.

Only by a careful examination of self, can a person who feels inferior over failure come to understand that he really conceives himself as superior. Thus, the self-concept may be brought into awareness with great effort, although usually it is hidden from appraisal. Self-understanding is difficult to achieve; otherwise psychotherapy would not be needed.

The Nature of Maladjustment

The nature of psychological distress as understood in the framework of client-centered therapy is that a person is experiencing things in life out of context with the way he perceives himself. Thus, he lacks integration. All of us are able to understand that failure or success is relative, one person's failure may be evaluated as success by another. The thing that causes distress, then, is not experience itself but the way one evaluates experience as compared to what one thinks of self. Shostrom and Brammer (20), among others, have described maladjustment as being a dissimilarity between experiencing self and the self-concept or between the real self and the conceived self. It is supposed that experience will be an expression of the real self or the true self. If a person is intelligent, he will obtain good grades, barring the development of neurotic or physical barriers. If neurotic or physical barriers do arise, these will be expressed as a difference between the real self and the experiencing self. The aim in client-centered therapy is to make the experiencing self congruent with the real self. If a person experiences only those things that are consistent with the way he feels about himself, he will be happy and comfortable; if part of his experience is contrary to the way he feels about himself, he will be unhappy and maladjusted. Lecky (6) impresses us with the necessity of self-consistency. Psychological adjustment is possible only if the system is unified.

Rogers (12) has made the clearest expression of the requirements of adjustment in his article entitled "Becoming A Person." The contention is that the struggle that all men are engaged in is the struggle to be themselves, to experience the world according to the way they conceive themselves to be.

Man's single goal in life seems to be to become what he has conceived of himself as being. Every act is related to the effort to maintain and to enhance self. Every moment is filled with evaluating the world and all that is in it in terms of whether or not all the perceptions, both physical and psychological, will create a threat to the fulfillment of self or will bring about a greater possibility of accomplishing self-realization.

As Snygg and Combs (23) have indicated, the most important things to man are the self, the goals designed to bring the self into full accomplishment, and the techniques designed to accomplish these goals. It is somewhat amazing that we can relate our every activity to the matter of bringing about a realization of what we have conceived ourselves as being. As the writer types this page, he may purport to have many reasons for doing so. Perhaps he may admit financial reasons, prestige reasons, service motives and others; but underneath and intertwined with these reasons is the goal to be reached in terms of becoming what the author has conceived himself as being, a good writer, a financial success, and a person whom people will regard highly. No price is too high to pay for the goal of becoming oneself.

If the aim of client-centered therapy is to make experiencing self the same as self-concept, the eventual question which arises is which must change, the self-concept or experience. The proper answer to this is that the self-concept must be changed initially. Research by Raimy (9) demonstrates that change in self-concept from negative to positive attitudes toward self is accompanied by improvement in adjustment. Usually it is true that experiences are a less than perfect portrayal of the real self because the tension which accompanies maladjustment prevents the person from experiencing in accordance with the real capacities. The person who makes a failing grade may have been capable intellectually of making passing grades of low level, but this ability is graded downward by the agitation that comes from experiencing below anticipation.

But still, the basic difficulty in maladjustment must be a faulty self-concept, and this must be the beginning point in treatment. As the self-concept is changed to come nearer the real and experiencing self, it will be possible for tension to be removed; this in turn will permit the person to function at or near the capacity of the real self. So both experience and self-concept must change in therapy. The person not only becomes satisfied with the products that evolve from the real self in action, but this satisfaction actually upgrades the performance of the real self to maximum efficiency.

What, then, has happened to the person who has become maladjusted? Is it that he wishes to become what he conceives himself to be and cannot do so? Is it that he is pursuing a goal and does not know how to go about achieving it? Or is it that he has set his goals too high and that realistically he cannot become what he wishes to become? It may be any of these things. The maladjusted person may have his goals above his possibilities of accomplishment, or he may have capabilities of accomplishing these goals; but he may be attempting to accomplish them by inadequate and amateurish methods. On the other hand, he may have become so defensive and engrossed in defending against failure that he is incapacitated in moving forward toward self-accomplishment— toward becoming the person he wishes to be.

Self-Theory and Tension

According to Snygg and Combs (23), tension arises from two related situations in experience. Every experience either enhances the self or is hurtful to it. Either enhancement or inconsistency to the self results in tension; but the enhancing tension may be thought of as basically pleasurable tension, while the fear of inconsistency or actual inconsistency brings about disagreeable tensions.

Let us suppose that a certain public speaker has a self-concept of himself as a public speaker of the highest type. If this is his self-concept, it follows that he will approach each opportunity to speak with a great deal of tension. First, he will have tension that is related to the opportunity he has of enhancing self, of proving himself to be what he thinks he is; second, he will have tensions of the type related to his fear of doing a poor speaking job and of making a fool of himself before his audience.

Every experience in life brings about some tension. The amount of tension will depend upon the clarity of perception as it relates to enhancement or threat to self. For instance, the concert pianist perceives his practice period as enhancing his concept of himself as a "great" pianist; but he does not differentiate this experience with as much clarity in terms of self-enhancement as he does the actual performance on the stage before an audience. The clarity with which a person perceives threat, however, does not depend upon reality. For instance, a clergyman may feel threatened because of a small audience since his possibilities of enhancing self are limited. An inexperienced speaker would be threatened by a large crowd because he cannot conceive of himself as a speaker. Neither large nor small crowds are really threatening in the objective sense.

In short, the amount of tension an experience produces is related to the awareness the person has concerning the possibility of the experience either to enhance or to threaten his self-organization. Every individual is striving each moment to protect himself from physical harm; he is trying with much more fervor to protect his self-organization from being shattered or destroyed.

A Concept of Neurotic Anxiety

In self-theory, tension has been explained as related to the threatening and the enhancing aspects of the phenomenal field. The same ideas concerning the figure and ground differentiation may be used to describe neurotic or free-floating anxiety. As an individual moves about, there are undoubtedly impressions both physical and psychological hovering in the background of perception, which come slightly into figure and recede again into ground, but which are never differentiated or brought into awareness at a higher level. These are often thought of as threats of an assiduous nature, not as severe and easily recognizable threats, but as unidentifiable and obscure threats which cannot be dispelled because they cannot be clearly discerned and differentiated into awareness.

Many of these peripheral threats to the self are residues of childhood which if brought into differentiation at a high level could be dealt with, but because of their lack of clarity cannot be dealt with. These remain as "ghosts" of the past and result in a steady but indistinguishable source of anxiety. A man who may think of himself as warm and affectionate in his relationship with women may have a peripheral threat occasioned by a rejecting grandmother which invades his phenomenal field as a peripheral differentiation each time he has a visual perception of an older woman. In such event, the man would be uneasy, suffering from threat to the self-concept without having the vaguest idea of why he felt anxiety. Such anxiety blocks his full development as the person he would like to become, because he is not able to deal with the threat that he cannot differentiate from ground into figure.

THE GOALS OF THERAPY

The goals of therapy have been stated by several authorities in different terms but with fairly common meaning; by Rogers (12) as aiding the individual to become himself—to become what the person conceives himself as being; by Lecky (6) as aiding a person to remove from his life all conflicting aims and desires—to become self-consistent and integrated; by Shostrom and Brammer (20) as bringing experience and self-concept into conformity; by Raimy (9) as promoting self-approval through reorganization of self-concept. Rogers describes most lucidly what occurs when psychological adjustment is achieved:

> It would appear that when all the ways in which the individual perceives himself—all perceptions of the qualities, abilities, impulses, and attitudes of the person, and all perceptions of himself in relation to others—are accepted into the organized conscious concept of the self, then this achievement is accompanied by feelings of comfort and freedom from tension which are experienced as psychological adjustment (16, p. 364).

The question that must now be answered is, "How is this psychological adjustment brought about?" Regardless of the manner of expression, all the goals quoted above are essentially the same and demand the same initial accomplishment; namely, a reorganization of the self-concept—a change toward a more realistic appraisal of self so that experiences do not threaten the individual by inconsistencies between what the person is and what he feels he is.

To effect a change in self-concept may be regarded by the uninitiated as a minor affair. It may seem to some observers that a change in concept of self should quickly follow insight into the unrealities of the self-picture. In the first place, insight into the faulty self-picture is not easy to bring about, since the individual is highly resistant to such insights. They bring about disintegration of that most cherished possession, the self-concept. But even after insight has come, the change in self-concept is difficult to effect because of the threat produced by the very thought of reorganization. The truth is that the individual is torn between two conflicting desires, the desire to change concept and effect psychological adjustment and the desire to maintain the self as perceived—both desires are strong but incompatible.

The Removal of Threat

The greatest effort in client-centered therapy, then, is toward the removal of the threat that arises as the self-concept is approached. This threat must be removed or the faulty concept will become more rigid and more incapable of change. The removal of threat is the chief target of all the methodology that has been derived for the practicing client-centered therapist. The reader should keep in mind that all discussion past this point is aimed at indicating the methodology of threat removal, but that this methodology cannot be revealed all at once. A fuller understanding of client-centered method dictates a gradual and careful approach.

TECHNIQUES IN CLIENT-CENTERED THERAPY

Thwarted Needs and Defenses

It has been postulated previously that the basic need of the individual is to maintain and enhance self-organization. When experience tends to disprove the validity of the self-structure, the organism immediately builds a bulwark of defense. Defense typically distorts the true problem; and, as defense is added to defense, the possibility of the client's breaking through to the real issue becomes more and more remote.

Many therapeutic disciplines emphasize the authority and superiority of the counseling person. In an atmosphere where the therapist proposes to examine the client and to diagnose and direct him toward his better adjustment, it is inevitable that the client will fall back upon his line of defense and lose the ability of self-examination.

The Underlying Drive for Self-improvement

Client-centered therapy has become strongly identified with the fundamental premise of belief in the integrity of the individual. The belief is that the individual has a strong drive toward health and that he not only can but *will* move toward better adjustment, provided there is an adequate atmosphere for his growth. The drive of the individual client is thought of as the motivating force behind all his improvement; and the role of the counselor is conceived as providing atmosphere and opportunity for the client to vault over his defenses and shake himself free of all inhibitions blocking his more perfect adjustment. Changes in adjustment are not brought about by the counselor; they are products of the client's own strivings for self-realization.

Choice of Clients

Obviously, the assumption that the individual has the ability to effect his own changes, make his own adjustments, and execute his own plans could not apply to every individual. Indubitably, there are individuals who have no such ability, and who may be unable to respond because of factors of age, intellect, or crippling mental deterioration. There are clients who respond well to client-centered methods just as there are clients who respond to other methods of therapy.

Rogers indicates that the client best suited for this type of therapy, based as it is upon the drive for health and the capacities for growth residing in the client, could be judged according to the following factors:

> From the material given in the previous portions of this chapter, it would seem that direct counseling treatment of the individual, involving planned and continued contacts, is advisable provided all of the following conditions exist:
>
> 1. The individual is under a degree of tension, arising from incompatible personal desires or from the conflict of social and

environmental demands with individual needs. The tension and stress so created are greater than the stress involved in expressing his feelings about his problems.

2. The individual has some capacity to cope with life. He possesses adequate ability and stability to exercise some control over the elements of his situation. The circumstances with which he is faced are not so adverse or so unchangeable as to make it impossible for him to control or alter them.

3. There is opportunity for the individual to express his conflicting tensions in planned contacts with the counselor.

4. He is able to express these tensions and conflicts either verbally or through other media. A conscious desire for help is advantageous, but not entirely necessary.

5. He is reasonably independent, either emotionally or spatially, of close family control.

6. He is reasonably free from excessive instabilities, particularly of an organic nature.

7. He possesses adequate intelligence for coping with his life situation, with an intelligence rating of dull-normal or above.

8. He is of suitable age—old enough to deal somewhat independently with life, young enough to retain some elasticity of adjustment. In terms of chronological age this might mean roughly from ten to sixty (11, pp. 76-77).

It has been asserted in previous contexts that the clergyman and other religious counselors are not able to chose counselees as others are able to do. For this reason, the religious counselor will not be able to use the client-centered method exclusively. It is possible and perhaps advisable that the religious counselor adopt the client-centered method as a basis for exploratory counseling. As the initial session progresses, the counselor may evaluate the client and his problem to determine whether or not he fits the conditions outlined by Rogers or unstated criteria set up by the individual counselor. If the parishioner fits the criteria, client-centered method may be implemented; if he does not fit, another method may be utilized or the parishioner may be referred.

Acceptance of the Client

The client must come to understand the inadequacy of his self-organization in terms of accounting for all his experiences. As long as he has experiences which he cannot accept into the conscious concept of self, he cannot become fully integrated. But there is no way that the counselor, by his own power, can bring about an awareness on the client's part concerning his erroneous and inadequate concept of himself.

The atmosphere conducive to self-evaluation and insight into faulty self-organization, as well as the atmosphere necessary to remove threat from the area of changing concepts, can be achieved only as the counselor is willing to accept the client as he is, to believe implicitly in the client's powers of growth, and to refuse to violate his autonomy and integrity. In such an atmosphere, the client is able to face himself honestly and squarely, perhaps for the first time; and he has no need to distort the picture with defenses. In all his human relationships he has found it necessary to present a "front" or a façade which has prevented adequate self-examination. There is no necessity for this in the permissive atmosphere, since the counselor presents an accepting demeanor regardless of events.

Acceptance of the client, in the language of client-centered therapy, means much more than the term does in other contexts. It means acceptance not only of the person as he is now, but acceptance of him as he may have been in the past and as he may choose to be in the future. The counselor makes no plans for the growth of the client; he simply endeavors to help him become free to grow in whatever direction he may choose.

It must be reiterated here that the clergyman often experiences extreme difficulty in accepting the client. Most clergymen are able to accept the client as he is; but some are unable to accept the client's decision to move in directions incompatible with religious concepts of proper living. The author makes no assertion that the religious counselor *must* accept the decision of the client to move in religiously and socially unacceptable directions; however, in presenting the psychological approach of client-centered therapy, the author is impelled to maintain the frame of reference of the clinical psychologists who have described the method.

Most clergymen work within a framework of convictions concerning the need of religious conversion and dedication, and they cannot logically be expected to allow people to leave the counseling session with avowed plans to move in directions perceived by the clergyman as contrary to the purposes and will of God. Most clergymen will depart from any planned therapeutic procedure in favor of what seems to be the leadership of God. The psychologist can only respect the rights of the clergyman to follow his conscience.

To accept a person without reservation does not come as an easy gesture to many people, even those outside the clergy. In fact, many people are *incapable* of such an act. Acceptance must be consonant with the over-all philosophy of life held by the counselor. He must believe that people are products of their heredity and past experiences and that they have been directed into whatever paths they have followed by events and circumstances largely beyond their control. The counselor must embrace a philosophy of life that assigns great value to every individual and recognizes the right of every person to choose for himself. If this is not the basic philosophy of the counselor, he will be unable to refrain from subtly directing the movement of counseling along lines that he has conceived as being desirable for the client (17).

The permissive atmosphere of the counseling scene has been described in another context but must be reiterated here. In therapy, the permissive atmosphere is more meaningful than in counseling for decision or for personal problems. The client feels warmth, responsiveness, acceptance, and understanding from the counselor (19). He feels freedom from pressure or coercion, and complete freedom of self-expression. There is no moral approval or disapproval. There is no praise or approbation; there is neither support nor antagonism.

Conveying Acceptance and Permissive Atmosphere

The client-centered counselor typically is envisioned as a person who says little and allows the client free expression. However, it is true that the counselor's simply refraining from talk does little in itself to convey the accepting atmosphere. The importance of the counselor's acceptance of the client has been emphasized; and it could be claimed that unless the counselor feels warmly toward the client, nothing he may do will convey the permissive atmosphere. However, counselor philosophy cannot be readily ascertained by the client unless the counselor has made some effort to make the client aware of it.

There is difference of opinion on the subject of telling the client about the atmosphere and plan of counseling. In the early stages of development of client-centered method, it was thought very necessary to explain the plan of counseling to the counselee; and this explanation usually included a description of the atmosphere of warmth and understanding. More recent evaluations emphasize the logic of promoting a warm atmosphere without the counselor's attempting to describe it to the client (11).

The counseling clergyman needs to give special consideration to the matter of initial structuring. Usually, he has been cast in a judgmental role before the client for considerable time. It is most difficult for the parishioner to accept the permissive atmosphere with his clergyman. The clergyman who utilizes client-centered methods should take time to speak with the parishioner concerning his need to be somewhat judgmental in the pulpit and his sincere desire to be accepting and nonjudgmental in the counseling chamber.

Such an assertion as this will not go unchallenged. There are psychologists who feel that nothing is gained by a counselor's telling a client that he is nonjudgmental. Some feel that the demonstrated warmth of the counselor will carry over to the client and that expressing the intended warmth will cause the client to doubt that the counselor can achieve it. Nevertheless, the clergyman is in a special category here; an explanation of the different role may be helpful.

Typical structuring activity may follow an approach similar to that in the following counselor remarks:

> I know that you must be wondering just what type of counseling we do here. Most clients do gain by having some understanding of this. Now, the counselors in our clinic do not believe the client is helped most by their assuming the responsibility for what is said and done. We believe that a client such as you has the ability to make his own decisions and to take the lead in talking about the things which are bothering him. I will just listen mostly and will be here to offer some assistance to you to help you clear up your ideas about things.
>
> We have found that most people can be helped by just talking out their difficulties and by gaining new ideas and attitudes. Since you are the only one who knows what you want out of life and out of this counseling experience, I am going to leave it in your hands not only to choose what we shall talk about but also to decide how long to continue to talk about your problems. Now why don't you begin by talking about the thing that troubles you most?

If the above could be regarded as good initial structuring, it would still be likely that structuring would have to be repeated every now and then in order to keep the plan before the counselee. It is not at all illogical to believe, as some counselors do, that the client will come into possession of the understandings necessary for client-centered counseling without any structuring being done at all. He would just come to feel the permissiveness and would accept his leading role in counseling because the counselor would cleverly lead him into these understandings.

Voluntary Client Expression

The theories of client-centered counseling place a great deal of importance upon the voluntary nature of the client's expressions and the maintenance of the lead by the client. Realistically, these theories do not always work to perfection and, perhaps, it may be said that they were not intended to be accepted as ironclad policies. At any rate, the aim in counseling is to keep the client expressing and exploring his attitudes with great freedom. As explained by Porter (8) there is little probability that the client may achieve his goals through counseling unless he can bring himself to express and explore the problems that face him. Sometimes the client may need a little help in getting started with his exploration. Some have envisioned the client-centered counselor as one who sits and waits until the client begins to express himself. The counselor may fear he will block progress by giving the client support. One critic describes the counselor's behavior as "stilted and inane" (25). Client-centered therapy is not basically a supportive therapy because support breeds dependency and defense; but this does not mean that the client-centered counselor refuses to offer support and help of various types toward getting the client started on his verbal conquests. To present a coldly refusing demeanor to the client would damage the maintenance of a permissive and warm atmosphere, especially in the religious setting; and the atmosphere is more important than strict adherence to theory. It has been suggested by some that "friendly conversation" is entirely proper to create warmth (22). Usually, when a client has been energized even from an external source, he is able to continue his movement from the internal source of energy.

In short, client-centered counselors usually find it necessary to build initial rapport with the client, utilizing all the methods commonly used in all types of interviewing. The maintenance of good rapport is essential, and may not always be best initiated or maintained by dogmatic adherence to rigid stereotyped counselor behavior. The permissive and nondirective atmosphere must be the ultimate aim; but realistically, they may best be achieved with some more reluctant clients by a reasonably high level of participation by the counselor during early stages.

Actually, it is possible to give support without being supportive (10). Supportive therapy has been identified with the efforts on the part of the counselor to place props under the client, to undergird him with the counselor's strength and wisdom. Encouraging the client to strike out on his own, giving assurance of interest and otherwise implementing the warm and permissive atmosphere, as well as allaying the slight embarrassment some clients have in beginning a strange experience are not actually supportive, although they are supporting.

Clarification of Feeling

The beginning counselor may be so concerned with "not directing" that he is blocked in his efforts to provide an atmosphere and "helping hand" for the client's freedom of expression, understanding, and integration of self. It is the considered aim of the client-centered therapist not to coerce, direct, or influence the client in his explorations of self and environment. Some methods for approaching this aim have been suggested. It is not realistic for the counselor to remain silent; this would create a threat for most clients. Granted that the typical counselor talks too much, it may also be possible for a counselor to talk too little. Once the true therapeutic atmosphere has been entered, the question may resolve into a consideration of what the counselor may say and do that would not be directive, coercive, or influential upon the client's movement and feeling.

In all that he does, the experienced counselor is less concerned with the possibility that he may be casting directive influence and is more concerned with helping the client find his way through the labyrinth of confused thoughts, motives, and attitudes that are his.

The most successful method of accomplishing this has been described in the literature as "clarification of feeling."

It should be remembered that the difficulty the client is experiencing is derived from an inability to perceive clearly the differences between his self-organization—what he feels himself to be—and the realities of self that are dictated by his inherent and acquired abilities and potentialities. The need is for the client to approach again and again his personal organization and reality factors until insight breaks through concerning the variations in these two. This can be done only if the client can examine his expressed feelings without resorting to defenses and other distorting phenomena.

In order to assist the client in this action, the counselor attempts to clarify feelings expressed by the client. Clarification may consist of restatement of the client's expressions with the belief that having the statements mirrored back may cause an understanding not present when the statements were uttered by the client. Further than this, the counselor may rephrase the content and feeling expressed in order to effect a deeper understanding on the part of the client. Combs (3) equates clarification of feeling with clarification of personal meaning. This is a worthwhile comparison, since what the counselor is really concerned about is helping the client understand what he means when he says something. It is typical of confused persons to say things that are fraught with meaning, but the true meaning has not been brought to the surface for conscious examination. The meaning is in the expression but not always understood by the client.

Toward the end of facilitating understanding of expression, the client-centered counselor often responds with such statements as "You feel that your brother doesn't like you," or "You think that you would have been better off if you had never started college." While clarification of feeling is undoubtedly the most important method in client-centered work, it is also a method which can be bent to the purposes of a counselor who really wishes to direct the client; and it is a method that deserves much study on the part of the counselor. It is the tendency of beginning counselors to think that any statement that begins "you feel" or "you think" is a desirable statement. This is far from true.

There are many considerations involved in making good reflections for the purpose of clarifying feeling. The event that follows such counselor statements should be a continuation of expression by the client. If a clarifying statement by the counselor causes the client to stop his train of thought, the statement is a poor one. Many counselors phrase their clarifying statements in such a way and speak in such a tone that the client must respond by agreement or disagreement. He must say, "Yes, that's right" or "No, that's not it." Usually, having to respond in this manner interrupts a continuing process of thought. The counselor's statement and tone should allow the client to concede, perhaps with a slow shake of the head, and then to continue his expression. Some counselors use clarification as an opportunity to interpret and to receive the approbation of the client for having stated the proposition fairly and squarely.

Statements by the counselor which pose as clarification of feeling may represent a very subtle interpretation and directiveness by the counselor (5). For instance, a client may be talking about his brother and the business deal which the two entered together. He may tell about the failure of the business and the ability of his brother to get out of the deal without being hurt while he, the client, was financially ruined by it. The counselor may say, "You feel that your brother treated you unfairly in this." Such a statement is directive unless the client by word, manner, or reflection has indicated some feeling in this direction. It becomes quite apparent that method does not make a counselor directive or nondirective. Method can be bent to serve basic philosophy. At the same time, the counselor who has every intention of allowing a client to control the interview may examine his notes or listen to his tape recordings and see how he has manipulated the clarification of feeling toward an interpretative direction for the client.

The following excerpt is taken from a recorded interview between an eighteen-year-old college freshman and a religiously oriented counselor. This excerpt is from the second interview. During the first interview a discussion of religion ensued; and it seems obvious that the counselor decided that the issue of religion was fundamental to the maladjustment of the client. The reflections are off-center in every case and indicate that the counselor was trying to return to the subject of religion and to direct the interview by his interpretative reflections. Only a small portion of the interview is given here. The section of the tape recording that follows this excerpt reveals a loss of rapport and a floundering until the end of the interview.

> C. I guess the reason I am so interested in the test I had in high school is that—well, back then the record was clear and everything was all right. I know everything was all right then, and now I don't know. So maybe we can go back there and go forward. Maybe that's the reason I'm so interested in that test.
>
> T. You mean, that the way you have it figured, something happened along about there.
>
> C. Well, no, I wouldn't exactly say that. It seems to me that at that time I was more settled and I knew what I wanted to do or something. Now, I'm just a mixed up kid.
>
> T. You feel like you are more mixed up now than you were when you were in high school.
>
> C. Probably so—could be the other way around though.
>
> T. You think that when you got out in the world away from the protecting influence of your home, you sort of got mixed up.
>
> C. Well, I don't know as I'd go it that strong. You remember last week we were talking about my religion and you know I never did tell you what my religion was. Well—ah, I've been thinking about that, and, well, I got to thinking maybe you thought I was an atheist or something like that. Well, maybe I am (laughs), but not quite.
>
> T. You think religion is one of the areas about which you are confused or which is responsible for some of your mixed-up feelings.
>
> C. Possibly that. But what I meant was that last week I was afraid you just didn't understand that I had some religious beliefs too. You know—that I'm really not an atheist.

Faulty clarifications of feelings such as those found in the preceding interview material emphasize the need for the internal framework in counseling. If a counselor finds that his clarifications, one after the other, are not being accepted by the client, he should be able to guess that he is not residing in the internal framework of the individual, but is attempting to clarify from the external point of view. This is typical of what happens when the philosophical directive counselor attempts to apply methods of client-centered therapy without changing his philosophy. He will be sitting there constantly evaluating the client, when he should be moving with the client in his internal framework. He should have strong identification with the client, with sufficient empathic understanding to get a strong implication of the client's feeling;

yet, he should have enough detachment to operate intellectually toward helping the client clarify his meanings.

The following excerpt is taken from an interview with a twenty-five-year-old salesman who was referred to the counseling specialist in the church. The parishioner came to the clergyman following divorce. His complaint was that he could not find the drive to return to his job following separation from his wife and children. He had not wanted divorce but acquiesced because his wife desired it. The reflections here are good and helped the client to gain some worthwhile insights.

C. Well, I guess I've been feeling as good as anyone would who has just been divorced. I guess it's just normal to feel kind of torn up. Isn't it?

T. You think it's just normal to feel a little badly under the circumstances.

C. Uh huh. That's the way I feel—but—I've been kind of encouraged. The only thing I do feel badly about is I still don't have any ambition to go back to work.

T. You still don't care too much whether you go back to work or not.

C. Yeah, yeah, I do! Well, it's not really the ambition, I don't guess. It's the drive. I'm sick of not working, being idle—but I don't, uh, well, I don't feel driven. Always before when I had the kids, doggone it—I'd just tie right into it. But now—well, I feel closer to it than I did. I tell you what, I just don't feel I have any self-confidence. And I just wonder what it means.

T. You feel like you are lacking in self-confidence but you don't know why.

C. I have periods now when I just want to take off and go to work. It's hard to explain. Actually, I want to work; I don't like to be idle at all. But it seems like I can't reach back and grasp the self-confidence I used to have—you know what I mean.

T. You feel like you had the self-confidence at one time, but not any more.

C. Uh huh, uh huh! Oh, I'm crazy about my job. I want to work. But I'm just wondering if I do go back to work, if I can hold out at it, or will it be the same thing over again.

T. You're just wondering if you do go back to work if you'll slack off and not be able to keep your quota up.

C. With the grasp I've got on the job—that I know I have, it just seems I'm ready and just waiting for the signal to go ahead.

T. You feel that you are just waiting for the light to turn green.

C. Yeah! Does that sound reasonable?

Clarification and Rapport

Good clarification of feeling presupposes that the counselor is able to maintain the internal framework of the client. But at the same time, it is necessary that the counselor move just ahead of the client and make judgments concerning the client's clarity of understanding of things being expressed. If the counselor believes that the client understands the full implications of his expressions, he will not feel that clarification is in order, but that a continuation of expression is better. So the counselor, although he is presumably in the internal frame of reference, must remain uninvolved, emotionally, to the extent that he is able to recognize the lack of complete understanding on the part of the client and to clarify it.

There is little question that the counselor must gamble to an extent when he attempts clarification. As is seen in many protocols, clarifications often do not work out. However, just because the client reacts negatively to a clarification does not mean that the clarification is incorrect; this might represent what the analyst calls resistance. As a matter of fact, a negative reaction may cause the client to work harder and may bring about a positive insight.

The technique of clarification of feeling draws upon the artistic abilities of the counselor to the utmost. He must stay near the client in his internal framework, and yet maintain his ability to judge rapport and to make decisions concerning the time and content of reflections. In the final analysis, a reflection aimed at clarifying feeling gambles with the possibility that the clarification may be incorrect. Such an improper reflection may stultify the therapeutic process. Yet, the determining factor involved in both the selection of feelings to be clarified and the manner in which such clarifications are attempted must be the perceived level of rapport. With good rapport, improper clarifications are simply shrugged off by the client, ignored, and not allowed to interrupt progress.

A good counselor does not gamble heavily upon arousing possible negative reactions to clarifications if he perceives a low level of rapport; if rapport is high enough, no clarification, regardless of its nature, will threaten the client unduly. Thus, the heavier odds may be accepted by the counselor.

For those who may object to these thoughts on the basis that they prevail too much on the judgmental qualities of the counselor, let it be said that the judgment of the counselor concerning what direction clarifications shall take are not directive unless the counselor is disposed to make them so. If the aim is indelibly one of helping the client to see himself and his relationships more clearly, then clarifications, which represent decisions on the part of the counselor and which are admitted to contain elements of chance, are not directive but exploratory.

What the counselor does or says in the interview is going to be influenced unavoidably by the rapport level. If rapport is good, even direct questions destined to open doors to understanding for the client may sometimes be in order. The counselor who is philosophically nondirective will not utilize any device for directing the client. He will be so engrossed in sponsoring a permissive atmosphere and freedom of expression of the client along lines of the client's own choice that he will not be tempted to exercise his own subjective and projected decisions. The counselor who is philosophically directive will direct no matter what methodology he uses.

Tests and Case Histories

The use of evaluative instruments and background information about clients is minimal in client-centered practice (13). Some counselors feel that it is an asset to know various background factors about the client as an aid to moving within his internal framework. Most therapists are content, however, to glean those background facts that might be helpful, from interview material. The thinking is that a client will reveal whatever is important and whatever he wishes the counselor to know about himself. On the other hand, if the client knows that the counselor has information about him at hand, he may be threatened by it and his freedom from the perceived judgmental attitude of the counselor may be impaired. Since many aspects of background and test information may be threatening, it is usually best to approach these facts only as the client becomes ready to do so.

Many counselors agree that prior knowledge of a client would impair their functioning in the client-centered interview. When everything is taken into consideration, background information would be more hindrance than help in therapy of this type. It is true, however, that counseling at lower levels with personal and choice problems may benefit from such information; and some counselors, operating within a broad philosophical framework of client-centered theories, use tests and background material in many ways to advantage. As Rogers (11) expresses it, client-centered counselors find tests most useful in counseling when such tests are suggested by the client.

Insight and Therapeutic Progress

Client-centered therapy may be called insight therapy. Insight is usually thought of as a clear understanding of some fact or relationship that had not been clearly understood before. It has been called the "aha" experience or the "now I see" experience. A concept that has remained difficult to defend in client-centered therapy is that of emotional insight. It seems that some insights may be brought about by astute interpretations of counselors who have a gift for exploring the dynamics of another and for deriving the correct explanation of behavior and feeling. These insights, derived by the counselor, are interpreted to the client and he perceives them intellectually. Intellectual insights may be forced upon the client; he may agree to the reasonableness of certain assumptions, but he may not fully accept them, or at least they may not bring about a change in behavior.

Insights develop in client-centered therapy in a different manner. They do not come through the astuteness of the counselor; they come through the free explorations of the client. He brings about his own insights. As a result, it is thought that these glimpses into reality are more meaningful; they occur at a strategic moment when the client is ready for them. As a result, too, the insights are usually tinged with emotion, the client feels them deeply, and they are more conducive to change in the self-pattern.

Rogers (18) designates these as "spontaneous insights." He equates insights with "self-understanding" and indicates a four-fold dimension of such understandings of self: (1) an acceptance of one's impulses and attitudes, good or bad, including attitudes previously repressed; (2) an understanding of the patterning of one's behavior, the perception of new relationships; (3) a fresh perception of reality made possible by this acceptance and understanding of the self; and (4) the planning of new and more satisfying ways in which the self can adjust to reality.

Under criticism concerning the claims for emotional insights, the client-centered people have difficulty explaining how insights can develop except through exclusively intellectual pursuit. Most client-centered authorities stand firm in their insistence that a different type of insight is developed by allowing the client freedom of thought and expression. It is thought that emotional insight produces change whereas intellectual insight does not do so in such a dramatic way.

Insufficiency of Insight Alone

Although client-centered therapy is known as an insight therapy, no one claims that insight alone is enough to effect a change in self-concept and in ways of evaluating experiences. Even emotional insight must have an ally to bring about so difficult a task as changing self-organization. It should be clear to the reader at this point that this other ally is the atmosphere of the counseling scene, emphasizing the relationship with the counselor which promotes the dissipation of threat and allows the insight to be felt deeply. Such insight and atmosphere as this allows the client to see himself, accept himself, and change himself to fit his new understandings of environment and its demands upon him.

Difficulty of Remaining Nondirective

Under the best of circumstances and with the most positive philosophy in terms of the client's control of the interview, the clergyman and his co-workers will find it difficult to maintain nondirectiveness and nonsupport of the client. Most clients will bid for counselor support and direction at every stage of the treatment in spite of frequent reminders from the counselor concerning the nature of the interview. Some clients are so eager for support and direction that they will set traps for the counselor; the average client feels that he understands and accepts the atmosphere of noninterference on the part of the counselor, but on the other hand he continues to seek support, interpretation, and direction unconsciously.

One of the ways the client bids for support is to ask the counselor questions. Parrying questions without giving direction or support is a constant challenge to the counselor. Some questions should be answered. Those that may be answered with factual information do not usually force the counselor into a supportive or directing role. Other questions may be turned back to the client for his answer, and some may be ignored. A common method for handling questions and also for moving therapy forward is to restructure the conversation back to some point and upon some subject that provided interest earlier but which was not exhausted at the time. The counselor might say, "Now, as I remember, we were discussing your relationship with your sister a while ago. I wonder if you have explored that as far as you would like?" Restructuring may serve to move away from a question which the counselor cannot answer nondirectively, or it may be used to bring an end to a long silence.

Other Reflective Techniques

Most of the counselor statements in client-centered therapy are reflective in nature; the counselor mirrors back to the client his statements, feelings, and attitudes. Clarification of feeling is a type of reflection and there are other uses for reflective techniques. Simple reflection and simple acceptance of client ideas are common techniques which serve to convince the client of a continued interest of the counselor. As the client makes a statement and watches the counselor for his understanding gestures, the counselor may simply say "Yes" or "I see." These are simple acceptances of what the client is saying and may not deserve the designation of reflection.

Simple reflections are usually concerned with the content of statements by the client. The counselor may say, "You saw your mother again last week." Such reflections or restatements merely allow the client to be sure that the counselor is following and give the client time to collect thoughts for the pursuance of expression. These expressions by the counselor should not be given with a dead-pan look and expression. The over-all result of reflections should be to cause the client to feel that he is being understood and that the counselor is quietly waiting for him to continue. Some reflections may serve the purpose of helping the counselor to be sure of the meaning of the client's statements.

Many counseling protocols of reflective techniques sound quite stilted and strained. It may seem that the counselor is simply echoing the words of the client. To the client and counselor, both of whom are engrossed in the client's explorations, the exchange usually appears very reasonable and devoid of triteness.

RELATIONSHIP IN CLIENT-CENTERED COUNSELING

It has already been said that the relationship between counselor and client should be one of warmth and friendliness, but this is not to say that these two people should develop an affectional relationship. It should be one of helpful friendship, but not an intimate one. Beyond this aspect is the fact that transference relationships as seen in analytical counseling are not encouraged in client-centered work. Actually, transference does develop, but is not utilized in therapy, and to a certain extent is guarded against. The thinking is that a person cannot feel the hoped-for permissiveness of the counseling relation if he perceives the counselor as some figure out of the past toward whom he possibly feels hostility or affection (26). Such a relationship would block self-analysis and self-understanding, because the client would be endeavoring to play a role before the transference figure. Defenses would likely spring up to obviate the complete freedom of the client.

Some authorities have suggested that the proper identification of the counselor by the client is that of a second self—the alter ego. The reflective techniques should accentuate this identification. Since the counselor voices all the feelings, attitudes, and ideals of the client, he may be unconsciously thought of as a second self. As the client talks to his counselor, he is talking to himself, but not to the self he has talked to before. This real self has been critical, judgmental, and unrelenting. The alter ego is accepting and unthreatening and, as such, may effect the withdrawal of defenses and make possible a full understanding of the inadequacies of the self-concept without the usual severe threat imposed by the fact that the self is inadequate to the demands of experience. As a matter of fact, the presence of the alter ego does much to allay the threat that accompanies any suggestion of change in self-organization. The self-structure may be visualized as a dark cavern which is frightening to the client and which he has not dared enter, examine thoroughly, and rearrange. With the comforting presence of this alter ego—this second self, who demonstrates no fear of the dark cavern of the self—it becomes possible for the client figuratively to turn the searching white light upon the self-structure, to ascertain that certain changes are essential in order to integrate self-concept and experience, and to make some revisions.

PACING THE INTERVIEW

Early concepts of the client-centered counselor who has no control at all of interviews are fading. The counselor must exercise some types of control; but they are all aimed at the maintenance of the freedom of expression of the client and his being able to gain from his own productions (1).

In this connection, it is considered a part of the artistry of the client-centered counselor for him to be able to pace the interview in order that the client may make the greatest gain. Some clients enter the interview situation with a strong compulsion to talk, others are very reluctant to do so. The compulsive talker may spend hour after hour expounding upon every subject imaginable, but with no profit. Some of these people talk excessively to keep from having attention turned to problem areas. They may feel that if they can just keep talking rapidly it will be possible to escape the pain of self-inquiry. The slow person may be using another approach to gain the same end. At any rate, there is an optimum rate or pace for each client which, realistically, must be set by the counselor. He may have need to slow down the fast pacer and to motivate the slow-moving person.

Pacing is best learned through experience, but the student may learn some things about it before having practice. The fast talker can be slowed down sometimes by the counselor's interrupting and making a statement of one type or another in a somewhat apathetic manner. The client will usually fall into the pacing of the counselor or at least will modify his own movement to correspond to the exaggerated pace of the counselor. The activity of the counselor in this sense may be compared to that of the choir director. By demonstration or by various physical movements he may slow things down or speed them up.

Handling and Utilizing Silences to Advantage

Because the handling of silences is such an individual thing, and because it draws upon somewhat intuitive and even subliminal impressions by the counselor in action, few writers have attempted to suggest general rules applying to different types of silence. We are made conscious that there are two divisions of the counseling interview, the verbal and nonverbal divisions. No one has yet been able to say which of these is more important.

Many writers have emphasized the constructive aspects of silences. The beginning counselor typically dreads silences and feels threatened by them. In order to overcome this threat, some writers seemingly have gone to great lengths to assure the student that silences are desirable and not to be feared. The truth is that silences may be desirable or they may be undesirable.

As a general rule, it might be said that silences that embarrass, confuse, or threaten either the counselor or client are undesirable. Contrary to the beliefs of some that benefit is derived from the counselor's allowing the client to sweat through a silence until he breaks under it and emerges with choice insights, this author believes nothing is gained from uncomfortable silences.

In keeping with this, silence handling is related to the rapport level in the interview. In the presence of good rapport, a silence may be maintained indefinitely without distressing either counselor or client. Valuable work is usually being done by the client during these silences in which he feels no threat or embarrassment. The counselor and client are like two good friends who do not have to fill the air with conversation in order to maintain comfort.

It is the duty of the counselor to maintain control of the silences; but good counseling never necessitates the breaking of them by a client because of the discomfort of it. The client should end most lapses in conversation because he has a new and meaningful expression. The counselor should be the guardian of uncomfortable silences and should bring them to an end when they become oppresive to the client.

All this means that shorter silences should be the rule during first interviews—during the time when strong rapport is being built. Indeed, oppressive silences are a hazard to rapport. All other things being equal, one would expect that the longer the acquaintance between counselor and client, the stronger the rapport will be; and the more deep-running the client's exploration, the longer the silences may be to his benefit.

Since the main part of the verbal interaction between counselor and client consists of expression by the client and reflection by the counselor, there are usually two different types of breaks in conversation; and, thus, there are two different opportunities for silence to develop. Following client expression, a silence may occur. Either the client continues, or eventually the counselor breaks the silence. If the counselor does begin speaking, it is apt to be with a reflection—either a simple reflection or a clarification of feeling. Since the simple reflection is primarily to inform the client that he is being understood, there need be no silence at all here. Simple reflections may follow immediately upon client expression, especially if pacing is fast. But in the case of clarification of feeling, there is likely to be a silence between client expression and counselor attempt at clarification. So much depends on rapport, pacing, and other factors that it is difficult to make broad statements about length of silences; but it may be said that the silence which follows client expression needs to be long enough to give opportunity for continued expression without interrupting the train of thought. The artistic counselor will learn from his interaction with each client when an expression is considered terminal by the client and when it is only left floating to be resumed soon by further expressions.

As a general rule, the counselor should never speak when he perceives that the client is going to speak. One obvious exception to this is the matter of slowing the pace of the effusive talker. As soon as the counselor perceives termination of expression, he usually feels that clarification is indicated.

Following counselor clarification is another potential silence, but different from the one following client expression. The client must have time to give adequate consideration to the reflection, and such consideration may profitably be quite lengthy. The silence, generally, should not be broken here until the client breaks it or until the counselor perceives definite discomfort. The client's comfort will be related to his anxiety. Anxiety fluctuates greatly during each interview and the counselor must take this into account in handling silences (7). It should be evident that proper handling of silences is of vast importance in therapy and that such handling depends greatly upon the artistic qualities of the counselor.

WHAT HAPPENS IN THERAPY

No one has adequately explained what happens in client-centered therapy. The explanation of how various therapies work is one of the greatest challenges to psychological research; but it is past argument that some very wonderful things do happen. Clients are vastly changed, are made more comfortable, and become better adjusted. These facts have been proved by research utilizing responses to various types of measuring devices before and after client-centered psychotherapy (14). Therapists who believe implicitly in the power of the individual to effect his own growth are prone to explain such changes in terms of a reorganized self-structure.

Much has been said about the drive to enhance and maintain self-organization. This drive is utilized in the final analysis to the benefit of the client, because what actually happens in therapy is that the individual becomes convinced that the only way to enhance and maintain the organism is to change it. No power could be great enough to bring about the frightening change in self-structure except the conviction that to change the concept of self is to enhance and maintain it. This is the undeniable truth: For the person whose self-concept is out of keeping with possible reality, there is no way that he may enhance the self, short of changing his concept of it.

An Illustrative Example

In Snyder's work (21) there is a case entitled, "The Case of Edith Moore" which affords an excellent example of the type of thing that happens in client-centered counseling. This case was counseled by Arthur W. Combs, and the religious counselor should study it thoroughly.

Edith Moore had a withered hand which she could not accept as a part of her. The hand had brought out shyness and a lack of confidence which may have been a basic part of her personality structure. At any rate, the malformed hand is useful in portraying the effects of client-centered therapy. Accepting the hand as a part of herself was for Edith very instrumental to her fuller adjustment. The withered hand may be utilized by the student as a symbol, a prototype of a dwarfed self, or a phase of self which cannot be accepted by the client. Understanding and acceptance of the part of the self which cannot be changed is one phase of therapeutic change; understanding of self and the garnering of courage to change what is changeable is a larger phase.

In Edith's case, she did need to accept a part of herself which could not be changed. Because the disability was physical, this helps us to understand about acceptance of self. While Edith had a physical thing to accept, many clients must accept their limitations in intellectual and even in social areas.

During the course of therapy, Edith experienced a gradual insight into her lack of acceptance of the hand. In the beginning, she kept it hidden from the counselor and also from her friends; but as she began to understand and accept herself, she began to display the hand unconsciously. This is symbolic of how clients are able to come out of the shells of defenses which they have built around the self. If a person fully understands himself with a deep emotional insight, he will either accept himself as he is without change or he will accept himself as he is with a change in self-concept to make all experience consistent with the changed self.

In Edith's case, the acceptance of the physical hand was a demonstrable effect of therapy, but we would be missing the point taught by this case should we assume that this is all that happened. Without knowing just what other aspects of the self-structure were affected, we may be sure that the change in self regarding the hand was accompanied by self-understandings in many areas of personality, and by changes in self-concept in some areas. After therapy, Edith was more comfortable in all her dealings with people, and she felt integrated and able to cope with her problems as they arose.

This case gives us an understanding that change comes about slowly and methodically, and at times, but not always, dramatically. Edith's rehabilitation was not complete when therapy ended and she knew that it was not; but she had experienced sufficient change to give her confidence needed to follow through without further help. In terms of acceptance of the physical handicap, human drama is captured in this case in the after-interview when Edith waved to the counselor with the withered hand that she had kept hidden during the first interview. Is it not possible that, along with the hand, she waved figuratively her entire new acceptance of the unchangeable aspects of herself as well as the changed concepts of self which together made up the new Edith Moore?

A paragraph from Roger's writing will sum up his concept of some of the recognizable events in client-centered therapy:

> In the final phase we know that this choice of new ways of behaving will be in conformity with the newly organized concept of the self; that first steps in putting these plans into action will be small but symbolic; that the individual will feel only a minimum degree of confidence that he can put his plans into effect; that later steps implement more and more completely the new concept of self, and that this process continues beyond the conclusion of the therapeutic interviews (15, p. 417).

Although the client-centered method has been widely acclaimed in religious circles, it should not be considered a panacea. The basic tenets and approaches seem to conform to common elements of religious concern. Clymer effectively translates the client-centered concepts into theological dimensions:

> . . . The inner force of integration is interpreted as the work of the Holy Spirit. Conflicts, anxieties, and blocks toward wholeness are equated with sin. The gaining of insight is salvation. Accept-

ance of the troubled person is love. To condemn not is to judge not. Acceptance of self is the proper love of self—as you love your neighbor. Acceptance of the neighbor is reconciliation. Establishment of rapport is the fellowship of the Holy Spirit. Acceptance of responsibility for change is repentance. Acknowledgment of guilt is confession (2, p. 153).

References

1. Allport, Gordon W., *Personality: A Psychological Interpretation*. New York: Henry Holt and Company, 1937.

2. Clymer, Wayne K., "Can the Counselor Be a Prophet?" *Journal of Pastoral Care*. Fall, 1956, pp. 150-160.

3. Combs, Arthur, "Some Dynamic Aspects of Non-Directive Therapy," *Annals of the New York Academy of Sciences*, October 8, 1948, pp. 878-889.

4. James, William, *Principles of Psychology*. New York: Henry Holt and Company, 1890.

5. Kramish, Art A., "Problems in the Non-Directive Therapist's Reflection of Feeling," *Journal of Social Psychology*, May, 1954, pp. 201-209.

6. Lecky, Prescott, *Self Consistency: A Theory of Personality*. New York: Island Press, 1951.

7. Mahl, George F., "Disturbances and Silences in the Patient's Speech in Psychotherapy," *Journal of Abnormal and Clinical Psychology*, 53, 1956, pp. 1-15.

8. Porter, E. J., Jr., *An Introduction to Therapeutic Counseling*. New York: Houghton Mifflin Company, 1950.

9. Raimy, Victor C., "Self Reference in Counseling Interviews," *Journal of Consulting Psychology*, 12, 1948, pp. 153-163.

10. Rogers, Carl R., *Client-Centered Therapy*. New York: Houghton Mifflin Company, 1951.

11. ————, *Counseling and Psychotherapy*. New York: Houghton Mifflin Company, 1942.

12. ————, *Becoming a Person*. Austin: The Hogg Foundation For Mental Hygiene. Reprinted, 1956. Copyrighted 1954 by Oberlin College.

13. ————, "Psychometric Tests and Client-Centered Counseling," *Educational and Psychological Measurements*, 6, 1946, pp. 139-144.

14. ————, "Recent Research in Non-Directive Therapy and Its Implications." *American Journal of Orthopsychiatry*, 16, 1946, pp. 581-588.

15. ————, "Significant Aspects of Client-Centered Therapy," *American Psychologist*, 1, 1946, pp. 415-422.

16. ————, "Some Observations of the Organization of Personality," *American Psychologist*, 2, 1947, pp. 358-386.

17. ————, "The Attitude and Orientation of the Counselor in Client-Centered Therapy," *Journal of Consulting Psychology*, 13, 1949, pp. 83-94.

18. ————, "The Development of Insight in a Counseling Relationship," *Journal of Consulting Psychology*, 8, 1944, pp. 331-341.

19. ————, "The Process of Therapy," *Journal of Consulting Psychology*, 4, 1940, pp. 161-164.

20. Shostrom, Everett L. and Lawrence M. Brammer, *The Dynamics of the Counseling Process*. New York: McGraw-Hill Book Company, Inc., 1952.

21. Snyder, William U., *Casebook of Non-Directive Counseling*. New York: Houghton Mifflin Company, 1947.

22. ————, "Warmth in Non-Directive Psychotherapy," *Journal of Abnormal and Social Psychology*, 4, 1946, pp. 491-495.

23. Snygg, Donald and Arthur W. Combs, *Individual Behavior*. New York: Harper and Brothers, 1949

24. Taylor, Donald M., "Changes in the Self-Concept Without Psychotherapy," *Journal of Consulting Psychology*, 19, 1955, pp. 205-209.

25. Thorne, Frederick C., "A Critique of Non-Directive Methods of Psychotherapy," *Journal of Abnormal and Social Psychology*, 59, 1944, pp. 459-470.

26. Wood, Austin B., "Transference in Client-Centered Therapy and in Psychoanalysis," *Journal of Consulting Psychology*, 15, 1951, pp. 72-75.

IX

Principles of Group Work and Applications to Religious Settings

Group work in the church-related institution is of profound importance. Although it has come into prominence in schools, business and industry, and mental hospitals, there is no sphere where group work is more appropriate or expedient than in the church program. This is true in the educational, promotional, and organizational phases of church work, as well as the phases that have specific pertinence to counseling.

The typical church sponsors a multitude of group situations. There are meetings of finance, evangelical promotion, teaching and training functions, women's and men's auxiliary work, and recreational and inspirational promotion for youth, to mention only a few. In larger congregations there is even more group emphasis.

In the modern church, there is a great number of emerging emphases that have importance to the broad area of counseling activity. The youth worker meets his charges in order to promote spiritual values, personal-social improvement, and wholesome fellowship. The specialist in counseling may hold group discussions with mothers of young children or with expectant mothers. The church-related clinic may sponsor groups for discussions of family problems. In addition, "group work with, and pastoral care of, older people are complementary ways by which the church and pastor minister to those in later maturity (11)."

A strong case has been made for the importance of group work in the large church. The closely-knit fellowship, which usually prevails in the small church, may dictate an even greater emphasis on the generation of a cohesive "we-feeling." No single individual in the religious setting utilizes group approaches more than the clergyman of the church so small that the clergyman is the only staff member. No single individual needs to study methods of effective group work more.

The clergyman's work must be considered predominantly group-oriented. As Maves and Cedarleaf say:

> The pastor, who is the ordained leader of the fellowship, spends the largest proportion of his time where two or three are gathered together. When there is special need, as we have already seen, he gives individual pastoral care. But the central function of leadership in the church is exercised through group relationship (11, p. 155).

Although this book emphasizes counseling aspects of group work, it may easily be understood that the same learnings concerning counseling implementation in groups carry over to good group production in every kind of assembly. Thus, those who direct committee meetings, conferences, panel discussions, small group discussions, or any kind of group effort may benefit from the findings of psychological research concerning group dynamics.

Group Work and Evangelism

A very large emphasis is developing in the modern church on counseling with new converts. Some churches have been negligent for centuries in supplying the new convert with support, instruction, and counsel until such time as he may be able to gain strength in the faith he has chosen and until he gains opportunity to serve as well as to train for service. This need has become apparent, in particular, among the traveling evangelists who win large groups of converts and must provide for their proper orientation to the Christian life or see many of them return to their former mode of life.

As a general rule, these group workers and individual counselors are selected and trained weeks in advance of the evangelistic campaign and continue at work long after the campaign has closed. In the "crusade" held in San Francisco by Dr. Billy Graham, over 4000 such counselors were used.

Varying Aims for Groups

There is no doubt that planning and implementation of activities that occur in groups will vary with the aims of the groups and the anticipated problems. In this sense, a group meeting may be thought of as discussion, counseling, or psychotherapy. When a group of psychotics is brought together in a hospital setting under a clinical psychologist, one may be sure that the intent is to implement group therapy. When the group situation involves high school students who have been guilty of truancy, one may suppose that the meeting will be more of a counseling than therapeutic nature; although the counseling may have punitive aspects, and some therapeutic as well as some educational values may evolve. When a group of young people meets in a church seeking to consider dating and courtship problems, one would be almost sure to speak of group counseling.

Varying implementation to accommodate differences in aims for the group will include such factors as group size, role of the leader, seating arrangements, the number of sessions, the presence of a recorder-observer, and the composition of the group, among other things. Even though group work may involve many variables in terms of aims and implementation, there are some principles that are common to practically all groups meeting for the purpose of solving problems of any kind.

Hinckley and Hermann state the broad principles of adjustment by means of group processes as follows:

> Persons poorly adjusted in a group are simply persons poorly adjusted. When failure occurs in social relationships, the inadequacy is a basic one because people fundamentally are gregarious beings who cannot survive without each other. Maladjusted persons have

not learned to capitalize suitably their own potentials, and they at once covet and resent qualities of adaptation in others.

To get along well with one's fellows by the process of contribution and acceptance is to become maturely self-reliant. For some people, however, life provides meager learning experiences, and the talents of such persons lie fallow. These are persons who are relatively static in the face of obstacles or who retreat from pressures instead of reweaving the fabric of behavior to meet the demands of reality.

When certain persons fail to achieve consistent social relationships—for reasons involving person-to-person contacts or the inner strife of conflictual desires—the specially arranged group offers a favorable medium for synchronizing personal resources. Group relationships can promote familiarity with social niceties, and there is security in knowing what may be expected in particular situations. Group relationships also help to coalesce disunified portions of behavior. In a sense, group interactions have a leavening effect on the total personality (8, p. 7).

The Scope of Group Work

Group work in a broad sense encompasses many areas of human endeavor. For instance, the major portion of all educational and recreational activities is carried on in groups. Even when one restricts the meaning of group work to an activity involving problem-solving, the field is still very broad. Large use has been made of problem-solving group methods in areas of business, community improvement work, parent-teacher groups, and religious promotion. Such groups usually attack problems related to a group of people or a community.

A more narrow concept of group work may be assumed in the area of religious, psychological, and social problems that individuals have and which become the object of attack in a group setting. These religious, psychological, and social problems of the individual become the emphasis in the concept of group counseling and psychotherapy. Admittedly, it is difficult to separate the values, aims, and implementation of religious instruction in Bible classes or youth recreational programs from group activities that are designed to solve individual religious, social, and psychological problems. Instructional and recreational activities aid in solving these same problems; however, there are many occasions when people come together for the explicit purpose of attacking their personal problems in a group. These meetings, because of their acknowledged intent, may be referred to as group counseling and/or group psychotherapy.

Many churches employ a "young people's director," who assumes a leadership role in assisting youth with their problems of religious and social nature. He accomplishes this goal by both individual and group counseling methods. Each summer thousands of young people attend church camps. Here, again, problems are solved as camp counselors promote individual and group counseling activities.

Activities similar to those sponsored by churches are carried on with groups under YM-YWCA auspices. While work in the YM-YWCA sphere has a broad religious basis and influence, it is true that there is more emphasis on socialization than in the typical church program. Group functions of all types are held under the leadership of "directors" or "counselors." These group meetings range from those having purely social and recreational aims to those planned specifically for formal group counseling.

Mental hygiene and family service clinics sponsor a wide variety of group meetings. These may include a "lonely hearts club," groups for aging people, and groups where expectant mothers share their feelings and problems.

The schools also promote group work of a counseling nature. Much of this work treats common problems of youth such as vocational choice and, in such case, is known as group guidance. Few schools differentiate between group guidance and group counseling. Actually, formal classroom work, group guidance, and group counseling appear as three points on a continuum moving from formality and common needs to informality and individual needs.

The use of group method as a special form of psychotherapy has roots leading back at least to the year 1907, when Dr. J. H. Pratt applied group methods in the rehabilitation of tubercular patients. Pratt was not strongly psychologically oriented but did conceive of his group work as a means of relieving anxieties he observed in his patients.

Although some progress was made in the field of therapeutic group work during the 20's and 30's, the major emphasis came during the 1940's when the needs for psychological treatment of war casualties and returning veterans became acute. Since World War II, emphasis on group treatment in psychotherapy has been great and has come to be a major area for psychological research and implementation through clinical psychologists.

GROUP DYNAMICS AND GROUP COUNSELING

A large area of research, study, and experimentation has been promoted in the last quarter century under the general title of group dynamics. Studies in group dynamics aim at providing a rationale for promoting experiments in group interaction and democratic processes in groups of all kinds. This work in group dynamics has not aimed primarily at providing a medium for counseling or therapeutic processes. The principal aim has been more in terms of helping people to work together in solving problems incurred in business and administrative fields, in solving problems involving community organizations, toward better functioning of committee action, and so forth.

Growing out of the general field of group dynamics have come some implications for group counseling and psychotherapy. In general, it is safe to say that any research in the field of participative action that provides a better means of cooperation among group members, democratic implementation of planning, motivation toward unanimous participation in group discussion, and the building of a warm and permissive psychological atmosphere has relevance to the field of group counseling. Accordingly, there follows a discussion of certain principles, growing primarily from the area of group dynamics, which prove invaluable in developing optimum conditions for group counseling and psychotherapy.

Atmosphere for Group Work

Atmosphere in a group situation has physical as well as attitudinal components, both of which contribute to a psychological attitude on the part of each group member and a permeating atmosphere within the entire group setting. As is true in the individual counseling scene, the physical setting has great bearing upon the atmosphere. Well-planned physical aspects may be expected to produce an atmosphere that will enhance the possibilities of group interaction.

One of the physical details which deserves consideration is the size of the room in which the group meets. Undoubtedly the size of the meeting place is dependent upon the size of the group. Gibb, Platts, and Miller state, "The effective problem-solving group has a physical atmosphere conducive to problem-orientation and is large enough to permit maximum experience background and small enough to permit maximum participation and minimal threat (6, p. 5)."

The student of religious counseling is reminded that the material in Chapter III emphasizes the provision of special quarters in the church for group counseling. Where facilities are meager, the challenge to create or improvise desirable meeting places is greater.

Naturally, the size of the group handled in any counseling situation will be a function of the type of counseling effort being made. For instance, when didactic methods of group counseling are being used, the group may be quite large, inasmuch as the audience does not usually participate and the lecturer is normally the only speaker. Where counseling technique is built around discussion of group members and when the intent is to elicit expression from each member in the group, the group will have to be kept quite small, with a maximum perhaps of ten people. Actually, the size of the group will be influenced by a number of factors including a consideration of the available meeting place and the purpose to be accomplished by the group. Gibb, Platts, and Miller say:

> There seem to be two major considerations in thinking about the size of the group. On the one hand it is clear that the functioning group should be small enough to allow each member to participate verbally in the group activities. Growth comes from full participation. It is equally important that the group be large enough to (1) represent all of the skills necessary for a functioning group, and (2) represent a wide variety of experience backgrounds so that an optimum frame of reference will be provided for consideration of problems that confront the group. Sometimes it is possible to satisfy both requirements by alternate large group discussions and sub-group discussions in the same meeting. The size of the main functioning group and the size of the sub-groups will depend upon the purposes of the group and the experiences of the members.

Many times small groups of 3 or 4 members will function more effectively than larger groups of 7 or 8. Training groups are encouraged to try several different grouping methods suitable to the group and its problem (6, p. 5).

Regardless of group size, the meeting place should conform to this size by providing room enough for comfort but without presenting vast open spaces which develop bad acoustics and a tendency to divert attention. Evidence is that people are able to attend to the conversations more easily in a room which neither presses in because of its smallness nor allows a vastness capable of diluting the atmosphere of closeness, fellowship, and togetherness. The meeting place should be considered with care and should be constant throughout the succession of group meetings, unless a fluctuation in number attending should dictate otherwise.

Another thing that contributes to the atmosphere within the group is the arrangement of seating. It is true that the emphasis upon democratic interaction will vary according to the type of counseling effort being augmented; in general, all types of counseling efforts benefit from the reduction of threat in terms of authoritativeness of leaders. Gibb, Platts, and Miller say:

> It may be helpful to think of the problem as one of analyzing the factors which inhibit group discussion and the ones which help it. In general everything that contributes to *threat* or inadequacy feelings on the part of group members will tend to cut down both the productivity and the enjoyment of the group. . . . For instance, if the people are all sitting in rows with all of the chairs facing the platform or the leaders, the situation may remind the participants of other formal situations in which they have been confronted by people to whom they felt inferior. They *feel* as if the very physical structure of the room contributes to the differences between them and the other fellow. Differences among members, then, contribute to threat. Arranging the chairs to get a feeling of *equality*, will help. This may be done by having the chairs all on the same level with the leader sitting among the members in a seat that is not accented in any way. It is best not to have group members raise their hands or have to be "recognized by the chair" (6, p. 4).

Practically every group situation benefits by the development of an informal atmosphere. Many things will contribute to this including both physical and psychological aspects of the environment. A circular seating arrangement not only adds to the informality of a group counseling scene, but also provides for a maximum number of eye-contacts—that is, allows every person to see the face of every other person. Clothing is a factor in informality. If the leader is disposed to decrease his own authoritativeness and add to the informality at the same time, he may set the pattern by removing his coat and loosening his tie, etc. The desire for informality in counseling will be dependent upon the depth of problems to be treated. In working with deeply-disturbed people, there may be an advantage in both a formal atmosphere and an assumed authoritativeness on the part of the leader. On the other hand, working with deeply disturbed people is seldom a function of the average religious counselor.

Where desirable, the informal atmosphere may be bolstered and interpersonal threat reduced at the same time by having each member of the group give a short self-history, telling about his interest, family situation, education, and so forth. As a general rule, people regard one another with a measure of aloofness and suspicion until they know something about each other. Once each person has revealed that he is just an ordinary human being with common traits, problems, and interests, it is far more likely that he will lose his power to threaten people. Use of first names also seems to dissipate threat. Ruch contributes as follows:

> Dress should be informal. . . . If feasible, light refreshments help to induce an informal atmosphere. . . .
> There are many reasons why people feel hostile or uncomfortable in the presence of other people. Feelings of insecurity are frequently brought out by the mere presence of strangers. Often, too, present situations and persons may remind us of past situations and persons that have aroused hostility in us.
> There are various ways of reducing threat, depending upon the size of the group. In groups of fewer than fifty members it is a good idea to give out tags. The first name should be in large letters so that it can be used comfortably without danger of getting it wrong. In smaller groups it is well, at first meetings, to have people tell about themselves in considerable detail. When time does not permit this sort of introduction, a good practice is to limit each member to three sentences—preferably humorous—that tell important things about him (16, p. 346).

The concept of informality and nonauthoritativeness is not likely to strike a responsive note with all clergymen. Some clergymen feel that their profession demands a dignity that should not be modified at any time. However, psychological research has revealed much greater interaction to be in essence among groups that are led informally. The religious leader who feels that the dignity of the clergy must be sustained even in group meetings may be correct in believing that such demeanor on his part serves the best interests of all. On the other hand, where religious leaders have no aversion to informal and nonauthoritarian involvement in a group, there seems to be merit in the informal atmosphere.

The informal atmosphere for group work suggested by psychologists should have many applications in meetings within a church that are led by clergymen and other religious workers. Events in which such atmosphere may be helpful include meetings of ministers with lay groups, such as deacons and elders in some Protestant churches, meetings of ministers of education with Sunday School leaders, and meetings of denominational leaders from the clergy with denominational lay leaders.

Numerous occasions arise in religious work where large numbers meet in conventions, associational meetings, convocations, etc. For the most part, such meetings bring strangers together; and methods of easy identification by name tags and other means become imperative.

Informal Atmosphere in Counseling

It should be clear that informality and nonauthoritativeness are appropriate in group-counseling situations where such important matters as religious conflicts, character-building, home and family difficulties, and some types of marriage problems are involved. Such counseling situations are very common in religious settings, social agencies, and young people's groups such as YM-YWCA. Where therapy as such is intended, informality and permissiveness may still be desirable to an extent, depending upon the basic philosophy of the therapist and upon the perceived nature of the problems of the group members. On the other hand, those therapists who depend upon transference to power figures of the past may find it desirable to maintain their roles as authority figures in the group-counseling situation.

Leadership and Group-Counseling

Practically every group-counseling situation begins with an assigned leadership. Some rationales of group movement are content to allow the designated leadership to continue. This is generally true in keeping with authoritative functioning in counseling and in administration. Few counseling situations develop in which the designated leader loses his identity completely. Most group-counseling implementation promotes a loss of designated leadership to an extent, together with a sharing of leadership by group members. Where authority is played down and where permissiveness and informality are accented, it is common that active leadership will leave the hands of the designated leader. In such case, leadership may move into the hands of an emergent authority figure from the group. Where participative action is the frame of reference for group activity, the designated leader is glad to give up the leadership; but he usually maintains enough control to prevent usurpation of the leadership by a monopolist in the group.

It is usually very beneficial for the youth leader in the church to allow his leadership to be lost in group interaction. Realistically, there are times when he must regain leadership. Although it may seem unfortunate, there are some things the youth leader does not dare have the young people discuss in an unrestrained manner. There are situations in which the clergyman may be forced to regain leadership not only in youth groups but also in adult group discussions.

Benefits that may be derived from *free* discussions are graphically presented by Douglass in his discussion of workshop techniques in the church.

> . . . Each person contributes from his experience; all learn from each. By patience, objectivity, and analytical insight the group "unfreezes" the opinions initially held by the members. The honest discussion opens up minds to the discovery of new ideas. Members become aware of the fact that no one person has all the answers, that each person's idea alone is inadequate and incomplete, that fragments of ideas contributed by all join together to produce a

more perfect design than any one member could develop by him-self. New facts and points of view set wrong ideas right and start minds moving in new directions. Out of the process and discovery emerges a synthesis. The group formulates a solution to the prob-lem which faces reality and which is adequate to the situation (4, p. 95).

Where possible, it is best for the leadership to be distributed among group members. In the first place, practice in leading is usually very beneficial to the participant. For this reason, each member should have opportunity to lead. It should be understood that it is seldom the policy for the leader to redelegate leadership to first one and then the other of the group members. Rather, the leadership passes from one member to the other as various themes, problems, or issues arise. In group counseling, the fluctuat-ing leadership is not usually consciously perceived by the group members. Ruch as well as Gibb, Platts, and Miller make contribu-tions to this thought.

> Experience is showing that groups can function effectively with-out formal leaders: the various functions of leadership can be shared by the different members of the group.
> Such a sharing of leadership causes an increase in the confidence that each person has in himself as a leader and also creates con-fidence in him on the part of other members of the group. The leader in the democratic group situation is not under the tension of the autocratic leader (16, p. 346).

> In the *participative* group, members work together to achieve high cohesion. The other three atmospheres (autocratic, paternalistic, permissive) are determined by the kind of leadership in the group. In the participative group the atmosphere is determined by the group. There is a maximum of emphasis upon the growth and de-velopment of all the members of the group. There is no one leader; the leadership is distributive. The group works on the principle of consensus, and attempts to get a high degree of pleasant interper-sonal relationships as a solid basis for the solution of its problems. Within the area in which the group may be participative all goals and activities are chosen by the group. All of the members of the group show a high identification with the group goals. This means that in the group situation there is a fairly even spread of the verbal participation. The threat to individuals is minimized through informality and through mutual acquaintance, through a maximum of knowledge of the background, interests, and skills of other mem-bers of the group . . . (6, p. 18).

Cohesiveness

The group therapist or counselor working in the religious setting will benefit from a study of the cohesiveness of groups in general. It is usually true that a group member gains from being in the group only if he is able to identify with the purposes and aims of the group—if he comes to feel a part of the broad entity, the "group." The counselor should realize that a number of people brought together do not of themselves comprise a "group." One may observe that certain activities planned for the participation of a number of individuals sometimes results in a feeling of "we-ness," whereas other planned activities fail to do so. There are definite reasons why one body of people becomes a "group" in the truest sense of the word while another body of people remains an unintegrated mass of physical bodies.

Almost everyone has been a member at one time or another of a group that turned out to be "going nowhere." Some groups exist because of certain demands for their existence which exist outside the need patterns of any of the group members. Other groups move concertedly toward a goal and everyone participates and enjoys the experience. One group has cohesiveness; the other does not. The counselor must be interested in this problem for at least two reasons. In the first place, if there is no cohesion, the group will not continue to assemble unless by authoritative command, in which case no tangible benefits may be expected to evolve. In the second place, a group lacking cohesiveness is listless, unmoving, and unbeneficial. To persist in meeting such a group is a waste of time.

Of interest to all counselors is the question of what causes group cohesion. Cartwright and Zander say:

> The general principle may be derived that the valence of a group will be increased by heightening the awareness of a member (or potential member) that he can fulfill his needs by belonging to the group. Since it is considerably more difficult, though not impossible, to change a person's needs, it is more common for organizations to attempt to strengthen various sources of attraction for the membership by dramatizing the value of the group's properties or the gains to be derived from belonging. An organization might increase interest in itself by emphasizing, for example, that many friendly people can be found there, that a strong union means higher wages,

that other people envy those who belong, that membership is the shortest route to heaven, that exercise is good for you, that the girls in this "chorus line" are beautiful, and so forth. The frequent use of appeals of this sort indicates that a group can be made more attractive either by making it more need satisfying or by reminding the members that it does satisfy needs. Various rituals carried out by groups seem mainly to serve this latter purpose (3, p. 80).

If the counselor may be assured that the cohesiveness of groups is based primarily on need fulfillment, he may still logically raise the question of how to make one group satisfy the needs of a number of persons. At least one means of doing this within the framework of youth counseling is to plan group work around basic problems of youth. If they come to the group for a definite, stated purpose, their cohesion should be insured, provided the stated purpose of the group meetings is carried out.

For instance, a youth director may announce a series of group sessions on "How to Get Ahead on the Job." If a number of young men should attend such a session, it would be evident that they had a shared interest and a shared need. Then, if the group should move into a discussion of sports, it would be logical that the cohesion would not develop unless everyone was interested in sports. It is often true that when the stated purpose of such meetings is not adhered to, members drop out saying, "Well, there is no use going; we never do anything."

The more common method of eliciting group attendance in the counseling field, however, is to announce group sessions for "talking over your problems." Actually, there is nothing wrong with this approach, except that it may be too vague. Any group of people have enough common problems to provide a basis for cohesion. The thing in question is the skill of the counselor to activate these problems and to keep discussion within bounds of the common problems of the group.

The best general approach for accomplishing this is for the counselor to take a place of nonauthoritative leading within the group, to open the discussion without posing a particular problem, to allow the group to originate, and to pursue the problem. It is generally true that the group will fail to follow a problem area opened by the counselor. They will, after having had an opportunity to dispel interpersonal threat through a get acquainted period, strike out on a problem area that is of sustaining interest to them.

After the group has become acquainted and has come to understand that the counselor is going to allow them to talk about the problems that really interest them, they will respond well to first one problem area and then another. Groups become cohesive through a democratic process much more easily than through authoritative manipulation.

Those who work in group counseling are constantly amazed at how quickly groups will cohere if a democratic framework is provided. Once cohesion is well established, both counselor and group members are surprised how easy it is for otherwise reluctant people to bring up problems that have been suppressed sometimes for many years.

The power of the group that has reached a state of cohesion to bring out deeply buried problem areas is amazing, indeed. Time and time again, group members will reveal highly personal problems and say at the end of the session, "I just never would have believed that I could talk like that about myself in front of people; but in here, well, it just seems like I couldn't hold it back."

The most valuable point of all concerning group cohesion is that once a group has been molded together by pursuing common needs, they then are disposed to maintain cohesiveness around the purpose of helping one another. If a troubled group member should open a personal problem of great import to himself as an individual during the first meeting, the probability is that the group would make small effort to help him with his difficulty. However, if, after the group has become closely knit through pursuing some common problems, one of the members opens up a problem of individual significance, then the entire group may rally to help the person with a problem.

This illustrates the value of developing a group over a period of time. Cohesion strong enough to sustain a group in pursuing individual problems cannot be promoted overnight. Another important implication for strong cohesion is the maintenance of a closed group. Once a group has become cohesive, the bringing in of a new member may disrupt this group feeling for several sessions; and even the loss of a member has an effect on the "groupness." In the absence of a member or in the presence of a stranger, the group is no longer the same entity. It is like a team of athletes;

when one member of the team is missing or a new member is introduced, the signals and other aspects of teamwork become confused. It is admittedly difficult to set up closed groups in religious settings.

OUTSTANDING VALUES OF THE GROUP METHOD

Economy

Group counseling and therapy received its original stimulation as a result of the necessity for economy. It was reasoned earlier that treating a number of individuals at once would be a more economical although a less effective means of accomplishing help for individuals. These economy measures were first utilized extensively in the schools in attempts to serve needs of the students.

Strong emphasis was given to group psychotherapy as an aftermath of World War II, when the need in the veterans' neuropsychiatric hospitals rose to such great heights. Simultaneously, with the advent of group therapy as a major means of treatment came the change in the role of the clinical psychologist, who until this time had served almost exclusively as a diagnostician and psychometrician.

Group therapy has been largely the domain of the psychologist. Even with increased staffs consisting of more psychiatrists, hospitals still do not have enough psychiatrists to do all the needed therapy either with individuals or groups. By and large, psychiatrists have taken over the role of drug and individual therapy and have left group therapy work to psychologists. Actually, resorting to psychologists as therapists and to group therapy in lieu of individual therapy were both emergency moves, but it can be reported now without reservation that they have resulted in better treatment of both the mentally ill and disturbed individuals. Group therapy, which was begun as an economy move, has proved itself worthy of a place among the most select means of treatment. It has been found that even without the value of economy, group therapy has values all its own; it would remain a most valuable method even though economy of treatment should become unnecessary. On the other hand, the work of the psychologist in group as well as in individual therapy has shown merits which assure that the psychologist will never return exclusively to his roles as diagnostician and test administrator.

Catharsis in the Group

Catharsis in analytical therapy has been discussed in Chapter VII. This is a pouring out of feeling which secures at least temporary relief for the client. If such relief may be gained through individual therapy, much more gain may be expected through catharsis in the group, but it could be debated which is easier. As reported earlier, most individuals who have not been a part of a cohesive group are inclined to believe that catharsis for them would be impossible under these circumstances. Experience has shown, however, that once a person becomes identified with the group, he is likely to experience less difficulty in revealing himself than to an individual therapist. Having poured out feelings and having felt the understandings of the group, it may be expected that cathartic release may be more beneficial in this setting. It has been evidenced that there are at least some people who can talk more freely in the group than with a single therapist. Whereas transference in the individual setting may be so strong as to render the individual incommunicative, the group reduces threat for some people and promotes expression. Hobbs, writing from the group-centered framework reports on this factor as follows:

> As a member of a group, the person learns what it means to give and receive emotional support and understanding in a new and more mature fashion. The self is redefined in a context not unlike that which initially created the need to distort the perception of the self, and of the self in relation to others. This is perhaps the most compelling quality of the group experience.
>
> Contrary to expectation, it is sometimes easier for a person to talk in the group situation than to an individual therapist, and this is a difference worth noting. A limited experience with several groups of severely disturbed veterans gives evidence on this point. The participants in the groups had all received individual therapy for varying periods extending up to a year, and they were referred for group therapy because they did not respond to individual treatment. Case records indicate that a few of the men who were unable to talk about their traumatic war experiences in individual

therapy gained from the group the stimulus and the acceptance needed to permit them to relive many of the terrible experiences that they were sealing off from awareness. Capital is here made of the individual differences in the ability to open up one's life. The group member most able to talk about himself may start, and thereby relieve pressure from more reticent members, who later take courage from his example and begin tentatively to follow his lead. Such expressions as these are common: "I've had that same experience, too," or "When that happened to you, did you have that same feeling that I had when . . ." Group facilitation, which has been studied by social psychologists in other contexts, operates. It is not to say all people will find it easier to talk in a group; while some may talk readily and others learn that it is safe to talk, a few may remain quiet, with no risks taken, throughout the sessions. But there is a possible gain in freedom, in the group, that is important (15, pp. 291-292).

The Effect of Many Therapists

The participative group provides not one but a number of possible therapists. Granted that the group members do not have training in therapy, the relationships and verbal exchange which spring up between different pairs and among different subgroups can be therapeutic. In the group, there are usually several transference figures. The given member may relate to several persons at the same time; the family constellation or a partial one may be symbolized in the group setting. The trained therapist has a difficult job endeavoring to keep up with all the developing relationships; but if he is well enough trained and experienced, he will be able to manipulate various transferences operating within the group to some extent. In addition to this, it is possible that among six or eight members, there will be nearly identical shared experiences. As one member reveals a problem, another may offer the information that he too has had that problem and has solved it after a certain fashion.

It is clear that such transferences as exist in the group situation are seldom as deep as those of individual therapy. The utility of the transferences and the therapeutic activity that is engaged in by the group members may not always conform to the standards of therapeutic practice held to be most valuable by the group therapist. At the same time, it is true that member therapists may be able to do certain things in the group which would not be thought wise in individual therapy, but which bring about good results in the group setting. For instance, sympathetic understanding of one group member for another may have beneficial results, whereas the individual therapist would be reluctant to offer sympathy.

A Laboratory for Training in Social Interaction

It has been suggested that the majority of human problems are concerned with human relationships. For this reason, the transference has proved very valuable in the therapeutic realm. In areas of personal and social problems, especially, the group method offers great opportunity for a working through of faulty patterns of social and interpersonal learning. For instance, a great many people suffer endless uneasiness simply because they do not know how to relate to others. Basically they are afraid of people. Indeed, it is the unusual case when an individual is not afraid of some people. The group method provides opportunity for training in social interactions. It is the medium through which shy people may learn to express themselves, the backward may feel accepted, and the overly effusive person may learn to control his complusiveness.

It is a real thrill to observe a group that has achieved a high level of cohesiveness as they join forces to help each other. If there is a shy person present, the entire group will make efforts to bring him into the conversation. If a person expresses a problem, every other member is eagerly anxious to lend a hand. And it is true that for the habitual monopolist, there are likely to be hostile remarks and innuendoes designed to slow him down and to help him find his place in the group.

The counselor or therapist may need to take some active part in socializing the group. It is not amiss for the leader to ask the shy person's opinion on a point of discussion. The leader should be diplomatic at all times, and his level of involvement will depend upon his philosophies; but he should not be passive to the extent that he fails to apprehend the problem areas of his group members.

The leader is usually unwise who presents his system of values to the group at any time during the sessions. Once these have been stated, the members will be unlikely to violate them by bring-ing up problems that may concern these value systems. For in-stance, if the leader is radical on the subject of alcohol use and says so, it is extremely unlikely that a member will bring up a drinking problem. Even so, it may be argued that values do have a place in counseling. It is especially true that in some types of youth counseling, values are a most important aspect. The point is that the group members may bring up points of value judgment for objective examination by the members without producing the same threat that would come from the leader's bringing it up.

The leader's role should be an accepting one. Except for situa-tions where certain subjects of discussion may be censored, he should endeavor to remain accepting to any expression by the group members. It should never evolve upon him to set group members "aright." Usually, if the member is far off balance in his thinking on any subject, someone in the group will set him "aright" in a way that does not carry the threat inherent in a statement by the leader, even though the leader may have lost his leadership role for all practical purposes.

Group Pressures for Change in the Individual

The power of the group to elicit expression for the individual through cohesive forces has been dealt with already. Cohesiveness of the group works in still another way to cause an individual to change either his values or behavior. Once the mem-ber has been allied with the group; and once the group members have indicated through their behavior toward him that they feel he should change, the pressure for change becomes somewhat un-bearable.

In a transference situation in the individual counseling scene, pressure from the transference figure for change of the individual may be resisted. When the group establishes a shared perception indicating needed change in the individual, he perceives the pres-sure as lying within the group; and rather than lose the identifica-tion he feels with the group and its purposes, the individual may conform.

This pressure is more than a summation of a number of opinions that the individual should change. In a sense the group has become a part of the individual, as he has become a part of the group. It is likely that the individual who needs to change attitudes, values, or behavior, but who does not do so, is taking dictation from the executive self or ego that lies within him. When the group exerts pressure for change, conflict will be great; but the probabilities are that the change will be made. Inasmuch as the change suggested by the group is more likely to be in keeping with the reality factors facing the individual, he should experience relief when he is forced to change.

It should be recognized that in the sense spoken of here, the group becomes authoritative. In order for it to do so, it is unnecessary for the group members to rise up en masse and suggest by verbal expression that the individual change. Instead, the group decision will be translated to the individual by means of varied communication media including facial expression, intonation, and bodily movement. The authoritativeness of the group may be defended more than the authoritativeness of the individual therapist. In the group, any decision for action that comes to the individual will represent a number of intellects in agreement upon a course of action as opposed to a single opinion by the counselor in an individual or group setting.

THE GROUP AND ITS MEMBERS

The Group Therapist or the Group Leader

The first requirement of the adequate group therapist is that he be skilled as an individual therapist. This is a necessity for many reasons. In the first place the group therapist must often do individual therapy with the same patients he sees in the group. In the second place, the same understanding of dynamics and technique so necessary for the individual therapist is needed by the group therapist. It goes almost without saying that the work of the group therapist is more difficult than that of the individual therapist. He must respond not only to one person but to several at the same time.

The group therapist must be aware of his own needs and his weak spots. McDanald says:

The most important person in the group at the outset is the therapist. To do relatively comfortable group work—no group therapist is absolutely comfortable—he should be at least intellectually aware of what most of his personal anxieties are about. For instance, the therapist may have prestige needs which create no problem for him in individual therapy, because he sees his patients one at a time. . . . An additional safety feature is that the patients he sees individually do not have opportunity to get together to discuss the fact that the spirit did not move him to respond effectively to the material they presented on such and such a day. In group therapy, an off-day for the therapist, especially in the early meetings, may cause him to be anxious about loss of prestige in the eyes of the group (12, p. 8).

Simply knowing his weak spots may not be sufficient for the group therapist. There are some weak spots which the therapist may cover up and defend against, if he is aware of them; there are others which, if possessed by the therapist, should remove him from consideration as a group therapist. The individual therapist from time to time will be the recipient of hostile reactions on the part of the patients. In group therapies, especially those that emphasize analytical procedures, the doctor will be the object of intense hostility from several patients at the same time. Powdermaker indicates that the value of hostility and the possibility of gain for the patients depend upon the doctor's ability to remain secure in the face of hostility.

If what he (the patient) expresses represents the feelings of several members, and if the doctor accepts them and is not made insecure, then the patient, and often other members, can proceed to new insights about these feelings. If the hostile patient lacks the support of the group or the doctor, his attempts to verbalize hostility lead nowhere, may block the process of therapy, and may result in the others' making a scapegoat of the dissident one, perhaps even driving him from the group.

We do not know whether there are conditions under which the group may work through its hostility toward the doctor despite his insecurity. It is conceivable that a well-established group, having a strong network of interpersonal relationships might feel secure enough to feel and express and resolve hostility together toward a new insecure doctor. . . .

On the other hand, the doctor's ability to remain secure in the face of hostility toward himself and to examine it impartially facilitated a therapeutically useful outcome (14, pp. 228-229).

The leader of a group, regardless of his orientation, should have a friendly manner. He should be able to ease tension and promote free expression. As mentioned in connection with the group-centered therapist, the leader must be able to "pour oil on troubled waters." The demeanor required of the group leader can come only through a thorough knowledge of human behavior dynamics, a thorough knowledge of himself, and a personality generally conducive to a calm pursuit of problems. He must *appear* unthreatened.

The most common fault of group leaders is the tendency to talk too much. Actually, the purpose of over-talking usually is to relieve threat that the leader feels. There are types of group treatment that utilize the lecture method, but where this method is not a part of the plan for counseling, the leader should seek to control his speech so as to allow member participation. When the leader does talk, he should attempt to avoid using stilted and technical language. Once the leader sets the pattern of leading-out in the discussion, the members will wait for him to open and expound upon every new topic. Naturally, the verbosity of the good leader will fluctuate over a number of sessions. In early sessions, he may have to talk more than he does after the group has unified.

The leader who over-talks will find that every member expression is "aimed" in his direction. He becomes a clearing house for all comments. All eyes of the members will be on him, and any response made as an interchange between the membership will tend to be routed through the leader. When he ceases to respond, the discussion quickly come to a halt. The good leader conducts himself and the group in such a way that the group may function without him, although in some settings the leader would never really absent himself from the group.

Douty offers an excellent and concise description of the functions of the leader in a church-related discussion group. As a matter of fact, this description would apply to the group leader in any setting.

> In the discussion the leader's job is to focus attention on the problem, throw it out to the group, and let them toss it back and forth. He re-enters the discussion if someone goes off on a tangent. The leader comes to the rescue of the person whose contribution

is in danger of being lost. He tries to draw out those who are slow to speak. Occasionally, where necessary he gives a quick résumé of what has been said. When the time is up or enough has been said, he tries to lift up what seems to be agreed on for the consensus of the group. It is important for the group to know that this is the function of the leader (5, p. 82).

The Observer-Recorder

Some groups utilize an observer-recorder, who sits apart from the group and does not enter into any discussion unless specifically invited. His duty is to keep a running record of events and topics under discussion, and he operates the tape recorder where one is used.

The observer may serve a variety of purposes for the group. He may at one time be a process observer, at another time a participation observer. He may be asked to keep charts on the amount of participation by each member, the fluctuating themes, the position of leadership from one time to another, or the patterns of spontaneous sub-groupings over a period of time.

In the analytical setting, especially, the observer may be asked privately to suggest new approaches for subsequent sessions with given members and he may be asked to point out various aspects of interaction, revealed dynamics, or resistances in individual patients. Because the observer usually does not participate in the discussions, he is able to be objective in his appraisal of the meetings. His chief utility is through conference with the leader after the sessions are over.

Observers may be graduate students in a university or interns in a hospital. They should be interested in group counseling and therapy, and they are better prepared for their tasks if they are well informed on the theoretical aspects of the subject.

Group functioning in the religious setting may benefit by having an observer. Sometimes a member of the group may sit outside the group and act as an observer; and at other times the youth leader may serve, while a designated group member assumes the leadership role.

The Group Members

The question of who should and should not belong to groups is settled largely in relation to the purpose of the group. In some groups there need be no exclusions. This is generally true of group-centered work on college campuses, inasmuch as the method allows individuals to exclude themselves if they perceive the group to be unsatisfying. In the social group, exclusion usually consists of refusing admittance to outstanding trouble-makers, but exclusions in church-related groups are rare.

In the analytical therapy group the matter of exclusion and the broader problem of composition have been studied closely. For a long period of time, it was thought that the chief determiner of group composition should be similarity of problems. Experimentation on this idea generally leads to the conclusion that having all members with the same type of disability would lead to a stalemate, a situation that might be compared to "the blind leading the blind." In general, it has been found that some diversification of problem area is beneficial.

A second trend in group composition has been to group those having similar situations. For example, if all members are factory workers it might be that the possibility of interaction and mutual benefit would be enhanced. Thus, widowers would be grouped together regardless of psychological problems. Age of the participants has been found to be a strong factor in composition among children where it is suggested that a large difference in ages be avoided. In the case of adults, some advantage has been suggested in having both old and young together, inasmuch as young adults may profit by the experience of their elders.

The most notable studies in group composition and exclusion have been made by the Maryland group under Powdermaker and Frank (14) and by Bach (2). The tendency of the Maryland group has been to play down the importance of exclusions to some extent. Among those excluded were psychopathic personality types who tended constantly to disrupt the group with their strong and insatiable hostility patterns. The other strong suggestion of this study was to segregate alcoholics and non-alcoholics. Indications were that little empathic understanding could be expected between these two divergent groups.

Bach (2) makes a stronger case for exclusion of certain types and for the importance of group composition generally. He sets up the objective for careful attention to composition as "the avoidance of some obvious sources of excessive tension and anxiety for all participants." Operating from a framework of group dynamics, Bach believes that group composition may well be among the most important considerations in the entire process of treatment. He observes, "group therapy is like a caravan—it travels at the speed of the slowest member."

Screening applicants for group therapy may be accomplished by intake interview evaluation, testing, or try-outs in the actual group setting. Bach (2) suggests four types of patients who should be excluded from group therapy.

The first exclusion is the patient with "insufficient reality contact." For the most part, these patients would be characterized as psychotic. The exclusion of these is for their own benefit, generally, since they would be disturbed by the contrast between their own functioning and that of the other group members.

The second exclusion is of patients who have "culturally deviant symptomatology." This type patient is exemplified by the person with a criminal record. Such deviants should be placed in a group of their own, since the ordinary group member would likely be hostile toward the culturally deviant individual.

The third exclusion is the "dominant character." This individual is best characterized as a monopolist of the conversation. He demands the spotlight in the groups and, in addition to arousing hostilities among group members, he does not allow other members to explore their own problems.

The last exclusion suggested by Bach (2) is the person with "psychopathic defense and impulsiveness." This individual disrupts the group by his hostilities as well as his violation of social rules of conduct in the group. Such patients seldom are able to enter into group activity unless the activity tends to magnify them in the eyes of the group. They are typically selfish, domineering, and anti-social.

There is little doubt that the matter of group composition is in need of a greater amount of study and research. Undoubtedly, much could be gained from having a somewhat compatible group of people placed together. Although it is largely impossible to determine just what the result of placing a given individual in a given group will be, the results of the entire process depend upon the quality of human interaction in the group. Group composition, admittedly a "skullcracking" problem, is too important to be relegated to a "gambler's luck" category.

Just as it has been apparent that the religious counselor has little choice concerning whom he shall counsel in individual sessions, so it seems plain that he is not able to screen members of groups as carefully as can others. Where groups are brought together for counseling pertaining to personal problems or for psychotherapy in the church setting, it is usually necessary to issue a blanket invitation to all who will come.

Even in the area of group attack on personal as opposed to therapeutic problems, some screening of group members would be advisable. When the religious counselor issues an invitation for church members to discuss problems, he has no way of knowing how many will come. If more come than can be handled in one group, wisdom dictates that the group be divided. Division of groups may offer a means of separating those who might be incompatible.

Much of what has been said about the composition of groups for therapy is pertinent for the assignment of committee members. Committee work comprises such a large segment of religious endeavor that it may be well for the counselor or clergyman to think specifically and carefully about committee composition. It is logical that any intelligent person would give thought to the disruptive qualities inherent in placing certain people together on committees.

A REVIEW OF SOME SPECIFIC TYPES OF GROUP COUNSELING AND THERAPY

Some group therapy may be planned and implemented in the religious setting. If the trend in religious work continues, it is certain that group approaches to personal-problem counseling will become a strong emphasis. A still larger need in religious work is the utilization of proper group methods in committees, Bible classes, and discussion groups.

A considerable portion of writing and research on group processes has been catalogued under the title "group therapy." It may be that in much of the literature the term "therapy" is more broadly applied than has been the intent in this writing. At any rate, much information that has been published under the "group therapy" label has pertinence not only to therapy in the church or religious setting but also to counseling with personal problems and to various types of problem solving by group approaches. The author chooses to maintain the terminology most commonly utilized in the literature, although it seems that the term "counseling" would serve better than the term "therapy" in many cases.

Repressive-Inspirational Therapy

Repressive-inspirational methods resemble supportive methods in individual counseling and therapy. Their utility is greatest with clients who have not experienced a deeply incapacitating type of neurosis or a mental deterioration. The method is very useful in treating disorders of short duration and especially those of traumatic origin. The basic idea is to repress anxiety and inspire ego strength through reassurance. McDanald says:

> Repressive-inspirational group therapy, as previously mentioned, was used in treating military personnel during World War II. The therapist made no effort to get the patient to reveal more than he could comfortably volunteer about the cause of his anxiety that led to his breakdown. As a matter of fact, the causes of his personal anxiety were explained away, insofar as possible, by statements to the effect that everyone was more or less homesick; that the normal person was afraid when subjected to active or passive conditions of combat stress; that each person has his breaking point. Emphasis was placed on the possibility that many who suffered from combat and other types of emotional exhaustion could still participate in the war effort in some capacity other than the one they were engaged in at the time of their breakdown. Importance was also placed on the ideal that each person in time of war makes more in the way of effort and sacrifice than he might be comfortable in doing, and that the extra effort and sacrifice were contributory to the preservation of our way of life. Many men with basically normal personality structures responded to the repressive-inspirational form of group psychotherapy in conjunction with rest, nourishment, and recreational and occupational therapy, and they elected, after a short period of time, to return to their parent organizations. Others

knew they would not hold up if they returned to the stress that precipitated their emotional decompensation and, quite wisely, chose reassignment to units removed from the areas of stress (12, p. 3).

Lecture-Discussion Techniques

As far as philosophy of treatment is concerned, there is really little difference between the lecture-discussion techniques and the previously discussed repressive-inspirational methods. Both methods utilize the idea of support and reassurance. The lecture-discussion methods, so well described by Klapman (9), emphasize a formal and intellectual approach to the task. The lecturer chooses a subject which he feels has merit in terms of common difficulties of the group. The intent usually is to encourage people by relating the universality of problems both general and specific. In the religious context, people are reminded of God's concern and the source of strength that lies in Him.

The leader typically opens the subject for discussion from the assembled group. Hadley says:

> Following his preliminary remarks the counselor encourages group discussion. He invites questions and asks for illustrative experiences. At first the subjects may be reticent in talking about their own experiences, showing many varieties of resistance ranging from complete silence to argumentative attacks upon the ideas presented by the leader. . . . If the leader maintains a permissive and interested attitude and avoids allowing himself to be drawn into defense of his own position, the subjects become increasingly able to speak about the things that trouble them. Once the process is started, it goes forward fairly well. Each subject is emboldened by hearing the others talk about their problems. Each has the valuable privilege, moreover, of remaining silent if he wants to; conversation is taken over by the leader or by someone else if his own talk begins to embarrass or frighten him (7, pp. 234-235).

The lecture-discussion technique may be compared to common religious approaches to problem solving. Typical sermons by ministers accent problem areas common to the congregation. However, in no sense is the therapeutic or counseling value all that may be found in the religious exercise. Spiritual values in conjunction with therapeutic values are the rule.

Lecture-discussion techniques are commonly implemented in

the church program, not only in counseling areas but in business and promotional areas. A chief danger in the use of the method is the tendency of the leader to usurp the discussion, leaving little time or opportunity for member expression. When the leader honestly believes in the power of the group to work out better decisions and plans than those he might originate, a democratic utilization of the lecture-discussion ensues.

Lecture-discussion may be varied and modified endlessly, and it may be used for a wide variety of problems. It works well for marriage problems and social problems of young people. For variety, the lecture may be modified into panel discussions, symposia, and the like. The Social Service Department of the Denver Area Council of Churches has utilized various forms of panel discussions in attacking marriage problems. Panels presenting ideas concerning problems of the home and family have been composed of physicians, social workers, and ministers.

Group-Centered Therapy

Arising from the theories and techniques of client-centered therapy discussed in Chapter VIII has come a group process known as group-centered therapy. One would expect that the basic philosophies embraced in client-centered work would find their counterparts in the group process. The student will recall that the primary philosophy of the client-centered practitioners is an implicit faith in the individual and in his ability to formulate his own plans and implement his own decisions, if set free from his psychological blockings. The author suggests that the group-centered method is highly applicable to most church groups, including committee meetings, Sunday School classes, and various counseling sessions.

Hobbs describes the function of the group-centered leader as follows:

> Essentially, what the therapist attempts to do is to reconstruct the perceptual field of the individual at the moment of expression, and to communicate this understanding with skill and sensitivity. The various terms that have been used to describe the kinds of statements that the therapist makes in individual therapy—such as clarification of feeling, reflection of feeling, restatement of content,

simple acceptance, structuring, and so on—are appropriate to the group situation as well, and there are other similarities that should be mentioned in passing. The concern with diagnosis is minimal, interpretation is not relied on as a therapeutic instrument, insight is not considered to be an essential change-agent in the process of learning, transference attitudes are handled just like all other affect-laden expressions, and the most effective predictor of possible gain from the therapy is considered to be the experience itself (15, p. 289).

The group-centered therapist finds himself in a position that is quite demanding. The ordinary group situation, even when made up of normal people, has explosive qualities. Although the therapist does not encourage it, transference hostilities will arise. Committed as he is philosophically not to intervene in the expression of client feelings, the group-centered therapist must be an expert diplomat. Although interrupting expression is foreign to his nature by virtue of his training in individual client-centered therapy, the therapist may be forced to interrupt discussions between individuals in the group when they become too heated.

The differences between the group-centered method and other methods, particularly those that have psychoanalytical basis, are that the therapist, having moved into the conversation between irate members, does not interpret their hostilities to them; he reflects and summarizes these feelings in an effort to bring the participants into awareness of their motives. Because the group-centered therapist must operate without the prerogatives of interpretation, direction, and authoritative control, he must be able to use diplomacy instead. In this sense, the group-centered therapist must be able to withstand the onslaughts of hostility toward himself without becoming disturbed by them or responding with hostility.

The role of the group-centered leader is a difficult one. The question may be asked as to the advantage of such attitudes and behavior on the part of the leader. It is generally conceded that the benefit which members derive from a group process is in direct relationship to the amount and quality of expressions and communications by the members. Those who utilize the group-centered method are convinced that communication is facilitated by the philosophies of the leader who believes in the worth and integrity of each member. The warm and permissive atmosphere which he endeavors to promote through his non-directing behavior is also seen as an effective stimulus to communication.

Theoretically, members will develop attitudes toward each other and toward the leader similar to those the leader holds toward the members. If the therapist is warm, friendly, accepting, understanding, and empathic toward each group member, it is conceivable that such an atmosphere will carry over into attitudes between group members. Since so much of the psychic disturbance of individuals is related to hostile attitudes among people, it is probable that, in a permissive climate, individuals may, for the first time, be able to relate to others without having to defend themselves. They may in this way gain valuable insight as well as relearning in the area of human relationships.

It should be clear to the reader that group-centered techniques would work better with certain types of individuals than with others. The presence of one or more members who could not under any circumstances yield to the accepting and permissive atmosphere of a group may stymie all possibility of gain. For this reason, group-centered work usually operates with open groups. Those who would logically disrupt the progress of group interaction, would not likely choose to remain in such a group. Those who have attitudes which, however divergent, are amenable to change probably will remain and receive maximum benefits.

A prerequisite to change for most people is being understood. Undoubtedly, techniques employed by group-centered leaders are conducive to an empathic relationship among members which in turn causes each to feel that he is being understood. Being understood promotes a type of security that provides a good basis for change where such change may be beneficial. The individual who has expressed his problem to the group and is accepted without reservation by it will have difficulty in preventing a change in himself if such change is clearly indicated by the group as being desirable. Group attitude and pressure toward change in an individual member become a powerful force, able in many instances to overcome the gains of deviant behavior for the individual.

The principles derived for group-centered therapy will generally apply wherever group expression is earnestly desired. These same principles have been broadly applied in business administration, and they may be broadly applied in church committee work. If committee leaders learn how to encourage a permissive atmosphere and how to play down their leadership roles, committee action will become representative of the true feelings of the members. With authoritative leading by the appointed committee chairman, committee action often becomes a decision by a minority.

Analytical Group Therapy

Analytical group therapy follows the basic tenets of individual analytical therapy discussed in Chapter VII. Within the broad analytical approach of group therapy there are several basically different emphases as revealed in works by Wolfe (20), Slavson (17), and Powdermaker and Frank (14). The present discussion will be concerned with the broadly conceived aspects of such therapy. This type of therapy is most often carried on by psychiatrists and clinical psychologists.

In general, there is an effort on the part of the therapist to maintain a role of authority. The therapist enters more freely into discussion than does the group-centered therapist, but he must maintain a firmer control because of the probability that the patients will be more inclined toward disruptive and destructive tendencies.

The two main avenues of approach to insight on the part of group members are the transference relationship and interpretation by the therapist of patient activities and expressions. The possibility of transferences is multiplied since the patients not only have the choice of transferring to the therapist but to each other as well. These transferences are usually encouraged, studied by the therapist, and interpreted to the patients.

Although the therapist assumes an authoritative role, he, nevertheless, places great emphasis upon client participation and expression. Within the boundaries of his control of the group processes, he likes to promote an atmosphere that is permissive and conducive to discussion. Hostilities are usually kept in hand by interpretation. The counselor may point out to one patient that the reason he is angry at another patient is that he is reacting toward him in the same way that he reacts toward his brother;

such interpretation usually keeps the hostility in check. The therapist often becomes the object of hostility from perhaps several members of the group at the same time, but most analytical therapists endeavor to maintain calmness under hostility from the members. They allow the hostility to progress up to a point and then interpret it.

According to Powdermaker and Frank (14), a major portion of hostility toward the therapist is displayed because the patients feel the doctor could help them if only he would. Other hostilities are direct results of transferences. Hostilities may be played out overtly or may become evidenced as resistances, which vary from refusal to talk to efforts to deny and gloss over revelations. Resistances usually indicate that insight is coming too rapidly for the patient to face. The therapist watches closely for resistances in the patient, seeks to understand their meaning, and at the opportune time interprets the resistances or defenses to the client. Thus, insight development in analytical group therapy becomes an end product of transference and interpretation. Hinckley and Hermann say:

> The process by means of which one reaches insight is called *interpretation*. Interpretation is a matter of explaining and giving meaning to behavior. *Insight* is the perception of relationships which have remained until this moment unconscious; it is a seeing of the "inner" nature of relationships, as it were, an unveiling and acceptance of what the patient has heretofore never suspected about himself.
>
> Interpretation holds an important place in therapy for two reasons, (1) The interpretation the therapist makes for himself does not coincide with what he offers the patient. Because the interpretation of another's behavior does not inflict pain on the therapist, he can afford to look at cause and effect clearly and fully. (2) For the patient about whom are gathered guilts and shames, the interpretation must be carefully limited and proportioned to the amount he can stand at a given moment. When patients are able to make associations similar to those the therapist formulates, they have developed some insight.
>
> There is, of course, no point at which one may say interpretation ends and insight begins. Both go along together. Because raising to a conscious level knowledge of relationships of which one has been unaware, can be exceedingly frightening, it is advisable in group therapy for interpretation and insight to be applied cautiously (8, p. 81).

It is rather commonly understood that catharsis, abreaction, and insight development are forerunners of re-integration of the ego and of conflictual behavior, but that these elements seldom are enough to reshape and implement new attitudes and orientations. As "working through" is used in individual therapy to facilitate readaptation to living, so must there be a similar therapeutic exercise in group therapy.

Bach (2) has labeled the last phase of group therapy as the Work Phase. Although not specifically allied to the analytical field of group therapy, the following quotation demonstrates some of the expected events in this as well as other types of group process.

. . . The group setting affords an opportunity to do therapeutic "exercises" and experiments in social field maintenance as follows:

1. Patients perceive some of the conditions of the social field which they can to some extent control.

2. Patients participate in the process by which the individuals in the group learn to free themselves from unconstructive leader-dependency. The professional group therapist makes it possible for the group better to self-determine its own development, including how to adjust better to the presence of himself, the expert.

3. Patients, by taking responsibility for the quality of their own group's culture, have new growth experiences. The therapist helps patients to recognize the crucial points in the stream of the group life at which the group by decision, sanction, or clarification can or could change the course and depth of its own social field.

The above "therapeutic exercises" are really training experiences in social field maintenance. . . . The patient gains strength and satisfaction through preparing this field of gratifying interpersonal relationships, rather than depending on others to provide contact considered "good" for him (2, p. 271).*

Group Work with Children

Among those who have done extensive work in the area of group work with children are Axline (1), Slavson (17), and Little and Konopka (10). Although there is disagreement on some of the interpretative aspects of child play and a variety of

---

* George R. Bach, *Intensive Group Psychotherapy.* Copyright 1954, The Ronald Press Company.

emphases on such things as "acting out" and doll play, the following description by Slavson embraces the most common aspects of
work with children in groups:

> Groups are supplied with simple arts-and-craft materials and
> tools to which the members have access and which they can use
> quite freely. No restrictions of any kind are imposed at the begin-
> ning of the treatment. The children also have free access to the
> total environment and can utilize the furnishings, and other ap-
> purtenances in whatever manner they wish. This is a *permissive en-
> vironment*. Limitations, control, and denial arise naturally as mem-
> bers infringe upon the rights and conveniences of others, and, at
> later stages in treatment, from the therapist as well.
>
> All sessions or meetings end with a repast of simple food, some-
> times cooked. Usually it consists of milk, fruit, and cake. At table,
> also, there is complete freedom. Children may eat with the group
> or take their share and eat by themselves. They may gulp or throw
> the food around (or at others) if they so desire. They may grab
> the victuals, stuff them into their pockets, share with the others,
> or try to take more than their rightful share. By their own sugges-
> tion and choice, the members of the group also arrange the trips
> to museums, parks, zoological gardens, industrial establishments,
> theaters and opera, and other places that may interest them.
>
> The purpose of these groups is to give substitute satisfactions
> through the free acting out of impulses, opportunity for sublima-
> tive activity, gratifying experiences, group status, recognition of
> achievement, and unconditional love and acceptance from an adult.
> Through the activities in the group, children overcome basic char-
> acter malformations, such as emasculation in boys, confused iden-
> tification in girls, feelings of impotence, and fear of expressing ag-
> gressive and hostile impulses. In such an environment and rela-
> tionships, the infantile and overprotected child can become self-
> reliant and act more mature, the exploited child becomes a more
> autonomous and self-activating entity, while the rejected child, with
> the broken-down, weak ego and a low degree of self-esteem, can
> be built up.
>
> The attitude of the therapist is permissive. The clients who come
> to these groups must be convinced that he is a kindly, unpunishing,
> friendly, yet positive individual. The group therapist is neither
> domineering nor pampering, nor does he exploit the child for his
> own emotional needs. Activity group therapists are individuals who
> have no love cravings or emotional drives toward children that
> would tie the children down and impede their growth. The chil-
> dren are set free to grow at their own pace through release and the
> restraint of the others in the group. The result is a new orientation
> toward environment and people (18, pp. 32-33).

Whether the purpose of group play techniques with children is therapeutic or evaluative, spontaneous play provides a nearly perfect medium. The child relates through his play activities more of his dynamics than could possibly be gleaned through his speech. If the therapist is analytically oriented, he will find abundant transference material to work with, because children transfer very freely. If the therapist is inclined to a more surface way of dealing with the child, he may observe the emotions and impulses of the child laid bare in the play scene. Nowhere are group methods more applicable or rewarding than with children.

Psychodrama and Sociodrama

Work with children has emphasized the values of acting out one's problems. From an observation of children at play, J. L. Moreno conceived the idea of the psychodrama. As Moreno studied the drama, he was impressed with the therapeutic possibilities of spontaneity:

> Inhalation and exhalation of the lungs is the symbol of disinfection. Through inhalation of oxygen the body is kept alive but by this the formation of the deadly carbon oxyde is precipitated. However, through exhalation the poison is removed from the body. One can say that through the process of living we inhale the psyche and we exhale it through the process of spontaneity. If in the process of inhaling poisons develop, stresses and conflicts, they are removed by spontaneity. Spontaneity permits the deepest level of personality to emerge freely. This free rising of the creative matrix does not take place by means of external interferences, but it is autonomous. Upon the relationship between the process of living itself and creativity and spontaneity its significance as a remedy is based. In place of depth analysis comes depth production and action emerging from the depths; in place of the physician self help. The intension is to make the disease visible. Paradoxically speaking, the purpose of spontaneous treatment is not to get well, but to get sick. The patient drives his disease out of himself. The magnification of reality into a drama makes him free from reality. It is a process of cure similar to the serum injection of smallpox to check the full breakout of smallpox. The patient acts like a dramatist who writes Hamlet to scare the latter away from him (13, p. 82).**

** From *The Theatre of Spontaneity,* by J. L. Moreno, M.D., Beacon House, Inc., Publishers.

Sociodrama differs from psychodrama in that the "acting out" pertains to conflictual situations which have social implications. On the other hand, psychodrama is a method used to tap deeper levels of psychic distress and is more apt to feature at least a symbolic abreaction. All in all, both methods are simply special adaptations of role-playing.

Psychodrama as worked out by Moreno consists of a fully planned approach to self-revelation and self-understanding. Therapists may participate in the drama with a client or may direct from an audience position. The undertaking is usually a joint one involving a number of therapeutic assistants.

Hadley gives the following description of the method:

> The participant first starts with himself (in the director's presence) and lives through situations that are part of his daily life. Later he enacts the roles of other people who are emotionally tied to him. Presentations may relate to experiences in any period of the individual's life, and he is helped by staff members to get started. These are the techniques of *self-representation*. Techniques of *spontaneous improvisation* are used when the participant acts out fictitious, imagined roles. He is instructed in doing this, to keep his personal character from interfering with the fictitious character. In this way his ego is presumed to be free to watch and record what goes on. The technique of *soliloquy* reflects the private reactions of players to their roles. These are spoken as asides. *Warming-up* techniques are used to induce spontaneous states. . . . The director may enter as a participant-actor, using his psychiatric knowledge to guide the drama (7, p. 241).

The sociodrama is more likely to be utilized as an adjunct of social group work and does not require psychiatrically-oriented directors. End products when used in social work are greater socialization and the elimination of objectional social conduct through insight.

Drama in one form or another has come into broad usage in the church. Douty (5) describes its application in many phases of church activity including kindergarten, women's societies and Sunday morning classes. "Whether our purpose be to entertain, instruct, challenge, or to lead, we can reach our hearers through drama as through no other medium."

Splaver (19), editor of Occu-Press, describes the use of socio-guidrama in the youth activity program of the church. These playlets deal with everyday adolescent problems such as going steady and understanding parents. "The modern church, like its forerunner of yore, recognizes the vast potential of the drama technique."

References

1. Axline, Virginia M., *Play Therapy*. Boston: Houghton Mifflin Company, 1947.
2. Bach, George R., *Intensive Group Psychotherapy*. New York: The Ronald Press Company, 1954.
3. Cartwright, Darwin and Alvin Zander, *Group Dynamics Research and Theory*. Evanston: Row, Peterson, and Company, 1953.
4. Douglass, Paul F., *The Group Workshop Way in the Church*. New York: Association Press, 1956.
5. Douty, Mary Alice, *How to Work With Church Groups*. New York: Abingdon Press, 1957.
6. Gibb, Jack R., Grace N. Platts, and L. Miller, *Dynamics of Participative Groups*. Boulder: University of Colorado, 1951.
7. Hadley, John M., *Clinical and Counseling Psychology*. New York: Alfred A. Knopf, 1958.
8. Hinckley, Robert G. and Lydia Hermann, *Group Treatment in Psychotherapy*. Minneapolis: University of Minnesota Press, 1951.
9. Klapman, J. W., *Group Psychotherapy: Theory and Practice*. New York: Grune and Stratton, 1946.
10. Little, H. M. and G. Konopka, "Group Therapy in a Child Guidance Center," *American Journal of Orthopsychiatry*, 17, 1947, pp. 303-311.
11. Maves, Paul B. and J. Lennart Cedarleaf, *Older People and the Church*. New York: Abingdon-Cokesbury Press, 1949.
12. McDanald, Eugene C., *Group Psychotherapy Methods*. Austin: The Hogg Foundation for Mental Health, The University of Texas, 1957.
13. Moreno, J. L., M.D., *The Theatre of Spontaneity*. New York: Beacon House, 1947.
14. Powdermaker, F. B. and J. D. Frank, *Group Psychotherapy*. Cambridge: Commonwealth Fund, Harvard University Press, 1953.
15. Rogers, Carl R., *Client-Centered Therapy*. New York: Houghton Mifflin Company, 1951.
16. Ruch, Floyd L., *Psychology and Life*, 4th ed. New York: Scott, Foresman and Company, 1951.
17. Slavson, S. R., *Analytic Group Therapy with Children, Adolescents and Adults*. New York: Columbia University Press, 1950.

18. Slavson, S. R., ed., *The Practice of Group Therapy*. New York: International Universities Press, 1947.

19. Splaver, Sarah, "Young People, Pastors, and Play Acting," *Pastoral Psychology*. January, 1957, pp. 55-60.

20. Wolfe, A., "The Psychoanalysis of Groups: Part I," *American Journal of Psychotherapy*, 3, 1949, pp. 525-558.

An Experience in Group Counseling

FOREWORD

The situation

Under the auspices of the University Psychological Clinic, nine people met twice a week for four weeks for group counseling. Each had his own problems, and four of the nine had engaged in individual counseling with the leader of the group sessions. Others probably had engaged the services of members of the clinic staff. All were taking some university work. There were six men and three women in the group and, in addition to the counselor-leader, a tenth person was present as observer-recorder for the counseling sessions.

Lloyd Powell at twenty years of age was a junior student and the youngest in the group. He was small of stature and very energetic. He was planning to become a school administrator. He was single, but serious about a girl also attending the University.

James Risinger was a senior ministerial student. He was having a great deal of difficulty passing his subjects. At twenty-one, he was unmarried and not serious about any particular girls. He said he got along better with girls who were already engaged. He was also unsure of his status as a ministerial student.

Sally Tucker was a quiet girl of twenty-one. Sally had been reared on a ranch, had four brothers and no sisters. She was not very social-minded because of her background. She revealed that she had not had a normal childhood and had been around adults all her life. She had no difficulty in conversing with young men but seemed afraid of girls. She had a steady boy friend, but he lived in another town at some distance.

Wilson McClung was a young married minister, serving a small church part-time while he went to the University. He would later attend the seminary. He had been married happily about a year.

Oscar Fleurs was the oldest of the group members. He was forty-two and was working full-time as a counselor in the regional

VA setting. His presence was probably a function of his interest in group work more than a desire for self-help. He was married but childless.

Harry Warrington like Oscar was a VA counselor. At forty years of age, Harry was married and had a daughter ten years of age. He did not enter into the conversations recorded here.

L. D. Pace was a minister of thirty-five, married, and he had a small son. L. D. was working on his Master's degree in psychology and preaching part-time. He was a very friendly sort and inclined to be a monopolist in the group situation.

Lurline Walker, a senior student, was planning a career of marriage. Her folks were in the wholesale grocery business. Strongly oriented religiously, she was not committed to a particular vocation.

Betty Rhodes was a senior student. Betty had held church-related jobs at various times. She was strongly religious and was engaged to be married to a ministerial student who had volunteered for foreign mission service. She was twenty-two.

Edgar Imsco was a senior student aspiring to the field of medicine. He had been reared on the mission field in South America. His father and mother were serving as missionaries in the Caribbean area at the time. Edgar was not a member of the group, actually, but was assigned the task of observer-recorder. He was twenty-three and single.

The counselor was a member of the staff of the Psychology Department of the University. His training in both group and individual counseling was extensive.

The following material is drawn from the second session.

GROUP COUNSELING

(COUNSELOR)   I think surely some of you have had some time to do some thinking now—to bring up some problem area that you would like to have discussed. So don't be bashful.

(JAMES)   I woke up this morning feeling mighty low. (group laughs)

(L. D.)   That's the situation for most of us. (more laughter)

(LLOYD)   It is Monday morning you know. (considerable frivolity)

(L. D.)   Yes, it sure is. (very long pause) Seems like I do all the palavering. I've run on to something I sure would like to hear somebody's ideas about. All my life I've been hunting for a nice way to say that all men are not born equal. I can't get over how well this man explains that. (refers to book)

(COUNSELOR) He really does a good job of it, doesn't he?

(L. D.) I'd be interested in everybody's reaction to that. I'm serious about that because it'd be worth something to me in my ministry. Sometimes when we have time I'd sure like to discuss it.

(COUNSELOR) Well, now's as good a time as any. Except now, James, did you have something particular in mind?

(JAMES) Well, I just missed my first period class. (laughs)

(L. D.) You just now got waked up, James? (group laughs)

(JAMES) No, I've been awake for an hour or two. Oh, it wasn't anything particularly serious. It was just that . . .

(L. D.) (to someone coming in late) We missed you this morning, too.

(COUNSELOR) Go ahead, James.

(JAMES) Oh, let's see now. I don't know what to talk about. What did we talk about last time?

(L. D.) We talked about my problem last time.

(BETTY) Well, I'll kick one off, then. (quietly and very seriously) Oh, I don't know exactly how to say it, but I wonder if anybody else ever thinks that they're thinking too much. You know like I'm thinking too hard on a subject. And you just wear yourself out trying to figure a solution— that, uh, doesn't seem to have a solution; and perhaps you just cloud your thinking because you are just trying to take all the aspects of the problem and be objective about a subject. What do you all think about that?

(JAMES) I agree with you. (long pause)

(LLOYD) That's not the first time I've heard somebody say some-

---

DISCUSSION: When several group members persist in being frivolous during opening stages, the counselor usually feels that several are strongly disposed to present their problems. It seems here that at least three people were in contention as to who would be first to bring his problem before the group.

James is highly motivated, but tries the humorous approach. He finally withdraws. L. D. proposes a philosophical question from which he probably hopes to move to a personal-problem area, if he finds the group accepting.

The counselor seems to see James as the person who should be encouraged. Previous experience has probably shown that L. D., a monopolist, will not likely produce more than verbal generalizations. At least one of the monopolist's problems is solved in being allowed to talk. The counselor seems to feel more can be gained by encouraging James.

thing about that—and especially in this department. I've heard two or three people say something along that train of thought. They thought that they were learning so much psychology, so far as they were concerned, that they were losing sight of their goals and everything else. They were spending so much time trying to figure out themselves and to figure out other people; and they were just getting too involved. (pause) I can see that it would be easy to do.

(BETTY)   I think it has a great deal to do with your maturity, but it seems to be a mark of immaturity when you get too involved. I don't know just exactly how to express being involved; but, oh, if you have a problem to solve and you just keep on thinking about it and then if the solution just doesn't come, then it should just be time to divert your thinking to something else or to just decide it's not time for that problem to be solved. Or what?

(COUNSELOR)   In other words you seem to feel, Betty, that sometimes a person can become obsessed and be compulsive in his approach to his own problem. He gets his mind on it and he's not making any headway on it at all. It just seems like this problem is going to maybe stay with him for the rest of his life; but somehow he just can't pry his attention away from it.

(BETTY)   Well, you realize that you've got to think the thing through and that sooner or later a solution will have to come. An intelligent person won't just pass it off; you've got to think it through. And, yet, maybe you think too much about it. Some people can have a problem and can do something about it; and, then, there are other people that just go around in circles.

(LURLINE)   It seems to me that, if you've had something like this going on for so long, if you give your mind a rest and put your thoughts on something else, you've thought about that so much already that it will go into your subconscious mind; and that your subconscious mind can be working on it while you are resting your mind on other things. Then, when you come back to it, you can see it

DISCUSSION: Betty moves in quickly and efficiently with her problem. The mood changes immediately to one of great concentration and seriousness.
    So many group members present their problems as some impersonal and vague generalizations until they are sure that they will find acceptance. Betty does this. Lloyd is trying to clarify Betty's feelings but is probably projecting some of his own difficulties.

DISCUSSION: The counselor is trying to clarify Betty's feelings. Actually, she hasn't had the courage yet to reveal what her problem really is.

clearer. Or you can see things after resting that'll help bring it out. (group agreement)

(BETTY) Sometimes you get so involved in thinking about it you can't see it.

(L. D.) You're too close to it.

(SALLY) I think sometimes we have a pressure for wanting to solve a problem; and, if we'll just wait a little while, it will probably solve itself.

(BETTY) How about this matter, though, that a lot of times hesitation causes you to miss an opportunity. You hear so many people say that just by a moment's hesitation they lose that opportunity. That's the trouble—it puts the pressure on. You wonder if you are doing the right thing by waiting.

(JAMES) Don't you usually think you make a mistake though when you let yourself get under pressure about a decision. I know I always have.

(LURLINE) I had an experience like that once, but in my case I was so swayed in one particular way; not that I liked that way particularly. I was just more or less pushed into it. I mean that, well, there was another way to go; but, ah, I know of one or two big decisions I've made and, ah, I wanted to go the other way so much but yet I didn't—I picked the other way I didn't want to go. I sure didn't have time to think about it then. It just worked itself out in the last four or five minutes.

(BETTY) I tell you right now my decision is just about equal. There's just no indication which one is better . . . that's when you nearly give up.

(L. D.) Sometimes you just don't know what to do.

(JAMES) That's when you feel like giving up.

(LLOYD) Well, I think a person ought to realize that they can't always make the right decisions.

(BETTY) But this is such a life-changing decision.

(LLOYD) So you make a mistake and your life changes, you can still make the best of that—you . . .

(L. D.) Well I—excuse me Lloyd, go ahead.

(LLOYD) I was just going to say that even if it is a decision important as to be life changing—you're going to make mistakes throughout your life I believe.

(WILSON) Surely there'll be many instances when you can never be sure whether you are right or wrong. I mean even . . .

(L. D.) Even after it's over with. (group agrees)

(L. D.) Then there's this hopeful viewpoint. There are some problems that no one has figured out how to solve, and so you might take the position that you are not going to be able to solve all of them.

(OSCAR)   That, I believe, is incorporated in the Alcoholics Anonymous prayer. It goes something like . . . Give me the wisdom not to try to change the things that can't be changed but to work hard at those that can be, and the ability to tell the difference.

(JAMES)   I have a question in this same regard. I wonder if this problem of making up your mind doesn't come from the basic problem of reconstruction of the basic foundations upon which we think and live. We've all been brought up to attach great importance to trivial things, and we may have lost sight of the really important issues.

(L. D.)   I guess that most problems look smaller when we look back at them than when we look forward to them. And because of my observation on that I just take some time during every day just to say that this is simply not as important as it seems. Whether it's true or not I have to say it for my own relief. I sort of automatically throw a switch around our place about supper time, and unless it's an emergency we don't consider anything serious from supper time on. I just don't bring problems home with me because, if I do, I start off tired and frustrated next morning. I just shut off the problem at night and say there isn't anything I can do about it until daylight.

(JAMES)   I don't know whether I agree that that's a good practice or not.

(L. D.)   I don't know whether it's a good practice or not; but I do know some couples who have broken up because they went through the strain of carrying their problems home with them—to the supper table with them, to bed with them; and they got up with them and they lived with them until they were nuts almost.

(BETTY)   That's what I'm talking about. You can think too much . . .

(L. D.)   And I just tell you—some of the most successful—I'm thinking in terms—I'm using a home illustration—in terms of

---

DISCUSSION: The group has grown so interested in the verbal exchange that they have forgotten all about Betty's problem. James shows evidence in his speech that he would like to work back around to his own problem.

DISCUSSION: The section beginning here with L. D.'s speech and ending with the next speech by the counselor offers material for a number of observations:

     (1) At this point, L. D. has become the emergent leader.

     (2) His leadership, being authoritative, creates resistances.

     (3) This type of leading is almost opposite from the group-centered leadership exercised by the appointed counselor.

	that, some people have even gone so far as to—they've butted heads over a problem. They've gone on separate vacations for example—husband and wife have gone in separate directions on a vacation, simply to rest. I think our bodies demand physical rest and our minds demand mental rest. And I don't know; but for me there has to be a time when I say, this isn't as big as it looks. I just tell you right now, I may be emotionally confused, but I have to do this.
(WILSON)	Well, I've never gotten to the place where I can do that with some problems. Some problems I just can't throw a switch. You might be able to quit talking about it, but are you able to put it out of your mind?
(L. D.)	Well, I tell you some people can be a success at it. For example, I go home every week-end to a full-time church —and I leave the University behind. I have to. If somebody asks me something about it, I make as noncommittal an answer about it as I possibly can—about my week at school and the program. And when we say "amen" on Sunday night, I leave that church down there. I just say it's in the hands of God until I get back on Friday. I just don't see how I could do what I have to any other way. It works for me.
(JAMES)	I don't suppose that applies to everybody. You have two areas—two or three separate areas of life. But some people have just one area of life—maybe inventors, or something like that, or musicians. They just have one major emphasis.

(4) The type of productions made by L. D., a minister, are instructional and perhaps even inspirational. It is a debatable issue; but, these productions may have real and lasting value for some of the group members. In fact, L. D.'s productions may be the most important aspects of the entire group experience. This type of leadership as opposed to the democratic, group-centered type may be somewhat typical of ministers. They are usually expected to be verbal and to offer instruction and inspirational counsel.

(5) On the other hand, L. D.'s monopolistic tendencies pose a problem for the appointed counselor in that he feels he should provide an atmosphere free from threat, an atmosphere in which each member has equal opportunity to express himself.

(6) The counselor has remained unusually quiet even for a person committed to the democratic process. Betty's problem has been lost in a philosophical maze, although the material offered is pertinent to her problem.

(7) The counselor feels that he should get the conversation back to the topic. He says that he is not certain whether or not Betty faces a definite decision. He probably uses this statement as a means of getting her to reveal the nature of her pending decision.

(L. D.)   But the successful ones develop a technique to rest
               from it.

(JAMES)   (Expresses doubt)

(L. D.)   Maybe you're not acquainted with them when they are
               resting from their problems. You do that with your eyes.
               You sit and read for an hour or two hours; then you'll
               look off, get up, and go to the window. We sit here and
               talk for an hour then take a break. The answer is to walk
               off from it, leave it alone. (Several in group seem to dis-
               agree)

(COUNSELOR)   Well, it seemed to me when Betty started talking over
               there, that—I just got the idea, Betty, that you were not
               talking about a decision to be made, a this or that propo-
               sition, an I will or I won't proposition. You were talking
               more in terms of yourself. But we've been talking mostly
               now since then about making decisions between this and
               that. Maybe that's what you *were* talking about.

(BETTY)   Well, it's hard to explain. See, there is a definite decision.
               I suppose every person faces it when they come to the
               decision about being married. And I guess a lot of people
               have a lot of things that enter into that question. But,
               there's things like that—well, I hate to get so personal
               with this; but it's so hard to explain, because it's really
               deep. And it's something that I've been thinking about
               for a long time. And I can't come up with an answer to
               it. And I know that sooner or later I've got to decide about
               this person. And, well, of course, it would change my life;
               but it's the calling that he has that makes it so much more
               difficult. He has surrendered for the foreign mission field
               and I don't particularly feel that that's my call. And yet,
               I know that there is a basis, a very strong basis for love.
               And all this enters into the decision. And, boy, it's just
               gotten to be terrific and perhaps I don't need to decide
               today but I know that sooner or later I will. That's just
               the surface of it.

(SOMEONE)   Whew! (Group laughs and all talk at once). In the con-
               fusion L. D. says, "You've got a real problem."

(BETTY)   I don't know just how it would sound. It can't be serious
               but a few words. Because—uh—the main thing is that I've
               never considered if I'm being selfish in putting my wants
               for, say, a home and security above the comparatively in-
               secure life that I would have on a mission field. In one
               sense, that would be selfish and it just points to the fact
               that, well, it's just not meant to be or I'm not the one for
               him and that perhaps I couldn't stand up under those cir-
               cumstances. Then on the other hand, we have such a

strong basis for this relationship. You just can't throw it
overboard just because . . .

(L. D.) Betty, do you know what part of the world he feels inclined to go to.

(BETTY) Well, uh, . . .

(L. D.) I don't know that that would have anything to do with it
or not . . .

(BETTY) Well it might, but any place out of the United States
would be the same thing for me; and it wouldn't . . .

(L. D.) There are some physical factors that would make a difference. For instance, I can give you some good illustra-
tions: our missionaries in Brazil, for instance, many of
them—the women are homemakers and they live in a relatively cultured community and they have the modern con-
veniences; whereas the mission wives in the bushland of
Nigeria are different, considerably different. And you indicated the word relative security. But as a missionary's
wife, one is not expected to do missionary work like her
husband.

(BETTY) Yes, I realize all that, about the differences in the areas
of service there. And yet, there is the other side of the
situation. If that was the only place I could be happy, it
would be worth it. Oh, all of the things have to be weighed
and decided upon. It's not just a matter of falling in love
and getting married; ah, I wish it were that easy. Sometimes I think it would be easier just to give up the whole
thing and find somebody else that will be here in the situation that I'm used to. Now that's what I mean by a decision that changes your complete life. And as we were
having a discussion this afternoon about—is that the difference in the greatness of men that they can make a decision
sometimes where you settle for something less, or perhaps
you sort of level off low. And just because you can't face
up, or you just can't quite see it through, there is something you give up—it's a sign of greatness. I guess I'm
sort of confused, but it is something I'm trying to think
through. Oh, and I have written down here something
and I've done some reading to develop this thought. If
you are part of a situation where you could, ah, you know

DISCUSSION: Betty's incoherence indicates just how serious she is about this
problem. A typescript such as this cannot communicate the emotional
overtones which are so important in group counseling.

DISCUSSION: Betty's confusion is great because of her tenseness. She starts to
read something and then abandons it. The fact that she came to the meeting with something written down indicates just how heavily this problem weighs upon her.

—that you have command of the situation—in other words say living in the United States. You feel like you could cope with almost anything. And yet, you feel that maybe my place is out there where the situation is entirely different. Is it right for you to put yourself in a situation like that? Just because you feel like perhaps that's where I'm supposed to be, where you would have to be completely readjusted. Is that—is that fair to yourself? Could you be of maximum service? Perhaps I'm getting too many things mixed up; I don't know what I'm saying.

(LURLINE) I think a lot of the missionaries who have gone—feel that way, especially the wives. If they had never been on the field before, they don't know what it's going to be like. And whether they admit it or not, there is no question but what they feel something like that. They've read about it and they know a little about it yet they've never witnessed it, and they say, I know that's where I belong—you know, but I bet underneath they feel different.

(L. D.) I can tell you from experience that some of them do. The ones I know personally have deep anxieties about it. There's always this business about what is best for their children.

(COUNSELOR) You started to read something there a minute ago.

(BETTY) Well, the question that I had written down here is that if a person is happy in his own situation and then he feels sort of compelled to do something for humanity, something very noble that would remove him to another situation that was completely reversed of what he's used to—is it fair to him to have to do that? Or would he not be happy if he stayed in his normal situation and just did his work?

(L. D.) Are you saying, is this demanded of him?

(BETTY) Well, I will just take a person—ah, he felt like perhaps his duty would be to go to another country as a foreign missionary. And yet, in a way it would be easier for him to stay here. Now, would it be better for him to give up what is easier for him, ah, living here in the United States,

---

DISCUSSION: Betty still didn't read what she had written down, but she is coherent enough in talking about it that the counselor and the group are able to understand her feelings and her conflict better. The point following Betty's first speech above is perfect for the counselor to attempt to clarify Betty's feelings. L. D. has such enthusiasm as to interfere with such an opportunity. The counselor should not be threatened by having the leadership taken from him. He should be sensitive to a situation like this where one person monopolizes, even though his productions may be considered very good and appropriate.

	or to go to another country? Is it duty or is it just a drive— a deep compelling love that I want to be of service to mankind?
(L. D.)	May I ask a question?
(BETTY)	Yes.
(L. D.)	I don't know whether I have a right to ask this question or not. Do you believe in a called ministry? Do you believe that God makes some sort of a peculiar impression on a fellow—that he'll know whether it's in reason or not that he's to be a preacher—do you believe that for missionaries?
(BETTY)	Yes, I do.
(L. D.)	Then I'm gathering from this conversation that your problem may revolve around your very strong belief that a missionary's wife must have a call too. Or else there are strong incentives in the same sense that the missionary feels.
(BETTY)	That's the basic contention between the two of us. Because, I say that a woman is called into the service of being a wife and mother and home-maker. And if she marries a missionary, her place is with him no matter where he goes.
(L. D.)	Well, now, the reason I asked that—I was already a preacher when I married my wife, and yet she never felt a call. I've heard girls say, I'm called to be a preacher's wife. But Jan has never said that. She says she's never had any peculiar sensation that she was supposed to be a preacher's wife. She felt she was supposed to be a good Christian—to go all the way within the limits of her ability and understanding. And she has always said that. You know when I was to be called to a church field and I would go and talk to her about it, she said, "Now that's between you and God. I cast my lot with you; you and He settle that." Now, that was after we were married, you understand.
(COUNSELOR)	There are many things that I could say on this subject, too, but I wonder if we might not invite our recorder to participate in this if he likes; inasmuch as his parents are both on the mission field now. Edgar, if you feel free to enter this discussion here, I think the group would invite you to do so.
(EDGAR)	Well, I was brought up on the mission field. I've thought of several things and it's been hard for me to sit here and be still. But, ah, I wish that you could read the biography that a lady is writing about my mother and her experiences in being called to the mission field. Daddy had his

call first—felt that he should go, but Mother didn't feel that way at all about it. She wasn't going to take her kids off to some heathen country. And it was quite dramatic the way that she finally did come to realize that her place was with him wherever he felt he should go.

(BETTY)   Well, I'd like to read it. I sure would like to get something first-hand.

(EDGAR)   Well, it's just in manuscript form. It's to be printed sometime—I don't know when.

(JAMES)   This kid needs it right away. (group laughs)

(L. D.)   Well, Edgar, let me ask you this. You have feelings concerning mission field service yourself, do you not?

(EDGAR)   No. No.

(L. D.)   Well, I was thinking that you were—I was mistaken.

(EDGAR)   As far as working somewhere on the mission field, I don't know. But as for actually being an active missionary, no, I don't think in terms of that.

(L. D.)   Were your parents already married when your father was called?

(EDGAR)   Oh, yes, he had pastored several years.

(JAMES)   Don't you think this kind of work requires a basic disposition? Like some people want to be social workers, for example. They get into social work and then they find they are not the kind of people who have the attitude of always going out to people that are miserable and destitute. And then, they find that that's just not the kind of work for them. And I wonder if there isn't something that a minister feels that he has to give and he has to go out even though he might be very content with pastoring a church at home where things are secure and where he has a television set and maybe a dishwasher and things like that that would make life pleasant. Or take a fellow that is going to school, he gets a degree and he knows that he can get a reasonably good job with a B.S.; and he knows he has the capacity to go on and maybe get a Ph.D. He'd have to work a lot harder. He'd have to give himself to that kind of work more or maybe he would become a teacher where he wouldn't get much money, but he would feel a sense of duty, a sense of calling. He feels that he needs to help people around here and he feels that challenge. Don't you think he'd be more content and he'd be more of a service to God and people if he accepted

---

DISCUSSION: The person functioning as recorder-observer usually does not enter the discussion. The counselor had observed his restlessness and felt sure he could add much to the discussion.

	the highest challenge he could accept even though it might not be as pleasant as the other?
(L. D.)	Might be the satisfaction would compensate for the undesirable things.
(JAMES)	Not compensate particularly that would be—that would be . . . this would be different and he would realize his—his highest possibilities and his highest desires to be of service to people and to work for something of real value.
(COUNSELOR)	In other words, James, you mean that if a person loses himself in service, he wouldn't regard his satisfaction as compensation for anything, since he would no longer feel that he had really sacrificed. He would be inclined to count the things he might presumably have given up as being of no value when compared to the things he had gained.
(JAMES)	Yes, that's it. Your real satisfaction would come from realizing you are striving towards a higher goal. It seems to me that the basis of the Christian message is to be outgoing to other people. Some people have this quality and some don't, some people have more, some people less. Some people have more chance to share with others. Take Christ, for example. He probably could have been a very successful carpenter, but he gave that up for a few years of rugged service to man.
(LURLINE)	(to Betty) You said a while ago that you believed the wife should resign herself and go anywhere with her husband. I mean—do you really believe that?
(BETTY)	Yes, I very definitely do.
(L. D.)	Only thing is Lurline, she's not his wife yet, that complicates the problem.
(BETTY)	Well, the thing to me that complicates the problem is—well, I just don't doubt that I love the person but there comes a question, would I ever hold him back. Now you were talking about how when you have a love for a job and you know the heights you can reach and you wouldn't be happy if anything kept you from reaching it—all right, now say something happened, say my health failed and he couldn't go as a foreign missionary. He would be miserable and he would feel like his life was just ruined. And it's things like this that I have to consider that perhaps I might be the cause of standing in the way.
(JAMES)	I think we will agree there though, that this is religious work where you just got to leave some things like that in the hands of God. Of course, now, if you just knew that you were going to contract malaria your first year out

that would be one thing; but if you just suppose, maybe, that's a different thing.

(BETTY)   Well, yes, that's just speculation, that's true.

(L. D.)   Those are "ifs" that we have to face every day. If you paid very much attention to the "ifs" in your life, you wouldn't get very far.

(WILSON)   You would find this true regardless of what kind of work you went into. If you were an engineer or something you couldn't afford to let "ifs" hold you back in that work.

(L. D.)   You wouldn't choose to have anything happen.

(BETTY)   Well, no, now we're getting sort of on the physical side there; but what I'm talking about is am I really capable of being a missionary wife. Do you know what it takes to be a missionary's wife in a foreign country where there are a lot of adverse conditions? And as I look at myself in the light of the background I have had—not a great deal of comfort and all, but comparative security and comforts, not riches. And I would be willing to give it up I believe; but, to me, you don't know yourself. Ah, when you find yourself in an entirely different situation, how do you know how you are going to react?

(EDGAR)   Well, you never know how you are going to react in a strange situation. But if you would make a good home-maker here; well, crossing a couple of hundred waves won't make any difference.

(JAMES)   But, is a completely different environment going to?

(COUNSELOR)   I think Betty probably feels that the environment per se is not as important as is her feeling about being away in a foreign country. None of us can really know how another person feels about things like this. A part of the environment is the way we feel about it.

(EDGAR)   The environment isn't going to be a lot different in the major portions of the world today. Unless it is in some of the remote areas of Africa or something—but in all Latin America and South America and the Hawaiian work . . .

(L. D.)   South Pacific work?

(EDGAR)   Yeah, those. You are not going to find a lot of difference.

DISCUSSION: At this point, Betty is fighting off a concerted attack by L. D., James, Edgar and Wilson. Lurline seems also to have expressed rather strong feeling relative to Betty's willingness to go with her missionary husband. The counselor's single speech in this section is given in an effort to remove some of the pressure. There is danger that Betty's unwillingness to go to the mission field will be broken down by the sheer weight of the opposition. The counselor feels that Betty can use some help, but hopes that any decision will come from within.

Our home life was very stable, very normal. And I think we were—my mother's whole drive was to see to it that our home was just as normal as it could be. She taught us; we grew up. The only companions we had were just in our family circle. That was her chief concern—but other than that, we had just as normal a home life I think as anyone could. But she still felt it her duty to bring us up in a home just as if she had stayed here.

(WILSON) Betty, I wonder if he doesn't feel really the same way you do in a lot of respects. He's going to have to give up something, and he's probably—there are probably doubts and puzzles in his mind just like there are in yours. I don't see how an individual could ever face anything like that without having thoughts such as you are having.

(L. D.) You have a similar sort of anxieties when you enter the ministry. I did. It changes, of course, as you grow older. I'd like to suggest this, now. It seems like Edgar has cast some wonderful light on the subject. But it might be helpful to make it a point to find some missionary wives. Just open your heart to them and ask them to give you a picture of what it was to them.

(EDGAR) If you find—I'll try to get this manuscript to you. The title of the book incidentally is *Whither Thou Goest.*

(BETTY) (laughs) Very good. (Pause) Yes, I would like to have it. (Pause) There is one thing I have tried to do. I think anyone has to be enlightened on a subject before they can make any sort of intelligent decision. And, yet, I have found that in some instances like, for instance, there was this piece in the paper about two missionaries, who had been in prison for about five years; and one of the women lost her sanity. Well, I have to stop and question if—if it's worth it. Now what have they really accomplished? Maybe they had accomplished a good deal before that happened; but I've got to be convinced beyond a shadow of a doubt before I will put my life into something that I think might wind up like that— Is it worth it?

(L. D.) (Above several others) Have you ever attempted anything at all without the shadow of a doubt?

(EDGAR) May I interject this, that a lot of these missionaries that go out independently certainly suffer. They go out and plan to preach their way—you know, let the natives support them, live off of roots and herbs and that sort of thing. And that is an extremely difficult thing. We have seen independent missionaries in South America who were in a bad fix. They were sick, their kids were sick, and there was forever and eternally something wrong with them. But when you are under the Foreign Mission Board or any of the Home Mission Boards like in Panama . . . when you are under these boards, they take care of your medical expenses—half of it, or a big portion of it. They pay you a salary that you can live on and the salary is calculated to the living conditions; and they pay you according to that standard. And they pay you your house rent and you are kept in good condition. And if something legal comes up, they give you help immediately. And that means a lot to the security—to know that the Foreign Mission Board, somebody with that much prestige is behind you and backing you all the way.

(L. D.) They won't let you get into these situations.

(EDGAR) You can get into them, but they are going to do their best to help you get out of it.

(L. D.) But they give you no assignments that look like they might lead to trouble.

(JAMES) Right! But that's not true of independent missionaries.

(BETTY) Yes, but I can't forget about these women in the newspaper.

(L. D.) I remember reading about the ones you are talking about.

(EDGAR) These were Ecuador women.

(L. D.) These five fellows that got killed in South America week before last. They were independents and were out there in some territory that good judgment and good Christianity might not have got them into.

(OSCAR) Well, I believe that more important than this consideration of physical hardships and such things as that—how compatible would you be with the person who has the attitude and sense of values that a foreign missionary must have? I think that if you are compatible in that respect the actual living conditions and physical hardship and so on—now that gets back to the question I guess of whether you are really called or not—but it occurs to me that the person who has the attitude or sense of value or standard of values a foreign missionary has is quite a bit different from what some of the rest of us have. Certainly it would be a significant fact in any marriage. It would be very significant.

(COUNSELOR) Betty, is it possible that you may be using this question of being able to stand the climate and so on as a reason for not accepting the young man's attention? Could it be that it is not the lack or desirability of living quarters and such that is scaring you at all, but some other things?

(BETTY) Well, to me, marriage—that doesn't pose a problem. When I think about the person, I think it would be very nice to

get married; but when I think about his work then that's
something else. Maybe my sense of values is out of focus.
Maybe I just don't realize what I would be getting into
by marrying him. But, honest to goodness, I have thought
it would just be easy to just forget the whole matter and
just find somebody and marry somebody that was going
to be here in the United States. Now, that's just the way
the situation has gotten to be.

(LURLINE)   But, Betty, you're so interested in religious work anyway.
At home, and all, you've been working as church secretary.

(BETTY)   Well, there's no doubt about that. Oh, I could be happy
in the work.

(LURLINE)   And seems like that if you loved him—if you really loved
him, that you would go anywhere with him. And do anything—and I believe you would be happy.

(L. D.)   Amen, that's my girl. (all laugh) Betty, you've only said
one thing that scared me in any sense and that's when
you said, I must know beyond a shadow of doubt. Frankly,
it's difficult for me to harmonize that with the Christian
concept. I've probably said the same thing. But, I believe
that that statement sounds a little hard—I'll say that.

(BETTY)   It just doesn't give . . .

(L. D.)   It seems to me that we are falling short of this noble ideal
of Christianity. Because if you didn't have doubts . . .

(BETTY)   Yes, but there are some people that are more analytical
than others—put it that way—and I suppose I have a
tendency to be too emotional about such things. Anyway,
for me it has to be in black and white where other people could just go right on in.

(COUNSELOR)   Then, it's really the uncertainty of the situation that actually scares you.

(L. D.)   I'm not saying God doesn't put things in black and white.
I think He lets us know many things for sure.

DISCUSSION: It seems obvious that the counselor welcomed Oscar's contribution. This changed the emphasis entirely and helped to lessen the pressure on Betty. The implication which was developing relative to the environment of the mission field was that Betty didn't want to go and was
using the environment as an excuse. This was too threatening to be con-
ductive to wise and prudent decision-making.

DISCUSSION: The question of compatibility raised by Oscar and then enlarged
upon by the counselor was resisted strongly. Such strong resistance may
reflect sensitivity to a factor which, up to this time, Betty has successfully
covered up. On the other hand, strong resistance such as this may rise
from a realistic assessment of the situation by Betty.

(OSCAR)   I might make this observation, too. I feel like this busi-
                ness of "I can go wherever he goes" has a good deal more
                glitter on it before the marriage than afterward. (all
                laugh)
(BETTY)   I'm glad you said that, Oscar. Yeah, it is easy to say, isn't
                it?
(L. D.)   It's not always realistic.
(LURLINE)   But, that would become such a waste, though I don't
                want to be so starry-eyed. But I've seen other cases where
                the person would have the same feeling that you have.
                Some are just that devoted. That would just be their life
                because that's what he did, that's what you would do. I
                mean—the Cooper family, now you all know them—and
                it's just natural for them. What Mrs. Cooper wants is what
                he wants. Of course, she's stayed out there so long as a
                missionary's wife, but . . .
(JAMES)   That comes from the wife having confidence. If she does,
                she'll just go down the line.
(COUNSELOR)   I think Betty has shown a lot of courage in giving us her
                honest feelings throughout this session. Some of these feel-
                ings are difficult to accept in oneself; but, in the long run,
                we never gain anything by holding back. I know that we
                all have very much wanted to say something that would
                help her. Actually . . .
(L. D.)   This is no easy problem, that's for sure. I hope Betty hasn't
                taken anything I've said too seriously. I think I know just
                how she feels.
(LURLINE)   Me, too. (others concur)
(COUNSELOR)   I was about to say that we've just about run out of time.
                We are going to have to defer discussion on this to an-
                other time. Now, before we come back on Thursday, we
                might all do some more thinking on this. But, on the
                other hand, maybe we can discuss other problems next
                time. We do seem to have spent most of our time on
                Betty's problem this time. (Group prepares to leave)
(BETTY)   And, thanks—everybody.

DISCUSSION: The counselor's efforts to turn the discussion into a new channel
    in keeping with Betty's remark about being analytical are thwarted.
    Oscar, who is an experienced counselor makes a second effort to bring a
    new approach which was designed to turn aside some of the criticism
    which threatened Betty.

EVALUATION

The counselor in the group setting has a number of primary duties. One of these is to keep the group moving, to aid in molding an atmosphere that elicits expression. Furthermore, he should endeavor to assure that each member has opportunity for expression.

The group represented in the foregoing material did not pose a problem for the counselor in terms of getting people to talk. They were strongly motivated to produce. There was considerable difficulty in distributing the leadership and in keeping the overly zealous members from talking too much.

It is probable that Betty could have gained more from a group that was not so strongly oriented to the concepts of evangelical religion. Three of the men were ministers or ministerial students. One of the women was highly motivated in religious service. One gets the feeling from this material that Betty was pressured too strongly toward accepting her place beside her prospective husband on the mission field. Perhaps the counselor should have intervened more often to relieve this pressure.

This group-counseling session may be somewhat typical, however, of group counseling in the religious setting. It does clearly demonstrate the power of the group to bring material into the open. It is a good example of the concern that people have for their fellows.

This counselor demonstrated the philosophy that the counselor should not express value-orientations. He apparently was committed to the idea that such expressions by the counselor result in a threat to the permissive atmosphere. The minister who serves as a group counselor may choose an entirely different philosophy. He may feel that his best contribution may come through his expression of a set of values.

Index

Index

COUNSELING:

A Modern Emphasis in Religion

by LESLIE E. MOSER

THIS practical and informative book presents religiously oriented counseling as an important and distinctive area of service to humanity. Written from the viewpoint of a Christian psychologist, the volume offers a wide range of salient implications from psychology, psychiatry, and other behavioral disciplines as points of departure and as guidelines of continued direction for counselors in the religious field.

Featuring group as well as individual approaches to problem-solving, the book describes such contemporary trends as the use of specialists and church-related clinics. Psychoanalytical and client-centered theories and techniques are treated thoroughly.

The book demonstrates lucidly how the contributions of religion and psychology may be integrated to help troubled people meet the strains and tensions of the modern and insecure world. It promotes scientific bases for understanding the psychodynamics of emotional disorders, somatic symptoms, and the roots of fear and anxiety.

The author reveals how counseling may help in the successful resolution of broad, surface-level problems of normal individ-

(Continued on back flap)